POLITICAL PARTY FINANCING IN CANADA

mcgraw-hill series in canadian politics

Paul W. Fox, *General Editor*

POLITICAL PARTY FINANCING IN CANADA

KHAYYAM ZEV PALTIEL

Professor of Political Science,
Carleton University, Ottawa, Ontario

Toronto
McGraw-Hill Company of Canada Limited
Montreal
New York
London
Sydney
Johannesburg
Mexico
Panama
Düsseldorf
Singapore
Rio de Janeiro

POLITICAL PARTY FINANCING IN CANADA

Cover design by Arjen F. de Groot.

Library of Congress Catalog Card Number 77-139244
ISBN 0-07-092829-0
1234567890 MB-70 9876543210

Printed and bound in Canada

FOREWORD

Since the financing of Canadian political parties has always been an intriguing mystery that has titillated the fancy of successive generations of students and citizens, one can predict with some confidence that this book by Professor Paltiel will evoke great public interest.

The attention will be justified for *Political Party Financing in Canada* not only answers many of the questions that have been asked continually about the incomes and expenditures of Canadian political parties during and between elections but it also raises and discusses many of the fundamental problems which are associated with the financing of political parties and which are crucial in a modern democracy. The author examines in some detail, for instance, the contemporary problem of the high cost of partisan campaigning by means of the mass media, especially via television.

Professor Paltiel presents a wealth of facts and figures on this previously obscure subject of how much our parties spend on various devices to try to get their candidates elected. But, fortunately for the reader, he has not stopped short with a mere recital of how many dollars went where, although that is certainly enlightening information in itself. He pushes on to examine a number of important aspects of the thorny subject of controlling campaign funds. Some of his findings may surprise readers. He points out, for example, that survey research shows that only a tiny portion of the public sampled (about five percent) was asked to contribute to party war chests in 1965 and that an even smaller percentage actually did donate. Professor Paltiel also reviews existing provincial and federal legislation dealing with campaign funds, of whose general *laissez-faire* nature he is very critical. However, he is impressed by Quebec's new system of public subsidization and control of election campaigning which was introduced in 1963 and which he explains carefully. The author also analyzes in detail the recommendations of the federal government's Committee on Election Expenses which reported in 1966. His concluding chapter is hard-hitting. Professor Paltiel does not hesitate to criticize both the traditional Canadian attitudes to the financing of parties and the gaps, as he sees them, in the proposals of the Committee on Election Expenses. He warns that, "Disenchantment with the failings of the electoral process has helped to promote the sense of political inefficacy that has contributed to the growth of extra-parliamentary oppositions of the Right and Left with their common proclivity to violence."

Professor Paltiel is well qualified for the task he has undertaken in *Political Party Financing in Canada*. If he will forgive an immodest remark, I think it is fair to say that he is one of the very few Canadian authorities on the subject of party financing. He has been interested in the topic for some years and he served as the Research Director of the federal Committee on Election Expenses which published, in addition to its final *Report,* a volume of related research studies that Professor Paltiel contributed to, supervised, and edited. He has also given a number of papers and published articles on the same subject. In this book he has drawn together his knowledge and reflections to present in brief compass an informative, provocative, and definitive work which fills a hitherto serious lacuna in the study of Canadian politics. His book, therefore, is a most welcome addition to the McGraw-Hill Series in Canadian Politics which is designed to be of use to both students of Canadian politics and of interest to the public at large.

April 17, 1970,   Paul W. Fox,
University of Toronto.   *General Editor*

To the memory of my father
Aaron David Paltiel
1880-1961

PREFACE

This book is both a description and an appraisal of the practices employed by Canadian political parties to finance their activities, and it is also a study of the legislation enacted to bring order to this aspect of Canadian political life. For this reason it appeared worthwhile to record the efforts of political leaders and fund-raisers as they have gone about trying to provide the wherewithal to fight election campaigns and to finance other party business. The answers to such questions as: what has been raised; how it has been raised; by whom and to whom money has been given; can help clarify the operations of our party system and governmental decision-making in Canada. An examination of efforts to control election expenses by legislation can be expected to reveal the willingness of the dominant parties to break with the past or the extent to which they are wedded to current practice. Inevitably a review of the flow of party funds and the attempts to control them casts light on the links between society and politics and government.

The field of political finance has always excited controversy. Epithets of bribery, corruption and scandal have been hurled at it continually, thus obscuring rational discussion of its influence and reform. Effective limitations on the abuse of financial power in the political arena must be based on knowledge of the motives and actions of contributors and the fund-raising processes in their relationship to political power.

In a sense my interest in political finance began during work on my doctoral dissertation which examined the structure of the Progressive Party in Israel. However, research for this book really started in 1965 when I was appointed Research Director of the Advisory Committee on Election Expenses. These studies continued in a series of articles and papers, the results of which are reflected in the following pages. In the course of this research, I have benefited from contacts with practical politicians and journalists in Canada, first met in carrying out my tasks for the Committee. I have also learned much from European and American scholars, such as Dr. Herbert E. Alexander, Prof. Nils Andrén, Chancellor Alexander Heard, Prof. Arnold J. Heidenheimer, Prof. Gerhard Leibholz, and Prof. Pertti Pesonnen.

I am grateful to Professor Paul Fox for his encouraging me to undertake the present book and for his agreement to write the Foreword. But without the persistence of Mr. William D. Crawley of McGraw-Hill, I doubt that it would have been completed.

Finally, I owe a considerable debt to my wife, Freda, for her critical reading of the entire manuscript and pertinent and sage advice at all stages of its preparation, and to my children, Ari, Jeremy, Candida and Ora, for their constant stimulus to flagging spirits. Together, they contributed not a little to whatever virtues are contained in the ensuing pages.

February, 1970,
Geneva, Switzerland.   Khayyam Zev Paltiel

ACKNOWLEDGMENTS

While the author bears full responsibility for the authenticity and reliability of the ensuing text, its preparation would not have been possible without the help of many individuals and organizations.

At the political level, particular thanks are due to: Senator John B. Aird Q.C., former National Treasurer of the Liberal Party; Mr. John R. Woods, Director of Finance, Liberal Federation of Canada; Mr. Edwin A. Goodman Q.C., National Chairman of Organization, and Hon. Richard A. Bell Q.C., former National Director, Progressive Conservative Party of Canada; Mr. Clifford A. Scotton and Mr. Terence Grier, the present and former Federal Secretaries of the New Democratic Party; and countless others at the party and parliamentary levels whose information was indispensable. On the administrative side, much invaluable data were provided by M. Jean-Marc Hamel, the Chief Electoral Officer for Canada; M. François Drouin C.R., the Chief Returning Officer of the Province of Quebec; Mr. D. L. Bennett, former Director of Program Policy, and Mr. Finlay Payne of the Department of Station Relations, Canadian Broadcasting Corporation; Mr. Ross Maclean, former Research Director, Board of Broadcast Governors, and Mr. W. L. Mahoney, Supervisor of Log Examination, Canadian Radio-Television Commission; and others in various capacities in the public service of Canada and its provinces.

The author remembers fondly and with gratitude the collaboration of his young assistants on the research staff of the Committee on Election Expenses, particularly Jean Brown Van Loon, Jill McCalla Vickers, James B. MacAuley and Reginald A. Whitaker; this publication may be viewed as the culmination of the work begun with their help. Similarly, the author is deeply indebted to Mrs. Pearl Fisher, Administrative Assistant of the

Department of Political Science, Carleton University, who with good humour, resourcefulness and efficacy supervised the preparation of the typescript in Ottawa from the manuscript written in Geneva.

A sabbatical year from Carleton University assisted by a Leave Fellowship from the Canada Council provided the leisure necessary to complete the manuscript. Carleton supplied additional aid by assuming the cost of typing.

LIST OF TABLES
AND CHARTS

Tables

Tables

Charts

Table

CONTENTS

PART I
THE SETTING

ONE

MONEY AND THE CANADIAN POLITICAL SYSTEM*

Political finance has always been enveloped in an aura of mystery. Its first students, the "muck rakers" of the early years of this century, were so moved by the piquancy of their discoveries and by a tendency to moralize that they frequently neglected to relate their findings about what they termed the "money power" to an understanding of the political system as a whole. Their sole monuments are scattered across the legislative landscape of the United States in the pages of the abortive and stillborn election expense laws which the Progressive Era was prone to produce.

It was not until the pioneering books of Pollock[1] and Overacker[2] appeared that the study of political finance entered the modern era; and with Alexander Heard's magisterial study[3] the subject may be said to have reached full scholarly maturity. Today, a host of scholars, like Theodor Eschenburg in Germany, Jean Meynaud in Switzerland, Richard Rose in the United Kingdom, and Herbert Alexander and Arnold Heidenheimer in the United States of America, are gathering systematic data and building a body of knowledge and theory which promises to be an important part of the study of politics in the contemporary period.

In Canada, until very recently, the subject has remained all but abandoned. Apart from the recondite and somewhat shamefaced references to

*This chapter follows closely a paper entitled *Federalism and Party Finance: A Preliminary Sounding* originally prepared for delivery at the 38th Annual Meeting of the Canadian Political Science Association, June 8-10, 1966 at the University of Sherbrooke. This paper was reprinted in revised form as Study No. 1 in Khayyam Z. Paltiel et al., *Studies in Canadian Party Finance*, Committee on Election Expenses, The Queen's Printer, Ottawa, 1966, pp. 1-21.

the more questionable activities of their subjects by the official biographers of our political worthies and the "tut tuts" of our journalists and editorial writers as they turned from the more sulphurous of Canada's long line of election fund scandals, little was done to clarify the nature of Canadian political finance. What outcries there were, prompted the enactment of even more ineffectual legislation, if that were possible, than some American statutes. Only one Canadian study deserves mention, an article by Professor R. A. MacKay, "After Beauharnois—What?", published almost four decades ago in *Maclean's Magazine,* October 15, 1931. But here too the focus was on the reform of election expense laws,[4] not the understanding of the political system. The only study of political finance which even remotely attempted to relate the problem to our party system in general was prepared as a doctoral dissertation for Alexander Heard at the University of North Carolina by Ernest Eugene Harrill.[5] The brute fact is that it was not until 1965-1966, when the then Secretary of State, Maurice Lamontagne, decided to establish the Advisory Committee on Election Expenses, that any effort was made to make a systematic study of party finance; it was this Committee's *Report*[6] and volume of supplementary studies[7] which provided Canadian scholars with information in the quantity and form appropriate to the task.

What follows is a Canadian gloss on Professor Heard's statement with respect to the United States, but which bears equally well for Canada, namely that our country

> is both a democracy and a pecuniary society that permits large concentrations of economic power. The interconnection of government with the rest of . . . society can be especially illuminated by the flow of funds from the rest of society into the channels of politics. The study of money in politics necessarily probes the organization of society in its relationship to the functions and actions of government.[8]

Canada is a federal state with a Parliamentary and Cabinet system of Government. These characteristics affect our party system. On the one hand, the Parliamentary and Cabinet systems place vast power in the hands of party leaders and, in the case of the party in power, in the Cabinet. This central role of the leaders in the structure of the major parties is reflected in the fact that each leader usually names the finance chairman of his party. Nor is this function belied by the fact that the leaders tend to disclaim knowledge about the sources and amounts of party funds; indeed the fate of the campaign fund is dependent on the leader's acceptability to the principal contributors. On the other hand, Canada's federal structure tends to fragment the leaders' authority by setting up competing power centres in the provinces and provincial party organizations.

The traditional methods of financing the two major Canadian parties, the Liberals and Conservatives, helped to overcome the splintering effect of the provinces and provincial party organizations. Integration was accomplished through a highly centralized system of party finance. This system rested on a common basis: the centralized corporate industrial and financial structures concentrated in Montreal and in Toronto. It is common knowledge that the two parties were financed largely from essentially the same sources—these corporate contributors numbered in the hundreds rather than in the thousands. Under this system, provincial and even municipal elections, as well as federal campaigns, were financed in the main from the central party funds and sources. The traditional system of party finance, despite all its failings, had important integrative effects which helped to overcome the centrifugal forces inherent in Canadian politics. This benefit was a by-product of the highly concentrated nature of Canadian industry and finance.

The emergence of third parties, continuing multi-partyism, and the breakdown of the two-party system since 1919, together with the resurgence of the provinces both politically and economically since the Second World War, have undermined the highly centralized nature of Canadian party finance. Much of Canada's postwar economic growth has been due to the development of resource and extractive industries which fall under provincial jurisdiction. In the same period, the rapid growth of spending on such items as highways and education has increased the share and enhanced the budgetary role of the provinces in the sphere of public expenditure. Large corporations, contractors and suppliers who are the principal contributors to Canadian political parties now seek access to and must deal directly with provincial governments and party leaders to satisfy their interests, whether the latter lie in the search for valuable concessions or lucrative contracts. This circumstance may have an additional dysfunctional effect on our federal system since, as the Hon. Walter L. Gordon has pointed out,[9] many of these corporate contributors are subsidiaries of foreign-controlled, non-resident companies whose proprietors and management are committed primarily to the self-interest of their parent companies and home governments.

In either case, substantial funds are now available to provincial, as distinct from federal, party organizations, notably in Western Canada. This is especially true, of course, when the party forms the Government, but it also applies to an increasing extent when a party is in Opposition. The consequences of this development are important for they have affected the structure of Canadian politics by influencing the articulation of our political parties. In fact the federal parties themselves have been affected. The provincial wings of federal parties, particularly in Western and Central Canada, are able to raise substantial sums on their own initiative. In addition, in Quebec, the "quiet revolution" contributed to the change by establishing a partial state subsidy system to help meet campaign costs. While ostensibly aimed at eliminating the abuse-ridden party finance devices of the Taschereau-Duplessis era, the new arrangement has in effect put the Quebec provincial parties in an independent position *vis-à-vis* their federal counterparts and their financial supporters. All these factors have tended to undermine the role which our national parties customarily played in the maintenance of traditional Canadian federalism. Some of the difficulties which have emerged in recent years in the sphere of federal-provincial relations may thus be attributed to these causes.

Several academic commentators, such as Professor Donald Smiley,[10] have argued that it is a mistake to exaggerate the role of political parties in the Canadian federal process and that attention must be paid to such other supports of Canadian federalism as inter-governmental administrative and financial arrangements and devices. However, even if this *caveat* be accepted, and its importance cannot be gainsaid, it cannot be denied that parties do have an important role in the maintenance of the Canadian federal system, as Professor John Meisel has shown, and that a breakdown in their cohesion has had a serious impact on the quality of Canadian political life.[11] One is led to agree with Riker that there is a "causal connection" between "variations in the degree of centralization (or peripheralization) in the constitutional structure of a federalism . . . [and] . . . the variation in degree of party centralization."[12] The argument advanced here is that recent shifts which have occurred in Canadian party finance have had a dysfunctional effect on Canadian federalism.

In the early post-Confederation period Canadian party finance reflected the legal framework of the electoral system which was characterized by open voting and deferred non-simultaneous elections, the dominant "ministerialism," and the weakness of partisanship.[13] The absence of permanent party organizations and the lack of specialized fund-raising structures put the burden of raising and distributing funds on the shoulders of the party leaders themselves. Thus, when the Pacific Scandal broke, the Conservative Party leaders, Sir John A. Macdonald and Georges Cartier, could not dissociate themselves from blame. At the same time, the fact that the leader of the Liberal Party, Alexander Mackenzie, was shocked by the suggestion that he help raise and provide substantial funds to assure the election in 1877 of his Quebec lieutenant, Wilfrid Laurier, only underlined his own naiveté and served to confirm the expected role of the party leader in such matters.[14]

It was only after electoral reform, the adoption of a modern voting system, and the expansion of the franchise that a coherent and continuous party structure, characteristic of modern political parties, emerged. The mobilization of the modern mass electorate required funds, and for this the parties turned to the one source which had large sums available — the business community. This evolution led to a specialization of function in the interests of efficiency and security. Party leaders were gradually relieved of the burden of soliciting funds directly. This function devolved upon specialized fund-raisers like Hon. Thomas McGreevy, M.P., as revealed in the result of the investigation into another of the long line of Canadian railway scandals.[15] The culmination of this process may be viewed in the light of the details revealed by the Beauharnois Affair. The specialized fund-raiser, who underwent several transformations and is still with us, had now become the full-time party professional in the form of Senator Andrew Haydon. Haydon had been general secretary of the National Liberal Committee in 1919. In 1922 he became the main treasurer and fund-raiser for election campaigns and was assisted by a "trustee" for Liberal Party funds in the Province of Quebec, in the person of the prominent businessman Senator Donat Raymond. When the Beauharnois Affair broke, Rt. Hon. William Lyon Mackenzie King managed to dissociate himself simply by asserting that he, as Liberal Party leader, was ignorant of the details of party finance. Although this argument was met with astonished incredulity by his Conservative and Socialist counterparts in the House of Commons, Mr. R. B. Bennett and Mr. J. S. Woodsworth,[16] nevertheless this stand has been generally adopted by party leaders ever since. Evidence gathered by political biographers indicates, of course, that King and other party leaders were and are bound in some way to be informed of the identity of the major contributors to their parties.

The Conservative Party's fund-raising structure in the twentieth century has followed a pattern somewhat similar to that of the Liberals, albeit subject to the vicissitudes of a less successful history. Specialized fund-raisers have emerged and full-time professionals have taken over party organizing and campaign functions. The differences between the parties, where they exist in this regard, are related to the fact that the Liberal Party's formal structure is more federalized, reserving a special place for its Quebec organization; while the Conservative Party, at least until Mr. Diefenbaker's accession to leadership in 1956, had a more centralized appearance. Also, the role and impact of the leader and his personality has had a greater effect on the fund-raising fortunes of the Conservative Party. Thus, the Rt. Hon. R. B. Bennett in effect personally became the main financial prop of his Party for about a decade, a benefit which his party scarcely survived. Also the policies and manner of leaders like the Rt. Hon. Arthur Meighen and Dr. R. J. Manion, not to speak of more contemporary personalities, have occasioned severe financial droughts for the Conservative Party.

It is perhaps a truism to repeat that the Canadian political system and modern election campaign styles turn on the existence of parties, their leaders, and the projection of the images of these parties and leaders. The role of the individual candidates in the constituencies and their local campaigns are corollaries of this fact. Yet the formal aspects of the Canadian electoral system and Canadian election law persist in the myth that parties have no existence.

Modern party and election finance are, as has been stated above, intimately related to the social system as well as to the Canadian party system and contemporary campaign styles. Canadian society is increasingly characterized and dominated by three great bureaucratic structures and their respective élites. Of prime importance and most pervasive and far-reaching in its influence is the industrial corporate structure, and the managerial business élite. The fact that the decision-making centres for the most significant portion of this sector are located beyond the borders of Canada,[17] and in the United States in particular, does not change the essence of the problem, although it must present special difficulties for the parties themselves and their internal or democratic decision-making practices; in addition, it has serious implications with respect to the policy outputs of governments headed by parties dependent on such support. Secondly, parallel and related to the industrial and business sector is a labour bureaucracy and trade union élite, whose close links with American parent bodies require a reservation concerning foreign influence similar to that just entered regarding the managerial structure. Finally, there exists the modern bureaucratic state and its various organs. There are sectors of our society which have not as yet been absorbed by the bureaucratic system but these are to a great extent archaic, traditional and, despite occasional upsurges, of decreasing political importance; even the expanding professions are less and less "free" and are increasingly dependent on and ancillary to the principal societal divisions. The three sectors and their élites are, or are becoming, the major providers of the financial wherewithal of the Canadian party system. Despite several efforts by the major parties, perhaps not persistent enough, and the repeated and sometimes partially successful efforts of several minor parties, it has not been possible for Canadian parties— including those which had the strongest ideological motives in that direction —to acquire the requisite funds by popular fund-raising without recourse to either one or a combination of the aforementioned bureaucracies.

Our parties require funds for three purposes: to fight election campaigns; to maintain a viable inter-election organization; to provide research and advisory services for the party's leadership and elected representatives at various levels. All the evidence indicates that only the first of these, the campaign fund, receives and gets the attention it deserves. Some attempts are made to provide the second, especially if the party enjoys the advantages of incumbency. But the last purpose has usually finished a very bad third, having been left to the voluntary freewill offerings of interested individuals and groups.[18] In the case of the two traditional major parties, this may have been a consequence of the fact that they began as and still are essentially parliamentary parties of the "cadre" type which Duverger has so well described in his studies of party structure.[19] Moreover, it is also true that while the minor parties began as extra-parliamentary movements, they never quite became parties of the "mass" type. In the case of the former Cooperative Commonwealth Federation, now the New Democratic Party, it may be said that the extra-parliamentary party or movement retains a strong influence over policy and organizational matters. Considerable amounts in the form of membership dues and donations are still collected from individuals, party clubs and other units; but the New Democratic Party is today largely dependent financially on affiliation fees and contributions from the trade unions. Only the Ralliement des Créditistes relies substantially on popular fund-raising. The moribund national Social Credit movement was financially not more than an appendage to the Alberta and British Columbia Social Credit parties which gather their funds from the same type of source as the two major parties, whether or not these are cloaked by such devices as the Social Credit Education Fund.[20]

In recent years the overall amount of direct campaign and related costs to parties, candidates and competitors for leadership at the federal level have ranged from $10 million to $25 million. Based on the information made available by the political parties and candidates and supplemented by their own inquiries, the politically experienced members of the Committee on Election Expenses calculated that in the 1965 federal general election it was

> reasonable to conclude that the national parties' organizations spend in excess of eight million dollars in a national election campaign. This estimated figure includes funds which are given by the national parties directly to support their candidates. Supplementary to this total should be added a similar amount raised and expended by or on behalf of the candidates themselves. The estimated total expenditures would approach $16 million. . . .[21]

Adopting a similar method of calculation, one may estimate that in the 1968 federal general election campaign parties and candidates spent well over $21 million. In addition, parties, delegates and competitors for the Progressive Conservative and Liberal Party leadership spent almost four million dollars prior to and during their respective party Leadership Conventions in September 1967 and April 1968. To complete the picture of the cash outlay on the federal electoral process, one would have to add the $13,841,484.08 spent by the Office of the Chief Electoral Officer in the 1968 general election,[22] as well as the expenses of the Representation Commissioner and the respective provincial commissions, plus the value of the free broadcasting time supplied to parties and candidates.

A detailed examination of the admittedly unreliable, incomplete and partially false declarations made by candidates under the provisions of existing Canadian legislation permits a partial analysis and comparison of party expenditures at the candidate level. Out of the 967 candidates who contested the 1968 federal election in 264 federal constituencies, 72 percent, or 700, filed reports indicating that they spent a total of $6,827,289.39,[23] one-third more than had been spent by the 758 reporting candidates in 1965. More than half this sum was spent by Liberals whose average expense was $14,270 for each reporting candidate. Well over one-third of the total was spent by Conservative candidates whose declarations averaged $12,508 in expenditures per constituency. Somewhat less than seven hundred thousand dollars was declared to have been spent by New Democratic Party candidates, of whom more than 100 did not report; the average for those who did report was $4,263 per candidate. Eighty percent of the 30 Social Credit candidates made reports indicating average expenditures of $2,065 per constituency, the only reduction recorded in comparison with 1965. Finally, less than half the Ralliement des Créditistes standard-bearers filed reports which revealed average constituency costs of $2,187.

The problems provoked by the need to raise such large sums are not simply those of amount, although these may be heavy enough since they have been compounded by the frequency of federal general elections recently, six campaigns having occurred in the past 13 years. Fund-raisers have been subjected to great pressures and, to achieve the required sums, the parties may have been tempted by tainted sources, as attested to by the Rivard Affair and the Dorion Report which followed.[24] However, the key question for students of politics is clearly the nature and shape of the influence which the sources, contributors, and canvassers exert on the selection of leaders and the determination of party policies. Attention must also be given to the impact of the distribution system employed to allocate the proceeds collected within the parties.

Historically the bulk of the funds for the two dominant parties came from individuals and corporations closely connected with the financial communities centred in Montreal and Toronto. In practice, these contributors hedged their bets by distributing their gifts in a proportion of sixty to forty between the incumbent and opposition parties.[25] The sums thus collected were transferred to other areas to support party organizations and candidacies in provinces outside Central Canada. However, in recent years, the British Columbia and Alberta wings of the federal Liberal and Conservative Parties have become largely self-supporting and contribute on occasion to the support of the Saskatchewan wing. Manitoba in the heyday of the Winnipeg Grain Exchange was self-supporting but now is a net importer of election funds. The rest of Canada, as far as the two major parties are concerned, are beneficiaries of transfer payments — they play the role of political colonies except when some grass-roots movement has swept a minor party into power or the provincial wing of a traditional party can exploit the advantages of incumbency by using office to gain funds for organizational purposes by fair or foul means. This process involving "toll-gating" and kickbacks on government contracts and concessions may, of course, be viewed as the exploitation of the third sector, the state organs and the government bureacracy, and as hidden governmental subsidies limited to the party incumbent in power.[26] Similar sources are exploited by the Social Credit Party in British Columbia and Alberta. In contrast to the old parties, transfer payments have moved from the provincial to the federal wing to assist the national spokesmen of Major Douglas's doctrines. Likewise, in the days of the old CCF, the national party was financially dependent on the Saskatchewan, British Columbia, and, in part, the Ontario provincial sections.

All the evidence suggests that very few people are involved in raising funds on behalf of the two major parties; the collectors and contributors together number no more than several hundred. Constituency organizations and candidates do, of course, raise funds with varying degrees of success depending largely on whether or not a strong local tradition or interest maintains this type of giving. This finding is supported by a survey of a scientifically selected sample of the Canadian electorate commissioned by the Committee on Election Expenses after the 1965 federal general election which indicated that only five percent of Canadian families had a member who had been asked to donate to campaign funds and that only four percent of the sample actually did contribute.[27] These data emphasize "the almost incredible degree to which parties do *not* seek funds from the citizens at large."[28] It is clear that the Liberals and the Conservatives make few serious efforts in this direction. The survey also bears out the observation that the New Democratic Party is far more active than its rivals. Apart from donors to the CCF-NDP, which gathers considerable financial support in the Province of Saskatchewan where it had for two decades formed the provincial government, the bulk of the respondents who reported having donated to Canadian parties were located in the Province of Ontario and Quebec.

The fund-raising structures of the Liberal and Conservative Parties have consisted customarily of finance committees in Toronto and Montreal with the Toronto chairmen acting as the seniors. Subsidiary committees may also be established in Ottawa, Hamilton and London. In the contemporary period, the Western provincial finance chairmen have risen in importance with the growing affluence of their areas. The chief solicitors are appointees and close associates of the party leaders. In practice they are not subject to the formal party organs. It would appear, too, that a solicitor of party funds normally does not hold elective office but will frequently be rewarded by appointment to the Senate. Usually co-opted by fellow fund-raisers, they often have literally inherited their party roles from older members of their families or business and law firms. In both parties the top solicitors and their chief aides appear to be prominent stockbrokers, investment dealers and corporation lawyers. The latter have commonly played a conspicuous brokerage role in Canadian political life — the appearance of the "political director" on the boards of Canadian subsidiaries of foreign corporations only serves to put new emphasis on this function.

There are some distinctions between the two major parties in the treatment of funds after these have been collected. In the more centralized Conservative Party, the funds appear to have been pooled and distributed centrally, often from the national office, not only for the national campaign and provincial headquarters but for the constituency organizations as well. Since 1956, when Senator Grosart assumed the position of national organizer of the Progressive Conservative Party, funds collected centrally are distributed to candidates through the provincial organizations. However, the attrition of the Quebec Conservative organization has necessarily implied closer national involvement in the affairs of that provincial organization than in the case of its rival. The financial operations of the Liberal Party have always been far more federalized, with the Quebec wing of the federal party retaining much of the funds collected and controlling expenditures at the provincial level to such an extent that Liberal finance chairmen are wont to disclaim any knowledge of financial operations in Quebec. As far as the rest of the country is concerned, due note being taken of the qualifications mentioned above, funds are collected, pooled, and distributed to the provincial organizations. But this reallocation of monies need not necessarily be in proportionate amounts as witnessed by the disaffection and consequent lethargy at the federal level of Saskatchewan Liberals in recent years.

While there appears to have been a peripheralization of major party and Social Credit and Ralliement des Créditistes finances, it is worth noting the growing centralization of the New Democratic Party financial structure due to the entry of funds from labour organizations, contributed in large part by the big trade unions located in Ontario with national and interprovincial interests. Whether this trend in NDP finances has consequences sufficient to check the centrifugal influence of the tendencies exhibited in the major parties, or the rise of provincially based minor parties, depends in part on the future success of that party at the polls.

A serious problem is posed by the question whether the solicitors are subject to party control, or whether they control the party themselves or on behalf of the givers. To use a useful distinction introduced by Alexander Heard: Are the solicitors "party oriented," or are they "contributor oriented"?[29] A definitive answer can be obtained only with full knowledge as to amount and source coupled with a comparison between party and government policy and appointments. At one time the Montreal financial community may be said to have held a veto on Conservative Party leaders and policy through the withholding of funds, as witnessed by the fate of Dr. R. J. Manion whose views on railway amalgamation were spurned.[30] Clearly, *quid pro quos* have been sought; our Royal Commission reports and judicial inquiries are replete with this information. Certainly what most givers seek, whether large or small amounts are given at the local or party level, is *access* to decision-makers at various levels. In addition, donors may wish to define the parameters within which decisions are made; this helps to explain the often heard appeal for funds to preserve the "two party" system. The proclamation of the New Democratic Party as "the political arm of labour" suggests that union gifts are not much different in this respect.

Regional variations in party and election expenditure come under the rubric of political culture as do the contrasts in campaign patterns between rural, urban and metropolitan areas. Surveys, interviews and examinations of expenditure records demonstrate that the Ottawa River[31] is an apparent boundary for many of these regional variations in attitudes and behaviour. East of the Ottawa, constituency expenses tend to be higher; the exchange of cash, liquor and other considerations for votes is more prevalent. Constituency campaign workers in Quebec and the Atlantic Provinces appear to be paid preponderantly in contrast to the prevalence of voluntary work in the constituencies West of the Ottawa River. Furthermore, very little by way of constituency campaign funds is raised at the local level in Eastern Canada — subsidies from central party funds tend to be high and cover the major portion of local costs. (Similar patterns may be discovered, however, in the more traditional Ontario counties.) West of the Ottawa, and particularly in rural Western Canada, volunteers are common and constituency campaign costs are considerably lower than in the rural East. These regional variants in Canada's political culture are not necessarily attributable to the federal structure of the Canadian state.

Money is a necessary political resource. Hence its flow has profound effects upon all our political systems (party, federal, governmental, as well as electoral). The reform of party and election finance must take account of the manifold ways in which money impinges on the polity. The sources of funds and campaign styles and expenditures reflect the nature of our society. Proposals for change must be rooted in an awareness of these factors. Faith in the honesty of the democratic electoral system may be damaged by ill-advised changes which encourage recourse to illegitimate sources and subject the parties to hidden manipulation. The following chapters are devoted to a detailed examination of these questions.

FOOTNOTES

1 James K. Pollock, *Party Campaign Funds*, Alfred A. Knopf Inc., New York, 1926.

2 Louise Overacker, *Money in Elections*, The Macmillan Co., New York, 1932.

3 Alexander Heard, *The Costs of Democracy*, The University of North Carolina Press, Chapel Hill, 1960.

4 See also Norman A. Ward, *The Canadian House of Commons: Representation*, University of Toronto Press, Toronto, 1963, chapter 16, *passim*.

5 Ernest E. Harrill, "The Structure of Organization and Power in Canadian Political Parties: A Study in Party Financing," unpublished Ph.D. dissertation, University of North Carolina, Chapel Hill, 1958.

6 *Report of the Committee on Election Expenses*, The Queen's Printer, Ottawa, 1966.

7 Paltiel et al., *Studies in Canadian Party Finance*, Committee on Election Expenses, The Queen's Printer, Ottawa, 1966.

8 Heard, *op. cit.*, p. 4.

9 Walter L. Gordon, *A Choice for Canada*, McClelland and Stewart Ltd., Toronto, 1966, pp. 120-121.

10 For his views of the relevance of financial and administrative arrangements to Canadian federalism, see D. V. Smiley, "The Rowell-Sirois Report, Provincial Autonomy and Post-War Canadian Federalism," *Canadian Journal of Economics and Political Science*, Vol. XXXI, No. 1, Feb. 1963, pp. 80-97. See also his Introduction to the *Rowell-Sirois Report*, An Abridgement of Book I of the *Royal Commission Report on Dominion-Provincial Relations*, Donald V. Smiley (ed.), The Carleton Library No. 5, McClelland and Stewart Ltd., Toronto, 1963, pp. 1-8.

11 For his views on the effect of the breakdown of Canadian party cohesion, see John Meisel, "The Stalled Omnibus: Canadian Parties in the 1960's," *Social Research*, Vol. 30, No. 3, Autumn 1963, pp. 367-390; and his "Les transformations des partis politiques canadiens," *Cahiers de la société canadienne de science politique*, No. 2, 1966, 54 ff.

12 William H. Riker, *Federalism: Origin, Operation, Significance*, Little, Brown and Co., Boston and Toronto, 1964, p. 129.

13 For details of the post-Confederation party system see Escott Reid, "The Rise of National Parties in Canada" reprinted in Hugh G. Thorburn (ed.), *Party Politics in Canada*, Prentice-Hall of Canada Ltd., Toronto, 1963, pp. 14-21.

14 Dale C. Thomson, *Alexander Mackenzie: Clear Grit*, Macmillan Co. of Canada, Toronto, 1960, p. 316, quoting a letter from Mackenzie to Pelletier, Nov. 1, 1877, *Letterbooks*, VII, p. 292.

15 For details of McGreevy's activities and functions see *Report of the Royal Commission in reference to certain charges against Sir A. P. Caron*, The Queen's Printer, Ottawa, 1893, *passim*.

16 Canada, *House of Commons Debates*, July 10, 1931, pp. 4379-4391.

17 The former treasurer of the British Liberal Party, for instance, has presented evidence recently of the practice of the Canadian subsidiaries of English companies, with the apparent approval of their head offices, of regular subscriptions "to two [Canadian] parties." See the articles by John Pardoe, M.P., "Paying for Politics," *The Times*, London, October 13 and 14, 1969.

18 In recent years the elected members of Parliamentary parties have been able to use the services of the research division of the Parliamentary party. But

more direct research aid was provided in 1968 to the Leader of the Opposition and the leaders of smaller parliamentary groups in the House of Commons budget. Canada, *House of Commons Debates,* Nov. 15, 1968, pp. 2790-99, 2829. This assistance has also been extended to members of the Government Party since the Spring of 1970.

19 Maurice Duverger, *Political Parties,* Methuen & Co. Ltd., London, 1954; John Wiley and Sons, New York, 1954, *passim.*

20 See the evidence of Mr. Einar M. Gunderson, the close colleague and principal fund-raiser for British Columbia's Social Credit Premier W. A. C. Bennett, in *Minutes of Proceedings and Evidence,* No. 16, Canada, House of Commons, Standing Committee on Finance, Trade and Economic Affairs, Tuesday, Oct. 18, 1966, pp. 694-696.

21 *Report of the Committee on Election Expenses, op. cit.,* p. 32.

22 *Statement as of December 31, 1968,* prepared by the Chief Electoral Officer, M. Jean-Marc Hamel.

23 This figure and the following statistics have been calculated from a report of the Chief Electoral Officer contained in Canada: Chief Electoral Officer, *Sessional Paper* (showing declared election expenses for each candidate in the General Election of June 25, 1968). A return tabled in the House of Commons, November 7, 1968. See Appendix A.

24 For details of this and other scandals see Richard Gwyn, *The Shape of Scandal,* Clarke, Irwin & Co. Ltd., Toronto, 1965; and *Report of the Honourable Frederic Dorion, Special Inquiry 1964,* Ottawa, June 1965.

25 Harrill, *op. cit.,* pp. 243-244.

26 For details of this process as perfected in the Province of Quebec in the Duplessis era, see, *The Report of the Commissioners concerning the purchasing methods used in the Department of Colonization and the Government Purchasing Service from July 1st, 1955 to June 30th, 1960,* Commission of Inquiry instituted by Order in Council, No. 1621, of October 5, 1960, Province of Quebec, June 1963 (commonly known as the Salvas Commission); and see also, Pierre Laporte, "Les Élections ne se font pas avec des prières," Montreal, *Le Devoir;* a series of 40 articles, published October 1-6 and October 10 - November 15, 1956.

27 John Meisel and Richard Van Loon, "Canadian Attitudes to Election Expenses," in Paltiel et al., *op. cit.,* pp. 23-146.

28 *Ibid.,* p. 53.

29 For a discussion of this differentiation see Heard, *op. cit.,* chapter 10, pp. 269-274 in particular.

30 See J. L. Granatstein, "Conservative Party Finances: 1939-1945," in Paltiel et al., *op. cit.,* pp. 257-315, *passim.*

31 See Meisel and Van Loon, in *Ibid., passim;* and Khayyam Z. Paltiel, Jill McCalla Vickers and Raoul P. Barbe, "Candidate Attitudes Toward the Control of Election Expenses," in *Ibid.,* pp. 459-594, *passim.*

PART II

MONEY
AND ELECTIONS

TWO

BUSINESS AND "BAG-MEN": THE LIBERAL AND CONSERVATIVE PATTERN*

A detailed review of the financial history of the Liberals and the Conservatives demonstrates that while there has been remarkably little change in the sources of party funds, substantial changes have taken place in the fund-raising structure of the parties since 1867. At the time of Confederation, the regular duties of leaders of the parliamentary parties included fund-raising and the allocation of campaign expenditures. Today, these tasks are usually carried out by party officials separate and distinct from the parliamentary leadership. This progressive differentiation of functions has resulted in increased specialization — the responsibility for budgeting and the allocation of campaign expenditures, and the raising of funds, have been divided — both tasks are clearly distinguishable from the party leadership. However, the extent to which these functions are separate and their relative degree of interdependence have varied from time to time within and among the two parties. This growing division of labour has permitted the modern party leaders to disclaim and escape some of the consequences of the occasionally illegal or illegitimate activities of their fund-raising specialists.

Changes have also occurred in the objects of campaign expenditures.

---

*For details of the financial structure of the dominant parties the author has had recourse to: Khayyam Z. Paltiel and Jean Brown Van Loon, "Financing the Liberal Party 1867-1965," and J. L. Granatstein, "Conservative Party Finance 1939-1945," in Paltiel et al., *Studies in Canadian Party Finance,* Committee on Election Expenses, The Queen's Printer, Ottawa, 1966, pp. 147-256 and 257-316, respectively. See also *Report of the Committee on Election Expenses,* The Queen's Printer, Ottawa, 1966, pp. 225-257.

Social evolution and technological developments have shifted the emphasis from the organization and mobilization of a relatively small number of voters at the poll and constituency levels to more sophisticated and expensive means of communication with a mass electorate. In the early years widespread corruption was engaged in and large amounts were spent to convey electors (or impersonators) to the polls. The dispensing of vast quantities of alcohol was a feature of all campaigns. Newspaper support was obtained either through outright ownership or suborned by way of patronage.[1] Greater reliance on the print media followed the expansion of the franchise, population growth and the spread of literacy. Organization was not neglected but increasing amounts were spent on communication particularly in the actual period of the election campaign. This pattern became prominent in the last generation with the advent of radio and television broadcasting.

Business has been and remains the prime source of funds raised to finance the activities of the Conservative and Liberal Parties. In the past century, there have been some shifts in the amount and proportion of funds derived by either party from one or another group and sector within the commercial, industrial and financial community, but nothing has occurred to end their reliance on such sources. Efforts by both the Conservatives and the Liberals to broaden their base of financial support have been a consistent disappointment. A relative handful of contributors remain the mainstay of the two parties. Incumbency, the beneficiary's prospects of electoral success, the acceptability of the party's leader and his policies all appear to affect the size of the donation made. But the business community is accustomed to hedging its bets and has tended to share its giving between the two parties — customarily 60 percent of a corporate donor's gift has gone to the party in office and the balance to the other.[2]

Inevitably the fund-raising structures of both the Liberal and Conservative Parties tend to reflect the nature of the sources from which they derive support. Party solicitors have been for the most part financiers, businessmen, corporation lawyers and members of "old" families with access to the firms and wealthy individuals on which the parties depend. However, greater success at the polls has permitted the Liberal Party to elaborate a more sophisticated financial structure than its long-time Conservative rival whose repeated leadership crises have estranged former supporters.

SECTION A — THE PRE-1920 PATTERN

Disciplined parties did not emerge until some time after 1867. Party lines had been blurred by the coalition ministry which had brought about Confederation[3] and their delineation was further impeded by the continued survival of "loose fish" or "ministerialists" who would back whichever group held office but whose support at the hustings could not be relied upon. The fundamental problem facing a parliamentary leader at that time was the creation of a stable working majority. One essential instrument was the allocation of funds raised by the party leaders themselves amongst their followers.[4] Such monies came from their personal resources and contacts in the business world, particularly those who had benefited or expected to benefit from government favour. The personal burden on Sir John A. Macdonald, for instance, was not inconsiderable. As one contemporary put it:

> He was pretty deeply in debt for a good many years, but I think his indebtedness was due to political exigencies and not to speculations or personal extravagance. I have heard him speak with much bitterness, and I do not doubt with much truth, of the scandalous way in which he was often pillaged by his political supporters and of the niggardly contributions he received from wealthly members of the party. But this is a very common experience with public men.[5]

Thus Macdonald and Sir Georges Etienne Cartier became involved in soliciting and collecting funds from government contractors, such as Sir Hugh Allan and the group bidding for the construction of the Pacific Railway. When the Pacific Scandal was revealed, the leaders' personal connection could not be repudiated and the Conservatives went down to defeat in 1874. But the last word in the matter should be left to Macdonald whose explanation to the Governor General best describes the financial structure of the parties in those days.

> It has been stated in the English press that I should not have mixed myself up in these money matters, but should have left it to our Carleton and Reform Clubs. This may be true, indeed is true, if such clubs existed; but, as a matter of fact, the leaders of political parties have always hitherto acted in such matters, and there can be no special blame attached to a leader for continuing the invariable practice on this occasion.[6]

The Liberals in this period found themselves in a similar position. The 1872 and 1874 campaigns were financed "with a very trifling expenditure of money"[7] according to party sympathizers but Macdonald estimated that the Liberals in 1872 spent more than a quarter-of-a-million dollars in the effort to oust the Conservatives.[8] According to George Brown the party depended almost entirely on a few members who "could come down handsomely";[9] amongst whom was the president of a bank which allegedly benefited from government deposits when the Liberals won. However, it was not until ten years after its defeat in 1878 that the Liberal Party was able to regularize its income and financial structure, the years of Mackenzie and Blake having been marked by a hand-to-mouth existence on a modicum of funds.[10]

In devising the National Policy of tariff protection and railway building in 1878 Macdonald found a program which appealed to the manufacturing interest and was designed to attract funds to the party coffers.[11] In the years that followed, fund-raising emerged as a specialized task of the party organization as disclosed in 1891 in the McGreevy Scandal, the second major Canadian railway scandal.[12] The charges involved members of the federal cabinet who were alleged to have diverted government funds allotted for railway subsidies to the support of government candidates in the Province of Quebec. From 1882 to 1887, Thomas McGreevy, M.P., had fulfilled the functions of principal collector and treasurer of the Conservative Party for federal campaigns in Quebec. Together with the federal Minister of Public Works and the Postmaster General (both posts traditionally having had vast sources of patronage at their disposal), McGreevy was a member of a three-man team acting on oral and written orders from his ministerial colleagues regarding the distribution of funds in the elections of 1882 and 1887.[13] This nascent specialization removed the leadership from direct contact with the fund-raising process, an essential step in the evolution toward the contemporary structure.

With Wilfrid Laurier's accession to the leadership in 1887, the fund-raising pattern of the Liberal Party took a similar turn. The unofficial group of party collectors typical of the period of Mackenzie and Blake gave way to organizers like Edgar and Preston in Ontario and Pacaud and Tarte in Quebec who were intimately concerned with provincial as well as federal campaigns and who devoted a major portion of their time to party political affairs.[14] When the party won power in 1896 these activities became centralized within the Cabinet; a pattern which was to be repeated in the latter years of the King régime. Like their Conservative rivals the Laurier Liberals learned to make their policies acceptable to manufacturing and railway interests. The incumbent Ontario Liberals under Mowat were, according to Cartwright, "all more or less mixed-up with the manufacturing element in one way or another."[15] The election of 1891 demonstrated that the program of commercial union with the United States alienated business. In 1891,

> They [the Liberals] faced an organized and aggressive campaign by the business interests which considered themselves in peril. Manufacturers . . . wholesalers . . . bankers . . . worked quietly and effectively in town and city. Most effective of all the anti-reciprocity forces was the Canadian Pacific. . . .[16]

> In every constituency but one — that of Marquette, where Robert Watson won a six-vote victory, wholly through oversight, Van Horne declared — through which the main line of the Canadian Pacific ran, a Conservative was elected.[17]

The Liberals turned to rival railway interests as illustrated by the Baie des Chaleurs Railway scandal in which Ernest Pacaud, one of Laurier's organizers, obtained $100,000 for the provincial party ($10,000 of which reached Laurier) from a railway concession.[18] Laurier's Cabinet included, amongst others linked with the business world, Sir William Mulock and the Hon. William Paterson who were well connected with Toronto banking and Ontario manufacturing interests.[19] Once it was in office, the Liberal Party did not hesitate to exploit all the sources of patronage afforded a party in power. In the words of a sympathetic observer, Laurier himself had "a large toleration for patronage."[20] Elsewhere the same commentator states:

> There was . . . a system of purchase of public supplies and distribution of public contracts which effectually excluded political opponents from any profitable access to the treasury. . . . From the privileged dealers in supplies subscriptions were taken, and from many contracts there was a generous return to the party fund.[21]

It should occasion no surprise that members of Laurier's Cabinet were denounced as "corruptionists."[22]

Under Laurier efforts were also made to systematize the organizational and fund-raising apparatus of the party. Around 1891, Joseph Israel Tarte began to switch his allegiance to the Liberals, joining the party at its first convention in 1893.[23] For four years prior to the victory of 1896, he worked as Laurier's full-time chief organizer in Quebec, raising funds, setting up a permanent office in Montreal and organizing Liberal clubs in the constituencies.[24] Although Tarte received only $1,200 of the $4,000 annual salary suggested on his behalf by Laurier, "his travelling expenses were high and his postal bill [from 1894 to 1896] alone was about $1,000."[25] After 1896, Tarte continued these activities from within the Cabinet as the salaried Minister of Public Works, organizing election campaigns and liquor plebiscites for the party in Quebec and New Brunswick.[26] His close involvement with these activities made it difficult to escape charges of corruption and he was forced to leave the Government in 1902.[27]

Once in power, the Liberals tended to divide organizational responsibilities on a regional basis among Ministers from the areas concerned. Thus Clifford Sifton took charge of fund-raising and organization in Western Canada with an occasional foray into Ontario.[28] Similar roles were played by Charles Hyman, W. S. Fielding, Andrew Blair, William Pugsley and Raymond Préfontaine.[29] In contrast to Sir John A. Macdonald's active role, however, the Liberal Party's fund-raising structure in the Laurier era was not concentrated under the party leader. Laurier was clearly aware of and occasionally assisted the activities of the fund-raisers.[30] But centralization occurred only at the regional level. Fund-raising remained in the control of the regional leaders with dire results for Laurier when he was abandoned by Sifton in the Reciprocity Campaign of 1911[31] and other leaders in the Unionist crisis of 1917. As a contemporary observer put it: "The former Liberal leaders of Ontario, New Brunswick, Manitoba, Saskatchewan and Alberta were members of the Union cabinet. The party organizations, the party rolls, and the party war chests had gone with them."[32]

The dependence of the two parties on the business community was reemphasized in the election of 1911, which returned the Conservatives to office under Borden. Aroused by Laurier's espousal of reciprocity, the financial community supported his opponents. The Canadian Pacific Railway headed by Sir William Van Horne threw its considerable weight against the Liberals,[33] and Sir Hugh Graham, publisher of the Montreal *Star,* employed the talents of his staff and about a quarter-of-a-million dollars on behalf of the Conservatives.[34] About $200,000 was channeled to the Quebec Nationalist leaders, Armand Lavergne and Henri Bourassa, in order to defeat the Liberals by splitting the French-Canadian vote.[35] Protectionism and big business had successfully asserted their power.

In the aftermath of defeat, the Liberals renewed the stillborn attempts to build an extra-parliamentary structure first broached at the convention of 1893. In 1912 a Central Information Office was created with William Lyon Mackenzie King as director with an annual salary of $2,500.[36] Publication of a monthly journal, the *Canadian Liberal Monthly,* began in 1914 but the development of the office was seriously hampered by wartime splits and the failure of the regions to supply the needed funds.[37] In 1915 a National Liberal Advisory Committee was established but it, too, proved ineffective. Finally in 1919 a National Liberal Organization Committee was established composed of representatives of the federal and provincial Liberal Parties. Andrew Haydon was elected Executive Director of the national office;[38] holding the complete confidence of the newly chosen leader, William Lyon Mackenzie King, he laid the groundwork for the party's return to power in 1921.

SECTION B—THE KING ASCENDANCY 1920-1948

Under Mackenzie King an effort was made to reshape the fund-raising structure of the Liberal Party by placing this task in the hands of party organizers and solicitors outside the House of Commons. A highly decentralized finance committee had been set up by the Convention of 1919 but this provision remained merely formal,[39] as did the proposal to finance party activities through the collection of membership dues.[40] The campaign of 1921 was like all those which followed since it was financed from business sources by such men as Haydon and his successors who had close contacts with the financial and industrial community.

King's acceptability to these groups had been demonstrated in the support he received in the 1919 leadership Convention.[41] In subsequent years, he was at great pains to preserve this backing, a fact that was revealed in his various Cabinet appointments.

[King] angled for the support of the Montreal business community when he made Gouin the minister with the greater prestige and bade Lapointe serve as Minister of Marine and Fisheries.[42]

King's diary in 1926 confirms this ongoing preoccupation.

Lemieux wd (sic) be the strongest man to keep the Montreal group with us, the Bank of Montreal, C.P.R. etc. to lose that group is to consolidate the Conservative Party give it new life & financial support . . . I do not want to lose Quebec support, much less incur active opposition of pwerful mffgs. (sic) interests. . . .[43]

Although King personally preferred the assistance of wealthy men such as P. C. Larkin of the Salada Tea Co., Vincent Massey, J. E. Atkinson of the Toronto *Star,* and Senator Donat Raymond of Montreal,[44] the party welcomed corporate donations: much of which came from oil companies, construction contractors, railroads, banks and manufacturers.[45] For the 1935 campaign the party was able to raise substantial sums from mining magnates in Toronto; and in 1939 the Hon. James G. Gardiner also received funds from the meat-packing industry to help defeat Duplessis and the Union Nationale in the crucial Quebec provincial election of that year.[46] King always attempted to blur his role in the party's financial affairs. At the 1919 Convention "provision was made for raising money for the party needs although, on King's insistence, it was expressly understood that he was to have nothing to do with the party funds."[47] However, he did participate by writing letters of appreciation to donors, requesting funds for support of the national office and encouraging such efforts by members of his Cabinet.[48] Nevertheless, the prime responsibility for raising campaign funds fell on formal and informal party officials like Andrew Haydon and Norman Lambert.

The structure of the Liberal fund-raising system during the twenties was laid bare by the Senate and House of Commons investigations of 1931 and 1932 into the most notorious corporate contribution of the period, known as the Beauharnois Affair.[49] Before the 1930 election the Beauharnois Power Company, which was anxious to obtain a hydro-electric power concession on the St. Lawrence River, through one of its promoters, R. O. Sweezey, had given the Liberal Party between $600,000 and $700,000; a sum of $200,000 offered to the Conservatives was turned down by their leader R. B. Bennett.[50] (Some funds from this source may have reached a prominent Tory official.) The money was collected on behalf of the Liberals by Senator Andrew Haydon, the party's national treasurer, and Senator Donat Raymond, its "trustee" for the Province of Quebec. The money was paid in several instalments, about half of it being used to defray Quebec requirements.[51] Mr. King denied any knowledge of the relationship between Sweezey and Haydon, despite his own connections with Senator A. W. L. McDougald, a member of the Beauharnois group, who had donated to the Liberals in 1921, 1925 and 1926 and had covered the party leader's hotel expenses in Bermuda in 1930.[52] Haydon's testimony, that he "made no explanations or disclosures regarding campaign funds to Mr. King, or to any of his Ministers or to anyone else,"[53] lent credence to the disclaimer.

In the House of Commons debate on the Affair, King asserted that his role as party leader involved no responsibilities for fund-raising whatsoever.

> There must be a division of labour in a political party . . . it is the duty of the political head of the party to see to matters of policy, to be able to discuss questions on the floor of parliament, and throughout the country; but . . . it is not his business to get out the literature of the party, nor is it his business to organize political campaigns. Such work belongs to the rank and file of the party and to those who will act on their behalf.[54]
>
> I would not care to have to deal with the questions with which this house has to deal and be possessed of an inventory of those who had contributed to the party funds. All the time that I have been the leader of the party I have never asked a single individual to make a contribution to a political campaign. I have had no knowledge of what the political campaign funds were.[55]

These ingenuous arguments did not impress his opponents. The Prime Minister R. B. Bennett retorted scornfully: "I have always held that the receiver of stolen goods was a criminal."[56]

The investigations illuminated several features of the Liberal Party's structure. Evidently, the party maintained two major campaign funds, one for Quebec and another for the rest of Canada; the size of its relative share revealed that in party finance, as in other features of party organization, Quebec enjoyed a special status.[57] Haydon's role as King's "most trusted political adviser"[58] demonstrated the two benefits of separating the parliamentary leadership from the fund-raising process. On the one hand the party profited from the activities of specialists and on the other hand the leader was able to dissociate himself personally from any discredit such as that which fell upon Haydon. Haydon had resigned as general secretary of the National Liberal Association in 1922 and had been named to the Senate in 1924. Holding no elected office in the party, he continued to be its mainstay as national treasurer. Because he had no official position, the public tended to assume that he was acting as King's personal agent. But King was able to escape much of the opprobrium which clung to Macdonald two generations earlier, and in his apologia paved the way for contemporary party leaders who have generally adopted his stance.

The Party's central office had been allowed to languish in the years of power. Active at election time, it received little money in other years.

Haydon and a few other "stalwarts" often advanced the necessary funds to keep the doors open.[59] The failure of a constituency quota system forced Charles Murphy, who had been paying office expenses from his personal funds, to lock up the office.[60]

After the Beauharnois Affair, King "imposed a central office with a permanent staff on the party";[61] it was to take on the organizational and fund-raising duties formerly undertaken by Senator Haydon. In 1933 the Hon. Vincent Massey assumed the presidency with Norman Lambert as party secretary. King wrote asking wealthy Liberals to contribute to a capital fund to assure the future of the office, but by 1933 only half the $50,000 goal was achieved.[62] A renewed effort to raise $200 per constituency for the national headquarters also failed. Ultimately, for inter-election revenue the party relied on the traditional sources of campaign funds.[63] The only successful "popular" appeal rested on a system of "associate memberships" in the National Liberal Federation. By 1933, 50,000 party supporters were said to have paid a $1 annual fee, receiving party publications in return;[64] but the fact that it was not resumed after the "political truce" of World War II suggests that administrative and production costs may have outweighed the financial returns from the system.

Campaign fund-raising continued to rest on the party's traditional foundations. "Informal Montreal and Toronto finance committees" were appointed for the 1935 campaign. "The National President, or the national organizer with advice from the party leader"[65] appointed collectors who solicited funds in the brief period before polling day. In 1936 another effort was made to reorganize the collection system.

> . . . Lambert made a Dominion-wide tour, talking to the key people in the various provinces. He then appointed a representative of the national party organization in each province. Sometimes this was the local provincial organizer . . . Lambert's scheme involved collections . . . at regular yearly intervals, thus building up a party reserve for election day. The funds collected were to be split on an equitable basis between provincial and national party organizations.[66]

By extending the period and defining the responsibility for collections, the process was to be made more efficient. But sources were to remain as unproductive as heretofore.[67] The system seems to have lagged during the war years and by 1953 had disappeared altogether.[68] Theoretically, the above changes were designed to create a fund-raising apparatus separate from the parliamentary membership. In practice, however, the return to office inevitably drew the attention of King and several members of the Cabinet to this phase of party work.[69]

Membership in the fund-raising structure of the party never became completely distinct from membership in the House of Commons, but

neither was it taken over by the parliamentary leadership. A much more
informal pattern evolved. Through the nineteen-thirties and forties the
group of fund-raisers expanded. Prominent persons with extensive business
connections, sometimes with a seat in the House or Senate, took on the
task of collection. Gradually the group assumed a recognizable structure:
two collectors in Montreal, two in Toronto and one in Winnipeg, Edmonton or Calgary, and occasionally Vancouver.[70] In 1945 the major fund-
raisers included five Senators (Daigle, Campbell, Raymond, Robertson and
Bouffard), two Cabinet Ministers (J. G. Gardiner and C. D. Howe), and
two present and future party presidents (J. Gordon Fogo and Duncan K.
McTavish).[71] Five key fund-raisers were members of the Liberal Party's
National Campaign Committee in 1945.

In the latter years of the King régime the party developed a modern
organizational structure. The office, which had been closed again during
World War II, was charged with the printing and distribution of party
literature. Paid officials were responsible for coordinating party activities in
the provinces. In the forties with the development of broadcasting the
Liberals made their first recorded use of advertising agencies in election
campaigns.[72] The National Campaign Committee, which included Cabinet
Ministers when the party was in office, supervised the allocation of funds
by organizers such as Norman Lambert.[73] In the 1945 campaign, the last
fought under King's leadership, the party spent well in excess of $3 million,
according to one reliable informant.[74]

SECTION C — CONSERVATIVE PARTY FINANCES 1920-1948

The financial history of the Conservative Party in the generation following
the First World War confirms the influence of business on the fortunes of
the two major parties. Arthur Meighen and R. B. Bennett felt this pressure
but the financial blockade of Dr. R. J. Manion established beyond doubt
the fate which awaited a Conservative leader whose policies outraged
finance and industry.

In 1911 these forces had combined to defeat Laurier and the Liberals on
the Reciprocity issue. Nor had they hesitated to make use of Bourassa and
the Nationalists in an effort to divide Quebec. Among these interests were
railway promoters like William Mackenzie and Donald A. Mann, of the
Canadian Northern Railway, and the Montreal financial community. Of the
former, the late Dr. O. D. Skelton stated:

> No little of the decline of the Liberal Party from its original ideals, no little of
> its overthrow of 1911 . . . no little of the Union movement in 1917, can be traced
> directly to the manoeuvres and exigencies of Mackenzie and Mann or of those
> who saw gain in their profit or in their emergencies.[75]

While yet a backbencher during the Borden government, R. B. Bennett had occasion to complain that these promoters were donating funds to both parties indiscriminately in the search for influence.[76]

After 1921, the issue of railways in politics returned to haunt the newly chosen and defeated leader Arthur Meighen. His so-called radicalism generated opposition from Lord Atholstan of the Montreal *Star* and other spokesmen of Montreal business interests. Anti-Meighen Conservatives received assistance, yet his own followers found it difficult to campaign because of the lack of funds.[77] Organizational work fell into disarray because of financial limitations[78] and proposals to build a sustaining fund from disinterested contributions were simply laughed out of court. As a prominent Conservative, Sir Joseph Flavelle, reported in 1927:

> I asked them [a group of influential Conservatives] if they would join me in creating the basis of a fund by subscribing fifty thousand dollars, with a pledge that neither we nor others who would add to the fund would seek for recognition from the Conservative party because we had contributed these sums. These gentlemen were too generous . . . to laugh. . . .[79]

Under the leadership of R. B. Bennett, the party's fortunes improved. The successful election campaign of 1930 was managed by the prominent businessman and veteran, Major-General (later Senator) Alexander Duncan McRae, with the fund-raising assistance of prominent financiers like the Montreal stockbroker and investment dealer, Brigadier-General George Eric McCuaig. More than half-a-million dollars was raised from about 50 corporations and individuals in Montreal, including Lord Atholstan and electric power magnate Sir Herbert Holt.[80] But the most remarkable feature of Bennett's leadership was the extent to which he personally financed the campaign and the party. One follower declared that the leader spent $750,000 of his own funds in the 1930 campaign.[81] His biographer has stated that:

> He [Bennett] had controlled the E. B. Eddy Company because he owned it. From 1927 he had controlled the Conservative Party organization because he was paying a large part of its costs, a state of affairs good neither for himself nor the party.[82]

Williams attributes much of the party's subsequent organizational weakness to this feature of Bennett's leadership which eliminated many former sources of support.

> R. B. Bennett must bear a large share of the responsibility for the declining ability of the Conservatives to obtain funds because he would not allow party organizers to accept money which he thought to be "tainted" and he attempted to provide most of the campaign funds himself with the aid of a few friends.[83]

By 1935 the Conservative machine was a shambles. The Depression had driven all of its provincial allies from office as unemployment undermined the party's electoral support. Bennett's "New Deal" legislation alienated business. With nowhere else to turn, the party became completely dependent on the leader and his resources. But in the aftermath of electoral defeat, this personal burden became too much to bear. As Bennett explained to a friend in 1937 shortly before his retirement:

> I am afraid you do not understand the difficulties that I have to meet in my present position. I am fairly well off and I am now convinced that no man of means can afford to be head of the party. They expect me to provide money for everything and I have reached a stage when I cannot reasonably be expected to do more. You will probably gather that I have a comparatively large income when I say to you that in the ten years I have been leader of the party I have paid income tax amounting to upwards of $600,000, and at the end of that time I have not only saved no money, but I still owe for party obligations $150,000. That certainly cannot continue. The results of the last election indicate that my services are no longer required and, while I have not arrived at any definite decision, I think it not improbable that I may make other arrangements for the balance of my life, be it short or long.[84]

And on that plaintive note sounding the failure of personal financing by the leader, he left a sorry inheritance to his successor, Dr. R. J. Manion, who was selected leader over the opposition of the Canadian Pacific Railway and its spokesman, Sir Edward Beatty, at the Conservative Convention of July 1938.[85]

Manion had aroused the antagonism of St. James Street because of his hostility to the C.P.R.'s plan to unify its management with that of the C.N.R. The plan would have meant substantial savings for the C.P.R.'s shareholders but for Manion it represented a "complete monopoly in the hands of one company of Canadian railway transportation. It would mean the building of huge voting power under one management. . . ."[86] He was urged to seek an accommodation with Meighen who was by now acceptable to the interests and he was warned by the mining promoter, Major-General D. M. Hogarth, that failure to compromise with the railway would result in a blockade by the "money bags."

> As things stand whilst they are almost unanimously against King this element will be unanimously for him with their money and influence in preference to you and the Conservative party. . . . I believe with all my heart and soul that this means disaster at the polls and that as time goes on many . . . who are presently behind you will be influenced by this element and you will be left holding an empty bag. You can't compete with the C.C.F. . . . Even if you should . . . King and laissez-faire will be seized upon as the house of refuge and security. I beg you to heed this warning in shaping your course of action.
> The railway problem is of course the key to the situation — the Montreal gang through various ramifications will freeze up the financial channels right across the country. . . .[87]

The results of Manion's refusal were reflected almost immediately in the paucity of funds collected the year before the outbreak of the Second World War. Manion had inherited a $35,000 deficit left over from the 1935 campaign and in addition there was a need for money to rebuild the party's shattered organization. Despite the efforts of Allan Ross and Harry Price, Toronto businessmen who had been authorized by Manion to collect funds, the sums raised were insufficient to cover expenses and retire the outstanding debt.[88] Fund-raising ground to a halt with the political "cease fire" declared in September 1939 and the party still owed approximately $22,500.[89] On the other hand, the Liberals had little difficulty in raising funds to defeat Duplessis in the Quebec provincial election of 1939.

The "snap" election precipitated by the unforeseen dissolution of January 1940 caught the Conservatives unprepared and in disarray, bemused by the political "cease fire," their offices closed, and the party tangled in debt, haunted by the railway problem and the revived conscription issue. Manion forcefully rejected suggestions that the situation could be retrieved by his agreement to withdraw from the leadership in favour of Meighen following the election.[90] Financial representatives were appointed to coordinate fund-raising in the provinces in company with the usual committees in Montreal and Toronto; the latter also served as a "little strategy group . . . [dealing with] . . . all kinds of political questions."[91] George B. Foster K.C., a prominent corporation lawyer and director of many companies and lynch-pin of Conservative fund-raising in Montreal for two decades, served as head of the Montreal group, along with Senator C. G. Ballantyne of the Sherwin-Williams Co. and Col. W. P. O'Brien, a prominent stockbroker. The Toronto Committee included another prominent stockbroker, Rupert Bain, leading provincial and federal Conservative politicians with business connections and Price and Ross (who served as National Treasurer).[92] But despite their efforts, Granatstein reports that "in 1940 the traditional methods did not work for the Conservative Party."[93] The threatened blockade had become real. Abandoned by the Montreal financial community, ignored by the C.P.R., the Montreal *Star,* the Bank of Montreal, and the power companies and heavy industry, the Party raised nationally far less than $250,000 from contributors of $1,000 or over, compared to the more than half-a-million dollars raised in 1930 in the Montreal area alone.[94]

The party ended the 1940 campaign with a deficit of $25,000 having spent only $500,000 on the entire campaign, with less than $100,000 available for Ontario.[95] The Liberals, on the other hand, were variously reported to have spent double to four times that amount; Senator Norman Lambert put the spending of his party in 1940 at $1 million.[96] Opposition to Manion and his philosophy, the attraction of contracts for munitions and Liberal prospects cost the Conservatives dearly[97] in an election which saw only 39 members returned to the benches of the Official Opposition.

In May 1940 the Conservative caucus chose R. B. Hanson to replace Dr. Manion. Acting as interim leader the former strove to keep the party alive in the face of a serious organizational and financial crisis which threatened the survival of the party and the maintenance of its staff and headquarters. As a last resort, Members of Parliament and Senators provided the minimum required. This appeal raised $3,350 for the latter half of 1940.[98] Fear of organized labour and the surging growth of the CCF roused Hanson and the then president of the National Trust Company, Mr. J. M. Macdonnell, to organize a meeting of party friends in Montreal in January 1941 "for the purpose of considering what they could do to assist the Party to resume the important part it has played in the maintenance of constitutional government in Canada."[99] Committees were established in Montreal and Toronto to raise $60,000 for a revitalized federal party. The Montreal committee consisted of the traditional stalwarts, Foster, Ballantyne and O'Brien; "none of the Toronto group was an experienced 'bag-man',"[100] but they were prepared to experiment with new devices such as fund-raising dinners. Half the required sum was raised, the Toronto committee providing twice as much as Montreal.[101]

The coup which installed Arthur Meighen as leader at the end of 1941 upset these arrangements and imposed another fund-raising structure under General McRae who had performed a similar function for R. B. Bennett prior to the election of 1930; but it was aborted with Meighen's defeat in the York South by-election of February 1942.[102] To retrieve the situation, Macdonnell, who had opposed Meighen, organized the famous "thinkers" Conference at Port Hope in 1942. The aim was to give the party a new image — no longer was it to appear as the captive of the "interests." Another step in this process was the choice of John Bracken, the Liberal-Progressive Premier of Manitoba, as leader at the subsequent Winnipeg Convention in December 1942 which saw the Party emerge with a new name as the Progressive Conservative Party.[103]

The culminating stage in this transformation was to be the "democratization" of the party's financial basis at the suggestion of Richard A. Bell, who was appointed National Director of the party by Bracken in April 1943.[104] Under Bell's direction a Popular Finance Campaign was projected in the Autumn of 1943 to raise $1 million through small donations of up to $25, the gifts to be acknowledged by certificates suitable for framing. The services of a prominent advertising agency were engaged. Door-to-door canvassing, backed up with publicity in the press, on radio and by direct mail, was carried on under the direction of a professional fund-raiser. Receipts, however, were "most disappointing," and failed to cover even the overhead costs of the drive.[105]

Notwithstanding the lack of success of such mass-based financing, Bell's organizational activities under Bracken were financially successful. Backed by the "Old Guard," party income in 1943 exceeded $173,000,[106] and expenditures in 1944 almost tripled, falling just short of half-a-million dollars.[107] The end of the Second World War found the party in the best financial position in almost two decades. Under the late J. S. D. Tory, Q.C., a leading Toronto corporation lawyer, who in 1944 had taken over the job of national finance chairman from the investment dealer J. H. Gundy, Chairman and President of Wood, Gundy and Co. Ltd., the party's fund-raising apparatus was rebuilt.[108] Prominent financiers who had been active in the past rejoined as active solicitors in the provinces. Although the party's popular vote fell in the June 1945 election, it did manage to increase its parliamentary representation to 67 seats.

The modest gains made in the 1945 election were not due to a lack of funds. One estimate places Conservative expenditures at $1.5 million.[109] Considerable sums were spent on "candidates' schools," publicity and gifts to soldiers overseas; the first recorded use of an advertising agency by a Canadian party was also made at this time. Large amounts were also contributed to support candidates in their local campaigns. On the other hand the Liberals, benefiting from their years of power and the fears of the CCF in the business community, were alleged by one Conservative source to have had a "slush fund" of more than $5 million for the campaign.[110]

The experience of the Conservatives under Meighen, Bennett, Manion and Bracken casts a lurid light on the Canadian party system. Clearly, no man, no matter how wealthy, can hope to control and finance a Canadian political party through his proper resources for any considerable period of time. On the other hand, no major Canadian political party has been able to raise sufficient funds for electoral purposes on a widespread popular basis. Lacking alternatives, Canada's two major parties were dependent on corporate business enterprise in a position to veto the ambitions of leaders and policies which ran counter to what these contributors considered their best interests. The continuity of the fund-raising structure throughout this period suggests that access to the business community was limited to only a few in either party. The subsequent history of both parties presents no evidence to disturb this picture.

SECTION D — LIBERAL PARTY FINANCE 1949-1968

The fund-raising pattern shaped in the preceding period continued unimpaired during the St. Laurent régime and re-emerged after the Diefenbaker interlude with relatively minor modifications in Lester B. Pearson's term as leader. The most recent federal general election campaign of 1968 under Prime Minister Pierre-Elliott Trudeau was financed in a manner similar to that of his predecessors. The system tended to evolve rather than change abruptly, becoming more sharply defined and stable during the nineteen fifties and sixties. The only significant breaks in the continuity of the structure affected the relationship of the Quebec wing with the Liberal Federation of Canada and the latter's ties with the Quebec Liberal Federation.

Business continues to supply the bulk of Liberal Party funds. In 1953 Harrill estimated that 50 percent of its campaign funds were derived from commerce and industry, 40 percent from businessmen linked to particular firms, and only 10 percent from private individuals.[111] One party official reported that 300-400 contributors donated the $7.5 million raised in 1957 at the national level.[112] Little is received from Members of Parliament, Senators, trade unions or private individuals, although local candidates may benefit from such sources. Substantial gifts "in kind" such as videotapes, broadcasting time, advertising space and other services are often provided by corporate supporters.[113] But cash is preferred. "It would appear that a donation of a thousand dollars is expected today from purely local firms and that for large businesses the scale rises considerably higher."[114]

The business centres of Ontario and Quebec are clearly the main source of national campaign funds. Some other provincial party organizations, such as British Columbia, Alberta and Manitoba, are more or less self-sustaining in federal general election campaigns; elsewhere provincial campaign committees are provided with funds from the national fund-raisers by transfer from Ontario and Quebec by the National Campaign Committee.[115] The Maritime committees receive larger subsidies from the national party than other provincial parties. Saskatchewan also benefits to a lesser extent from such inter-party transfers; however, friction between the provincial leadership under Premier Thatcher and federal spokesmen in the province have often inhibited this relationship. It should be noted, too, that national party fund-raisers and contacts have often been employed in financing provincial election campaigns notably in the Maritimes and Western Canada.[116]

There is a close correspondence between the party's fund-raising machinery and those to whom it makes its principal appeal.

> The traditional practice has been to have standing Finance Committees, staffed by trusted party supporters in the corporate and business world, in the major cities — Montreal, Toronto, Winnipeg, and Vancouver. The Montreal and Toronto Committees are the most important because these cities are in the areas which are the sources of most of the party's funds.[117]

The activities of these committees were directed by the National Treasurer of the Liberal Party of Canada. This post is distinct from the formal position of Secretary-Treasurer of the Liberal Federation of Canada, filled in recent years by Gordon R. Dryden, Q.C., of Toronto, a symbolic position concerned mainly with the ongoing work of the Federation as distinct from the campaign fund. The National Treasurer, appointed by the Party Leader, has been the party's key fund-raiser. The most recent holder of this post was Senator John B. Aird, Q.C., who was named to the upper house by the Rt. Hon. Lester B. Pearson and who continued as Party Treasurer until July 1968, resigning after the last election campaign. Since that time the Liberal Federation has appointed a Director of Finance to coordinate fund-raising activities, but it is too early to judge whether the party can dispense with such figures as the Party Treasurer. It is clear, however, that in the recent past the party had a parallel financial structure, a formal one for the Federation and another which carried out the essential task of collecting campaign funds; it is the latter which concerns us here. The "first string" fund-raisers in Montreal, Toronto, Winnipeg, Calgary, Edmonton and Vancouver are often Senators, Cabinet Ministers, Members of Parliament or simply prominent Liberal supporters.[118] Under these key men are those who do much of the collecting; about twenty men, for example, performed this task in Ontario during the 1965 campaign.[119] The most useful are those who have established contacts in business circles.

> In the 1950's the Presidents of the Federation, Fogo, Woodrow, McTavish and Matthews also engaged in collecting funds for the party. . . . However, this is not normally the function of the President. Fund raising happened to be the **forte** of these Presidents, especially the latter two, and it would have imposed some hardship on the Party had these men terminated this activity upon assuming their new position.[120]

The apparent independence of the fund-raising structure and its continuity, even when the leadership of the party changes, are maintained by its method of recruitment no less than by its function and focus on a narrow social sector. New collectors are recruited informally by those already active in the field from among rising young businessmen and lawyers identified with the party; sometimes participation is a family tradition. This capacity for self-renewal helps explain the autonomous character of this aspect of party activity.

However, the fund-raising structure is far from monolithic. Federal arrangements within the party provide for considerable decentralization at the provincial level. Provincial party organizations are not required to submit detailed reports to the National Treasurer.[121] Thus, the fund-raising structure of the federal party in Quebec enjoys a special status autonomous of both the national and provincial party organizations. In June 1965 the late Guy Favreau, then leader of the federal Liberals in Quebec, announced a "democratization" of the Quebec-wing.[122] Traditional fund-raisers such as Senator Louis Gelinas were replaced by a four-man Finance Committee under the chairmanship of a prominent Montreal stockbroker, M. Jean Ostiguy, a nephew of one of Laurier's key solicitors, Senator Marcellin

Wilson.[123] The chairman was to choose the other three members of the Committee which was responsible to the National Leader through the head of the Quebec wing.[124] Parallel steps were taken by the heads of the provincial Quebec Liberal Federation to endow itself with its own financial apparatus. Three persons closely connected with Montreal banking and investment circles — Roger Letourneau of Quebec City and René Hébert and Peter Thompson of Montreal — were authorized to receive funds between elections; others were to be accredited during election campaigns by the treasurer of the QLF. But accountability was to be limited to the provincial party leader, who was to receive a report of the amounts available (not including the names of the donors) to the party.[125] Other provincial party organizations, such as that in Newfoundland, have developed their own methods of pooling and allocating campaign funds.[126]

Central direction and regional execution also characterize the campaign planning and budgeting process of the Liberal Party. The National Campaign Committee always includes at least one fund-raiser, a representative of the Leader, and one from the national office; the three main aspects of party activity, policy-making, finance and organization are thus represented.[127] The Committee includes the National Campaign Chairman, appointed by the National Leader, and the provincial chairmen selected on the advice of the provincial associations.[128] The national office estimates its needs as do each of the provincial committees. Alternative advertising and spending programs are determined to fit varying prospects of campaign income. Allocations and disbursements are made by persons specially appointed in each province as revenues flow in by means of cheques written on "trust" accounts. The national budget covers national advertising outside Quebec, surveys, leaders' tours, special events, radio and television costs and the supplementary costs of the national office. Provincial committees may decide on additional advertising. Grants to candidates and an alternative lump sum payment to Quebec are also included in the budget.[129]

Here, too, Quebec is a special case. The National Campaign Committee decides the general direction of the campaign, but in Quebec funds are collected and expended by the Quebec committee which also has charge of campaign advertising in the province.[130] On the other hand, the Ontario provincial office ceases to function during federal campaigns and is taken over by the National Campaign Committee which absorbs all costs until the week after polling day. In the Maritimes there are few distinctions between federal and provincial party organizations. In Western Canada this relationship varies from election to election with the personal links between federal and provincial party leaders in each province.[131]

Campaign expenditures in the contemporary period clearly demonstrate the growing emphasis by the Liberal Party on communication and national advertising in the mass media. Financial aid to candidates has also continued to absorb a large share of the campaign budget. Various estimates are available for the global sums spent by the party in the two decades under consideration. Prior to the 1949 election the Liberal Party, according to Hon. C. G. Power, spent more than $3 million at the national level, and another $3 million at the constituency level in support of candidates.[132] Party literature distributed in that election was estimated to have cost approximately $750,000.[133] Liberal costs in Quebec alone during the 1953 campaign were stated by Power to have been $2 million;[134] others calculate that the national party's total costs in that campaign were in the neighbourhood of $6 million.[135] Aid to Liberal candidates in 1953 was not less than $3,000 per constituency, according to the late Senator Lambert.[136] Harrill calculated that both major parties in the 1950s allocated their national campaign budgets in the following manner: tours of party leaders, 10%; headquarters organization, 10%; national advertising, 40%; individual candidates, 40%.[137]

For the 1957 campaign the Liberals amassed one of the largest warchests in the party's history. Twenty-two years of uninterrupted power permitted the party to raise close to $8 million from a relative handful of contributors. One writer suggested that the Liberal national office spent about three times the sum spent by the Conservative office in that campaign.[138] Aid to candidates absorbed about one-third of the budget; leaders' tours and associated events cost more than half-a-million dollars. Expenditures on national publicity soared with the introduction of television which was used for the first time in this campaign.[139]

Liberal expenditures from 1958 to 1965 do not appear to have reached the heights attained in 1957. The years in the wilderness, the need to rebuild a shattered organization and morale, and the frequency of elections imposed their respective restraints. In the aftermath of defeat, a new leader, Lester B. Pearson, was chosen. The party, nearly bankrupt, faced the threat of closing some of its offices. A suggestion by the new leader that a national system of membership fees be instituted was rejected as impracticable.[140] In 1958, however, the federal party in Ontario established a sustaining fund known as the Liberal Union, consisting of a group of about 400 supporters who annually contribute $100 each. The Century Club in Manitoba fulfills a similar function by raising money through the sale of tickets to dinners, a practice which has since spread to other areas.[141] Occasional mailed appeals for funds were less successful; one such appeal in 1961-62 cost $4,000, yielding only $6,800; another resulted in a net loss of $500.[142] Useful as such devices might be for rallying the faithful and providing a modicum of sustaining funds, they were clearly insufficient to provide for proper campaigning. The party continued to rely on the business community, but the Rivard Affair attests to the temptations which beset a party which is short of funds.

Several sources report that Liberal resources in the 1965 campaign were less than adequate.[143] However, all the evidence indicates that the party suffered no shortage in 1968. In 1965 disenchantment with the Conservative leader, John Diefenbaker, worked against his party, but similar misgivings seem to have affected the Liberals because of the Hon. Walter L. Gordon; the latter's purported economic nationalism allegedly alienated certain sections of the business community which limited its giving to the Liberal Party in that campaign. No such inhibitions affected contributors in 1968. Party officials in admittedly partial and incomplete estimates state that national and provincial campaign committees spent approximately $3.5 million and $4 million in the 1965 and 1968 campaigns, respectively.[144] Substantial portions of these sums were spent by the Quebec campaign committee which "runs its own campaign." The expenditures of the National Campaign Committee in 1965 and 1968 (other than expenditures by the Quebec and other provincial committees) are summarized in Table 2-I.

Table 2 - I
LIBERAL NATIONAL EXPENDITURES
FOR THE 1965 AND 1968 CAMPAIGNS

Item	1965	1968
	$	$
Radio Time and Production	70,000	80,000
Television Time and Production	200,000	261,000
Newspapers and Publications	55,000	40,000
Printed and Other Material	75,000	75,000
Leader's Tour	30,000	94,000
Other Travel	10,000	5,000
Administration	45,000	52,000
Other Expenses	40,000	50,000
Total	525,000	657,000

Sources: Letter from Senator John B. Aird, Q.C., National Treasurer to the Chairman of the Committee on Election Expenses, January 26, 1966; and letter to the author from Mr. John R. Woods, Director of Finance, Liberal Federation of Canada, January 7, 1970.

In addition to the amounts spent by the national office there are other substantial costs; in 1965 these included the retirement of the accumulated deficit of the Federation amounting to $250,000.[145] Other large items are the sums allotted to the provincial committees and financial aid to the constituencies. In Ontario more than $405,000 was distributed for the latter purpose in 1965, compared to candidate allocations of $447,000 and

$457,000 in 1962 and 1963 respectively.[146] Candidate grants in 1968 were sent out in four "waves," ranging from $750 to $1500 each, and totalled almost $800,000 including about $360,000 turned over to the Quebec organization as a lump sum.[147] An additional $190,000 collected in Ontario and Quebec was transferred to provincial fund-raisers in Western Canada and certain Atlantic provinces.[148]

Expenditures by provincial committees, given the present dearth of information, can only be guessed at from descriptions of their respective campaigns. Clearly such special events as the rallies held in Hamilton and Victoria in 1968 are very costly even with the financial participation of the national office both directly and by way of general subsidy.

Official statistics confirm that Liberal expenditures rose by more than one-third at the candidate level from $2.6 million in 1965 to $3.5 million in 1968.[149] Other data suggest that similar rises occurred at other levels. Thus, total expenditures on the broadcasing media rose by more than 13 percent,[150] most of the increase being represented by expenditures at the national level.[151] Similar increases occurred in the costs of the leader's tour in an obvious attempt to capitalize on the charismatic attraction of the newly chosen party leader Pierre-Elliott Trudeau.

Between election campaigns, the national office of the Liberal Federation maintains contact with the provincial organizations and the membership through meetings, bulletins and *The Journal of Liberal Thought*. The operating costs of the office, according to Regenstreif rose from $45,000 in 1945 to over $150,000 in 1960.[152] In 1966 the National Treasurer wrote that "a minimum of $200,000 is required annually at the national level to maintain both the party and the Federation. . . ."[153] According to the present Director of Finance:

> The cost of maintaining national headquarters over the past year [1969] ran to about $363,000. Broken down, this would be as follows:
>
> | | | |
> |---|---|---|
> | 1. | administration | $ 67,000 |
> | 2. | finance | 20,000 |
> | 3. | organization | 46,000 |
> | 4. | communications & public relations | 30,000 |
> | 5. | policy research | 30,000 |
> | 6. | student liberals | 20,000 |
> | 7. | premises | 50,000 |
> | 8. | national meeting & special project | 100.000.[154] |

In this period the party has also had to meet the costs of three national leadership conventions at decennial intervals in 1948, 1958 and most recently in April 1968. Such functions involve two types of cost, the organizational expenses for the Convention proper and the costs incurred by the various aspirants for the leadership in rallying support. The latter are similar to campaign expenses and are financed by supporters of the various nominees. Some of the seven main aspirants in 1968 are alleged to have spent about $400,000 each in seeking the leadership; it would not appear far-fetched to estimate that approximately $2 million was expended by the aspirants in cash or in kind on travel, telecommunications, organization and entertainment prior to and during the Convention.

Party expenditures are given in Table 2-II.

Table 2 - II
LIBERAL LEADERSHIP CONVENTION EXPENDITURES — 1968

Item	Amount
	$
Transportation and Reception	31,000
Hall and Decorations	162,000
Communications	5,000
Program	5,000
Printing	13,000
Simultaneous Translation and Interpreters	11,000
Administration	10,000
Miscellaneous Expenditures	5,000
Total Expenditures	242,000
Income from Registration Fees	181,000
Net Cost	61,000

Source: Letter from Mr. John R. Woods, Director of Finance, Liberal Federation of Canada, January 7, 1970.

For purposes of comparison, the costs of the Liberal leadership Convention may be set beside those for the federal New Democratic Party Convention in 1969. The latter's expenditures on facilities and administration amounted to $35,000, and revenues from registration and souvenir program advertising came to $25,000; this left a net deficit of $10,000 to be covered by the federal party.[155]

SECTION E — PROGRESSIVE CONSERVATIVE FINANCE 1949-1968

Since the Second World War the fund-raising structure of the Conservative Party has shifted to Toronto from its former stronghold in Montreal — the structure usually consisting of finance committees in Toronto and Montreal, with the national chairmanship located in Toronto. Other persons selected by the chairman solicit funds in Hamilton, London and Ottawa.

According to Mr. R. A. Bell, the fund-raising and the budgeting functions were separated except where donors earmarked funds for particular regions. The national director of the party was responsible for the allocation of campaign funds, subject to the supervision of the finance committee.[156] As in the case of the Liberal party, most provincial party organizations benefited from transfers of funds from the two main financial centres. The heaviest subsidies went to the Maritimes followed by Saskatchewan and Manitoba; only the British Columbia and Alberta parties maintained a relative degree of self-sufficiency.

In the 1949 election Conservative expenditures at all levels amounted to more than $3 million.[157] Under the leadership of the former Premier of Ontario, George Drew, who was most acceptable to Bay Street, money was more forthcoming than under Bracken or Manion. A reliable source places national party expenditures in the 1953 campaign at nearly $2.5 million, the average constituency receiving a grant-in-aid of $4,000. Apart from Quebec which received a lump sum for redistribution, specific grants were decided at national headquarters by the national director.

Under Mr. Diefenbaker's leadership after 1956 the allocation system changed. The new national director, Allister Grosart, pooled the funds which had been collected. Provincial committees were given sums proportionate to the number of seats in a province, the basic amount being $3,000 per constituency. The provincial committees could allocate these sums at their discretion.[158] This ended the traditional centralization of Conservative budgeting and made for more effective campaigns but led to charges of discrimination against Quebec. Cries that the Conservatives were trying to govern without Quebec representation followed this attempt to put allocations in that province on a footing similar to the others.

The upset victory of 1957 was financed at minimal cost, with national party income variously estimated as ranging between $1 and $1.7 million (or a mere third of that available to the incumbent Liberals).[159] Most of this money was used to subsidize candidates, the rest being spent on Mr. Diefenbaker's triumphal tour, administrative expenses and a bare minimum of paid advertising. Only in the latter part of the campaign were sums of "considerable magnitude" made available by the business community which had been counting on a Liberal success.[160] The situation was reversed in 1958. Benefiting from incumbency, Conservative Party revenues increased, permitting grants of approximately $6,000 per constituency to each provincial committee and expenditures of $100,000 on the leader's national campaign tour. Estimates of Conservative national spending in the 1958 campaign, which produced the greatest electoral landslide in Canadian history, range between $2.7 million and $3 million.[161]

The 1962 Conservative campaign followed the pattern of its two predecessors but with even greater resources. Allocations per constituency increased in some cases to $9,000 and helped bring spending at the national level to well over $3 million. In 1963 the wheel turned full circle and income shrank. Some observers assert that unspecified amounts of the sums collected were withheld from the national party organization in favour of local or provincial party organizations.[162]

According to information provided by party officials total expenditures by the national headquarters in the 1965[163] and the 1968[164] campaigns were approximately the same, $1.95 million and under $2 million respectively. A similar breakdown of major expenses was also supplied; about $1,250,000 in constituency grants, $500,000 to $600,000 for all media advertising, and $165,000 to under $200,000 for the leader's tour, travel and headquarters administration.

Be that as it may, it is clear that Mr. Robert Stanfield's selection as leader of the Conservatives restored business confidence in the party. Far larger sums were available at the local level in 1968 than in the previous election as evidenced by the 39 percent rise in spending by reporting candidates.[165] Furthermore, party expenditures on the broadcast media rose by almost 60 percent from 1965 to 1968; on television the Conservatives actually outspent the Liberals.[166]

CONCLUSION

The most obvious generalization to be made about the finances of Canada's two older parties is that they look almost exclusively to business for the supply of their campaign funds. Both the Liberals and the Conservatives have tried with varying degrees of enthusiasm to widen their base of financial support. To date these efforts have been a failure. On the other hand electoral success and greater income stability has allowed the Liberal Party to develop a more sophisticated fund-raising structure than its long-time rival. The Conservatives still depend on the part-time efforts of volunteers whereas the Liberals have made the breakthrough to professionalism with a full-time Director of Finance, accompanied by a more elaborate system of budgeting and allocation. Large sums continue to go in direct aid to candidates, but increasing shares of party funds are spent on communications and the mass media at the national level as the electronic media and the airplane tour replace the newspaper and stump meetings of former years.

FOOTNOTES

1 See Chapter 5.
2 Ernest E. Harrill, "The Structure of Organization and Power in Canadian Political Parties: A Study in Party Financing," unpublished Ph.D. dissertation, University of North Carolina, Chapel Hill, 1958, pp. 243-44 and 269-70.

3 Hon. Sir George Ross, *Getting into Parliament and After,* William Briggs (now The Ryerson Press), Toronto, 1913, pp. 17-18.

4 Donald Creighton, *John A. Macdonald, The Old Chieftain,* The Macmillan Co. of Canada Ltd., Toronto, 1955, pp. 47ff.

5 Rt. Hon. Sir Richard J. G. Cartwright, C.M.G., P.C., *Reminiscences,* William Briggs (now The Ryerson Press), Toronto, 1912, p. 49.

6 Cited in Joseph Pope, *Memoirs of the Right Honourable Sir John Alexander Macdonald, G.C.B.,* The Musson Book Co., Toronto, 1894, p. 553.

7 Cartwright, *op. cit.,* p. 192.

8 Creighton, *op. cit.,* pp. 140-141.

9 *Regina v. Wilkinson* (H.T. 40 Vict. 1877) Quoted in *Upper Canada Queen's Bench Reports,* Vol. 41, 1878, p. 11.

10 Khayyam Z. Paltiel and Jean B. Van Loon, "Financing the Liberal Party," in Paltiel et al., *Studies in Canadian Party Finance,* Committee on Election Expenses, The Queen's Printer, Ottawa, 1966, pp. 152-154.

11 W. T. R. Preston, *My Generation of Politics and Politicians,* Rose Publishing Co., Toronto, 1927, p. 126.

12 *Report of the Royal Commission in reference to certain charges against Sir A. P. Caron,* Queen's Printer, Ottawa, February 6, 1893, Sessional Papers, No. 27.

13 *Ibid.,* pp. 161-164.

14 Paltiel and Van Loon, *op. cit.,* pp. 176-182.

15 *Laurier Papers,* Letter from Cartwright to Laurier, October 15, 1887, quoted in W. R. Graham, "Sir Richard Cartwright, Wilfrid Laurier, and Liberal Party Trade Policy, 1887", *Canadian Historical Review,* XXXIII, No. 1, p. 12.

16 O. D. Skelton, Life and *Letters of Sir Wilfrid Laurier,* Vol. I, Oxford University Press, Toronto, 1921, p. 416.

17 *Ibid.,* p. 418.

18 *Royal Commission of Inquiry into the Baie des Chaleurs Railway Matter, 1891,* Reports, Proceedings and Depositions, Quebec, 1892, pp. 51-65; see also Joseph Schull, *Laurier, The First Canadian,* The Macmillan Co. of Canada Ltd., Toronto, 1965, pp. 254, 257.

19 Paltiel and Van Loon, *op. cit.,* pp. 156-157.

20 Sir John S. Willison, *Sir Wilfrid Laurier,* Makers of Canada series, Oxford University Press, London and Toronto, 1926, p. 468.

21 Sir John S. Willison, *Reminiscences, Political and Personal,* McClelland and Stewart Ltd., Toronto, 1919, pp. 280-281.

22 *Ibid.,* p. 277.

23 Laurier Joseph Lucien Lapierre, "Politics, Race and Religion in French Canada: Joseph Israel Tarte," unpublished Ph.D. dissertation, University of Toronto, Toronto, 1962, pp. 242-50.

24 *Ibid.,* pp. 303-304, p. 311.

25 *Ibid.*

26 *Ibid.,* p. 366, p. 398.

27 *Ibid.,* p. 526. Tarte is responsible for the deathless phrase "Les élections ne se font pas avec des prières" — Prayers do not win elections.

28 John W. Dafoe, *Clifford Sifton in Relation to His Times,* The Macmillan Co. of Canada Ltd., Toronto, 1931, p. xiv.

29 Willison, *Reminiscences Political and Personal, op. cit.,* p. 277; Schull, *op. cit.,* pp. 458-9.

30 Paltiel and Van Loon, *op. cit.*, pp. 181-182.
31 Skelton, *op. cit.*, Vol. II, p. 372.
32 Schull, *op. cit.*, pp. 591-592.
33 *Ibid.*, p. 523; see also Dafoe, *op. cit.*, p. 364.
34 Mason Wade, *The French Canadians*, 1760-1945, The Macmillan Co. of Canada Ltd., Toronto, 1955, p. 602.
35 *Ibid.*, p. 598. See also Robert Rumilly, *Histoire de la province de Québec*, Éditions Bernard Valiquette, Montréal, 1948, v. XVI, p. 75.
36 Samuel Peter Regenstreif, "The Liberal Party of Canada; A Political Analysis," unpublished Ph.D. dissertation, Cornell University, 1963, pp. 124-126. Reissued in Xerox (63-4827) by University Microfilms Inc., Ann Arbor, Michigan, 1965.
37 *Ibid.*, pp. 127-128.
38 *Ibid.*, p. 136.
39 Harrill, *op. cit.*, p. 256.
40 H. Blair Neatby, *William Lyon Mackenzie King: The Lonely Heights*, University of Toronto Press, Toronto, 1963, p. 327.
41 H. S. Ferns and Bernard Ostry, *The Age of Mackenzie King: The Rise of the Leader*, William Heinemann Ltd., London, 1955, pp. 295-6, 331; R. MacGregor Dawson, *William Lyon Mackenzie King: A Political Biography, 1874-1923*, University of Toronto Press, Toronto, 1958, pp. 298ff.
42 Steven Muller, "Canadian Prime Ministers 1867-1948," unpublished Ph.D. dissertation, Cornell University, 1956, p. 562; Gouin held directorships in 14 "major" corporations in 1922.
43 As quoted in the diary of William Lyon Mackenzie King, cited in Neatby, *op. cit.*, p. 14.
44 Regenstreif, *op. cit.*, p. 423, n. 90.
45 Harrill, *op. cit.*, pp. 236-237.
46 J. L. Granatstein, "Conservative Party Finances: 1939-1945," in Paltiel et al., *op. cit.*, p. 272.
47 Dawson, *op. cit.*, pp. 326-327.
48 Harrill, *op. cit.*, p. 262; Memo, King to Cabinet 1939, cited in Regenstreif, *op. cit.*, p. 198; Neatby, *op. cit.*, p. 331.
49 Canada, House of Commons, Special Committee on Beauharnois Power Project, *Minutes of Proceedings and Evidence, 1931*; Canada, Senate, Special Committee on Beauharnois Power Project, *Report and Proceedings, 1932*.
50 Canada, House of Commons, *Debates*, July 31, 1931, p. 4399.
51 Senate, *op. cit.*, p. 243; House of Commons, *op. cit.*, p. xx.
52 Neatby, *op. cit.*, pp. 371-373.
53 Senate, *op. cit.*, p. 189.
54 Canada, House of Commons, *Debates*, July 30, 1931, p. 4380. Reproduced with the permission of the Queen's Printer for Canada.
55 *Ibid.*, p. 4384. Reproduced with the permission of the Queen's Printer for Canada.
56 *Ibid.*, p. 4382.
57 Neatby, *op. cit.*, pp. 328-329.
58 *Ibid.*, p. 331.
59 *Ibid.*, p. 330.
60 Regenstreif, *op. cit.*, pp. 134-135.
61 Neatby, *op. cit.*, p. 385.
62 Regenstreif, *op. cit.*, pp. 168-169.

63 Neatby, *op. cit.*, p. 388.
64 Regenstreif, *loc. cit.*
65 Paul Henry Heppe, "The Liberal Party of Canada," unpublished Ph.D. dissertation, University of Wisconsin, 1957, p. 145. See also J. W. Lederle, "National Organization of Liberal and Conservative Parties in Canada," unpublished Ph.D. dissertation, University of Michigan, 1942, *passim.*
66 Lederle, *op. cit.*, p. 192.
67 Interview with Senator Norman Lambert, cited by Harrill, *op. cit.*, p. 236.
68 *Ibid.*, p. 257.
69 Paltiel and Van Loon, *op. cit.*, pp. 188-189.
70 Confidential interview, cited *Ibid.*, p. 189.
71 Regenstreif, *op. cit.*, p. 212.
72 *Ibid.*, pp. 186-187.
73 Lederle, *op. cit.*, p. 193; and Regenstreif, *op. cit.*, pp. 212-14.
74 Harrill, *op. cit.*, p. 181.
75 Skelton, *op. cit.*, Vol. II, p. 419.
76 Ernest Watkins, *R. B. Bennett*, Bellhaven House Ltd., Toronto, 1963, p. 84; see also Roger Graham, *Arthur Meighen*, Vol. II, Clarke, Irwin & Co. Ltd., Toronto, 1963, pp. 72-82.
77 *Ibid.*, pp. 338-339; and Grattan O'Leary, "When Can We Escape This Deadlock?", *Maclean's* XXXIX No. 4, February 15, 1962, p. 45.
78 John R. Williams, *The Conservative Party of Canada: 1920-1949*, Duke University Press, Durham, N.C., 1956, p. 149.
79 Letter quoted in Arthur H. U. Colquhoun, *Press, Politics and People: The Life and Letters of Sir John Willison*, The Macmillan Co. of Canada Ltd., Toronto, 1935, p. 111; see also *Ibid.*, p. 287.
80 Granatstein, *op. cit.*, pp. 259-260, citing the Manion Papers.
81 F. W. Turnbull (Cons. M.P. Regina) *Regina Leader-Post*, Sept. 28, 1932, p. 1.
82 Watkins, *op. cit.*, p. 167.
83 Williams, *op. cit.*, p. 145.
84 Quoted in Watkins, *op. cit.*, pp. 230-231.
85 For a description of Beatty's efforts, see Granatstein, *op. cit.*, pp. 262-267.
86 From Manion's speech at Smiths Falls, July 24, 1939, cited *Ibid.*, p. 264.
87 Hogarth to Manion, June 7, 1939, quoted *Ibid.*, pp. 267-268.
88 *Ibid.*, pp. 269-270.
89 *Ibid.*, p. 272.
90 *Ibid.*, pp. 275-276.
91 The National Treasurer, Allan Ross, in a letter to Manion, March 7, 1940, quoted *Ibid.*, p. 276.
92 *Ibid.*, pp. 276-277.
93 *Ibid.*, p. 278.
94 *Ibid.*, p. 280-281.
95 *Ibid.*, p. 279-280, citing a letter from Ross to Manion, April 29, 1940.
96 Harrill, *op. cit.*, p. 180.
97 Granatstein, *op. cit.*, p. 281.
98 *Ibid.*, p. 283.
99 *Hanson Papers*, Macdonnell to guests at meeting, January 13, 1941, quoted, *Ibid.*, p. 285.
100 *Ibid.*, p. 286.
101 *Ibid.*, p. 288.

[102] *Ibid.*, pp. 288-291.
[103] *Ibid.*, pp. 292-293.
[104] *Ibid.*, p. 295.
[105] *Ibid.*, pp. 297-301.
[106] *Ibid.*, p. 301.
[107] *Loc. cit.*
[108] *Ibid.*, p. 302.
[109] *Ibid.*, pp. 303-304.
[110] *Hanson Papers,* R. B. Hanson letter to H. A. Bruce, June 14, 1945 quoted *Ibid.*, p. 305.
[111] Harrill, *op. cit.*, pp. 251-252.
[112] Confidential Source. See also James Scott, "Political Slush Funds Corrupt all Parties," *Maclean's,* September 9, 1961, p. 13ff.
[113] Paltiel and Van Loon, *op. cit.*, p. 171.
[114] Harrill, *op. cit.*, p. 236.
[115] Letter from Senator John B. Aird, Q.C., National Treasurer of the Liberal Party to the Chairman of the Committee on Election Expenses cited in *Report of the Committee on Election Expenses,* The Queen's Printer, Ottawa, 1966, p. 248; and letter from Mr. John R. Woods, Director of Finance of the Liberal Federation of Canada, to the author, dated January 26, 1966 and January 7, 1970 respectively.
[116] Paltiel and Van Loon, *op. cit.*, p. 193.
[117] Regenstreif, *op. cit.*, p. 211.
[118] See *Ibid.*, p. 212 for a list of persons who have been important fund-raisers in recent years.
[119] *Globe and Mail,* Toronto, October 11, 1965, p. 7.
[120] Regenstreif, *op. cit.*, p. 175.
[121] Letters from Senator Aird and Mr. Woods see footnote 115.
[122] *Star,* Montreal, June 7, 1965, p. 3.
[123] *La Presse,* Montreal, September 1, 1965, p. 28.
[124] Jean-Pierre Fournier, "La Vieille Garde Libérale Croule," *Le Magazine Maclean,* October 1965, p. 56.
[125] Premier Jean Lesage, "Cartes sur Table," speech delivered in Quebec City, May 26, 1965.
[126] Letter, Hon. J. W. Pickersgill, P.C., M.P., to the Committee on Election Expenses, January 22, 1966, cited in *Report of the Committee on Election Expenses,* The Queen's Printer, Ottawa, 1966, p. 239.
[127] Paltiel and Van Loon, *op. cit.*, p. 192.
[128] *Ibid.*, pp. 203-204.
[129] *Ibid.*, p. 205.
[130] *Ibid.*, and Fournier, *loc cit.*
[131] Paltiel and Van Loon, *op. cit.*, pp. 205-207.
[132] Cited by Harrill, *op. cit.*, p. 181.
[133] Blair Fraser, "Our Illegal Federal Elections," *Maclean's* LXII, August 15, 1949, p. 85.
[134] Harrill, *loc. cit.*
[135] *Ibid.*, p. 182.
[136] Cited in Lois E. Torrence, "The National Party System in Canada, 1945-1960," unpublished Ph.D. dissertation, The American University, Washington, D.C., 1961, p. 453.
[137] Harrill, *op. cit.*, p. 202-203.

138 John Meisel, *The Canadian General Election of 1957*, University of Toronto Press, Toronto, 1962, p. 173. This study contains a full description of the campaign.

139 *Ibid.*, pp. 67-72.

140 Paltiel and Van Loon, *op. cit.*, p. 173.

141 *Ibid.*, p. 174; and *Report of the Committee on Election Expenses, op. cit.*, p. 188.

142 Paltiel and Van Loon, *loc. cit.*

143 For example, reports in the Ottawa *Citizen*, November 13, 1965, p. 17, and the Toronto *Globe and Mail*, September 30, 1965, p. 10.

144 Letters from Senator Aird and Mr. Woods, see footnote 115.

145 Letter from Senator Aird, see footnote 115.

146 See footnote 318 in Paltiel and Van Loon, *op. cit.*, p. 254. The total Ontario committee budget in those years was $610,000, $630,000 and $517,000 for 1962, 1963 and 1965. *Ibid.*, footnote 320.

147 Confidential document in possession of the author.

148 Letter from Mr. Woods, see footnote 115.

149 See Appendix A, p. 166.

150 See Table 5-XI, p. 90.

151 See Table 2-I, p. 38.

152 Regenstreif, *op. cit.*, p. 192.

153 Letter from Senator Aird, see footnote 115.

154 Letter from Mr. Woods, see footnote 115.

155 Letter to the author from Clifford A. Scotton, Federal Secretary of the New Democratic Party, November 17, 1969, which puts personal expenditures by delegates at $300,000.

156 Interview with Mr. R. A. Bell, June 1965.

157 Williams, *op. cit.*, p. 143.

158 Confidential source cited in *Report of the Committee on Election Expenses, op. cit.*, p. 255.

159 The larger figure is cited by Meisel, *loc. cit.*, p. 173.

160 *Ibid.*

161 Confidential source cited in *Report of the Committee on Election Expenses, op. cit.*, p. 256.

162 *Ibid.*

163 Information provided by the National President, Dalton Camp, and the National Campaign Organizer, Edwin A. Goodman, Q.C., cited in *Ibid.*

164 The 1968 figures are derived from a confidential letter addressed to the author by a highly placed officer of the Progressive Conservative Party, dated October 2, 1969.

165 See Appendix A, p. 166.

166 See Table 5-XI, p. 90.

THREE

THE GRASS-ROOTS AND LABOUR: THE FINANCES OF THE COOPERATIVE COMMONWEALTH FEDERATION AND THE NEW DEMOCRATIC PARTY[1]

The New Democratic Party and its forerunner, the Cooperative Common-wealth Federation, had their beginnings in the fragmented farmer and labour movements whose union in 1932 was precipitated by the Great Depression of the nineteen thirties.[2] The new party (called CCF for short) adopted a constitution and a program, the "Regina Manifesto," drafted by a group of academic intellectuals, known as the League for Social Reconstruction, at its first national convention in 1933. Party organization was to reflect and serve as an instrument for the political realization of social democratic ideology. The radical concept of party organization shared by the party's leaders helps to explain the financial history of the CCF. In the matter of political finance, the CCF sought to develop a microcosm of economic democracy: a party financed at the "grass-roots" by small contributions from a broad base of citizens who would give freely as individuals.

But herein lies the paradox of the financial history of the CCF. The practical difficulties involved in operating on a grass-roots financial basis meant that the party was continually starved for essential funds. Only when associated with some organized form of giving through trade unions or farm groups was this form of fund-raising successful. Formally, such donations were made by individuals; however, since the funds were collected through organized groups, the term "individual" is somewhat ambiguous. Only in the special ambiance and political culture of the agrarian movement in Saskatchewan can "grass roots" fund-raising be said to have been successful; for clearly the impersonality of the trade

48

union "check-off" system is characteristic of highly structured collectivities rather than of individual acts of free will.

Having begun as a federation of local and provincial groups, the NDP retained a highly decentralized structure inherited from its predecessor the CCF.[3] Although most apparent in the early days of the party, this organizational pattern has dictated an upward flow of party funds: from the constituencies and their clubs to the provincial offices and parties and finally to the national or federal office and party. Fund-raising, budgeting, campaign expenditures and intra-party transfers between levels and provinces have all been shaped by this decentralization.

Given its doctrines and ideology, the finances of the CCF rested on its capacity to attract dedicated members at the provincial or federal constituency level. The first five years of the party were marked by valiant efforts to establish a "national office" and organizing staff but the absence of adequate financial resources had a debilitating effect on these plans.[4] It was only toward the end of its first decade, particularly after the appointment of Mr. David Lewis as secretary of the national office in Ottawa in 1938,[5] that the party's structure was consolidated. Increasing membership and the consequent growth in party revenues made possible continuous organizational work based on the activities of full-time organizers in place of the previous dependence on the part-time help of volunteers and the sacrifices of busy party officers.[6]

CCF EXPANSION 1938-1945

Despite uneven gains centred largely in Saskatchewan, British Columbia and Ontario, party membership in 1942 reached 20,000[7]; elsewhere, outside Cape Breton Island, progress was minimal. In 1941 the CCF became the official Opposition in British Columbia; in 1943 it achieved a similar status in Ontario; and its mass following in Saskatchewan swept it to power in that Province in 1944. But despite the cries of alarm spread by the supporters of free enterprise in the two traditional parties, the CCF surge had begun to recede by 1945, although the party tripled its representation in the House of Commons in the 1945 federal general election from eight to twenty-eight. By this time CCF membership reached its historic peak ranging between 80,000 to 100,000 in the period 1942-45.[8] After the Second World War membership fell sharply, never rising above 40,000 from 1946 to 1961 when it was transformed into the NDP.[9]

Like mass-membership parties elsewhere the CCF raised its campaign funds from members or supporters. The election efforts of 1935 and 1940 were financed by fees of one dollar per member and relatively large donations from the party's sitting Members of Parliament. Additional sums were raised also from supporters during the campaign. Collections were the responsibility of clubs[10] and constituency organizations and the proceeds were shared between the three organizational levels, local, provincial and national. This system put the prime burden of providing party funds on the constituency level which received little or no help from the national or provincial organizations. The support anticipated at the outset from farm, cooperative and labour groups did not materialize; only one trade union affiliate, the Cape Breton Local No. 26 of the United Mineworkers of America, provided financial assistance in the period between 1932 and 1940.[11] National office expenditures in the federal election years of 1935 and 1940 amounted to a mere $1,745 and $11,547 respectively. Given such wretched sums, no effective campaign budgeting could take place beyond an effort to provide some printed literature and display materials and advances to cover candidate's deposits in areas where even such modest sums were beyond the capacity of the local party.

The shifting financial fortunes of the CCF are indicated in the sums available to the party's national office. As recorded in Table 3-I below, income rose slowly from 1932 to 1938, followed by sharp increases during the Second World War; it hit its highest plateau prior to the 1949 federal general election. The nineteen fifties record a slow decline checked only in the election years of 1953 and 1957; the rise in the final year simply records the increase in trade union giving in anticipation of the foundation of the New Democratic Party.

The period of the Second World War was marked by the substantial growth of CCF provincial party organizations, notably in Saskatchewan. At the same time a system of provincial quotas was established to help maintain the national office by supplementing the latter's share of membership dues. These quotas were met with funds raised in special drives at the constituency level directed by the provincial offices concerned. But success depended on the existence of viable local organizations, as in Saskatchewan. Lipset has described how extensive community organizations evolved in rural parts of the province through which farmers participated in making decisions concerning their economic and political life. A broad and responsive system of communications developed linking the farmers and their leaders who were influenced by the ideology of the CCF; this grass-roots network facilitated the mobilization of mass support for the party.[12] Saskatchewan party membership attained 31,858 in 1945. This mass base was the primary source of the funds required for provincial election campaigns and for party activities in the inter-election period. Furthermore, the Saskatchewan party organization then and since has been a principal supplier of funds for national and federal party activities and campaign purposes.

To a lesser extent, the same period saw a strengthening of party organizations in British Columbia, Manitoba and Ontario. Even in Quebec,

Table 3 - I
CCF NATIONAL OFFICE RECEIPTS AND EXPENDITURES 1932-1960

Years	Receipts	Expenditures
1932-33	759.24	712.81
1933-34	1,475.28	1,312.26
1934-35	1,745.50	1,435.22
1935-36	2,832.36	2,244.80
1936-37	2,217.38	2,694.56
1937-38	3,442.93	3,266.48
1938-39	9,157.45	8,157.34
1939-40	11,547.45	11,544.77
1940-42*	16,497.99	17,164.92
1942-43	17,172.81	12,727.62
1943-44	28,320.92	33,355.08
1944-45	35,928.88	34,535.16
1945-46	38,166.46	29,820.57
1946-47	37,846.40	43,034.74
1947-48	49,507.80	49,959.27
1948-49	49,584.86	53,005.34
1949-50	31,242.00	48,417.00
1950-51	25,679.38	30,692.62
1951-52	29,980.14	29,759.93
1952-53	42,632.97	43,240.52
1953-54	36,921.61	41,123.92
1954-55	36,772.00	35,257.00
1955-56	35,261.00	32,763.00
1956-57	33,960.74	34,173.27
1957-58	36,498.00	32,852.19
1958-59	28,547.00	42,483.00
1959-60	48,994.00	44,117.00

*N.B. The figures for 1940-1942 cover the receipts and expenditures for two years.

Source: Based on yearly audited financial statements of the CCF National Office presented annually at the Meeting of the National Executive.

where the clerical "ban" against the party was lifted in 1943, membership almost reached 1,000 by 1945.[13] Fund-raising for the 1945 election began some two years earlier in the form of collections from individual supporters and members for a "Victory Fund." The biggest sums came from the large British Columbia, Saskatchewan and Ontario organizations which raised $78,048.50, $107,108 and $37,027.39 respectively, for the support of all party levels.[14] The Victory Funds in seven provinces provided a total of $83,822.38 to the National Office for the 1945 campaign. The sources were as follows: British Columbia $15,488.25; Alberta $7,120; Saskatchewan $42,491; Manitoba $6,812.50; Ontario $6,151; Quebec $100; and the Maritime Provinces $685; direct donations came to $5,015.[15] Other than a small donation from Local 26 of the U.M.W. included in the Nova Scotia quota, it appears that all these sums were raised in local financial and membership appeals. Although national office receipts exceeded original expectations by more than 60 percent, the overall 1945 campaign budget of $569,000 was not achieved;[16] estimates place the final figure of party expenditures at all levels in the 1945 election at slightly more than $300,000.[17] At the national level, major expenses included the following items: campaign publicity $47,126; subsidies to Nova Scotia, New Brunswick, Prince Edward Island, Quebec and the Yukon $6,690; organizers' salaries $10,229; organizers' expenses $3,129; campaign expenses of national officers $5,364; general office expenses $2,954.[18] Spending at the constituency and provincial levels in 1945 amounted to approximately $200,000, which covered the costs of campaign literature, display and newspaper advertising, and candidates' deposits in British Columbia, Saskatchewan, Manitoba and Ontario. Politically and financially, the 1945 election constituted the high point in the history of the CCF at the federal level. The deterioration of the party's position in the subsequent period, 1946-1960, was the prime impetus which led to the formation of the New Democratic Party.

CCF DECLINE 1946-1960

Declining membership and revenue in the last 15 years of the party's existence precluded budgeting on the scale of the 1945 election in any of the four campaigns which followed. Indeed, much of the money spent nationally and in the eastern provinces was raised in Saskatchewan where the party had held power since 1944 and where membership never fell below 6,500;[19] for example, the Hon. M. J. Coldwell reports that in the 1953 election campaign approximately $10,000 of the $13,000 raised in his constituency of Rosetown-Biggar was transferred by the Saskatchewan office for use in the national campaign.[20] In addition to Saskatchewan, only British Columbia and Ontario (at the constituency level) were able to maintain and carry the costs of presenting candidates.

Various devices were attempted in order to provide predictable amounts of funds to permit forward campaign planning at the national and provincial levels. In 1946 a "national membership fee" was instituted; enrolment of members remained a provincial responsibility but automatic remittance of one dollar per member to the national office was instituted. The modest receipts from this system are demonstrated in Table 3-II.

Table 3 - II
PROCEEDS OF NATIONAL MEMBERSHIP FEE
CCF NATIONAL OFFICE RECEIPTS 1947-1960

Year	Receipts
1947	$29,820.00
1948	38,782.00
1949	29,261.00
1950	20,238.00
1951	24,176.00
1952	24,204.00
1953	25,046.00
1954	18,273.00
1955	19,751.00
1956	24,771.00
1957	27,586.00
1958	24,852.00
1959	23,022.00
1960	29,097.00

Sources: CCF Records, Vols. 2 and 3, Public Archives of Canada, Reports of the Meetings of National Council on occasions when the annual Audited Statement was submitted 1947-1958. The Report of the 16th National Convention, Regina, August 9-11, 1960 contains the figures for 1959 and 1960.

The second attempt to increase the party's financial resources followed the sharp downturn in the 1949 federal general election, in which the CCF lost 18 of its 28 seats. This disaster had been presaged by financial stringencies at the national and provincial levels. Prior to the election the national executive had drafted a national office budget calling for expenditures of $60,000 on the campaign.[21] Despite two downward revisions first to $55,000 then to $42,000,[22] slightly less than $35,000 was received from all sources by the national office; the bulk was spent on radio and newspaper advertising, pamphlets and a subsidy to the Quebec CCF.[23] At the provincial level, the plight of the Manitoba party in 1949 was typical; less than $15,000 was expended by the constituency organizations and the provincial office spent about $2,000 or less than one-third the comparable figure for 1945.[24] These difficulties led directly to the "National Three-Year Expansion Programme" set up after the election.[25]

The Programme called for the establishment of a federal election fund, based as usual on a provincial quota system, and sought to put membership drives, membership renewals and financial appeals on a systematic basis, to achieve a goal of $175,000 over the three-year period. The response was tepid, netting only $9,656 or 11 percent of the projected goal at the end of the first year. Revised downward, the plan generated an even more dismal response in 1951 raising less than $5,000. It was finally laid to rest in 1953.[26]

Another effort to expand party revenue was attempted by the Ontario CCF. The "Ontario 500 Club," a group of more affluent members who pledged sums of money beyond their regular membership dues, provided somewhat more than ten percent of national office revenues in the last six years of the party's existence. Since 1961 the previously localized Ontario 500 Club reappeared in the NDP's national accounts in the form of the very lucrative item known as "sustaining membership" fees or contributions.[27] It should be noted, however, that although this device was reasonably successful in the affluent urban Ontario environment, it was less productive when transferred to the rural areas of Manitoba where it was known as the "5,000 Club" (1951-1953); collecting one dollar regularly from 5,000 members proved to be a financial and administrative nightmare and it was abandoned in 1953 as a complete failure.[28]

From 1953 onwards it was downhill all the way. The national office managed to raise and spend just over half the projected 1953 federal election budget of $40,000.[29] As in 1949, the largest sums were raised in British Columbia, Ontario and Saskatchewan, the latter supplying about half the sums received. The 1957 campaign was more dismal. Only $21,000 was raised for national office expenditures in Saskatchewan, Ontario and Manitoba; but $8,000 was provided from trade union sources.[30] At the provincial office level, 1957 was equally uninspiring. Saskatchewan continued to be the best financial source of all the provincial parties; but with the assistance of the labour movement, much of it in indirect form such as the payment for services, newspaper advertising and deposits for CCF candidates, the Ontario party spent close to $100,000 at the constituency and provincial office level.[31] The 1958 federal general election, the last to be contested by the party as the CCF, saw the party's representation in the House of Commons cut by more than two-thirds to a mere eight seats, and a further worsening in the financial position of the national office. Provincial support of the national campaign fell to a mere $8,500 derived from the British Columbia, Ontario and Saskatchewan organizations. Only the increasing financial participation of trade unions which donated $13,232 permitted the national office to match the meagre expenditures made on the previous campaign.[32] The only mitigating factor counterbalancing the deterioration of the party's financial position in this period was the increasing support received from the trade unions in British Columbia and Ontario. In the latter province it has been estimated that at least half the funds spent at the constituency and provincial office levels by the CCF in 1957 and 1958 was contributed by sections of the labour

Table 3 - III

CCF/NDP NATIONAL OFFICE INCOME (BY SOURCE) 1947-1969
(campaign funds not included)

Year	Total Receipts	National Member-ship Fees	Affiliated Member-ship Fees (Trade Unions)	Ontario 500 Club	Sustaining Member-ship Fees	Direct & Sundry Contri-butions
	$	%	%	%	%	%
1947	37,846	78.7	—	—	—	21.3
1948	49,507	78.3	—	—	—	21.7
1949	49,584	79.8	—	—	—	20.2
1950	31,242	72.5	—	—	—	27.5
1951	25,679	—	—	—	—	—
1952	29,980	85.3	3.5	—	—	11.2
1953	42,632	—	—	—	—	—
1954	36,921	49.7	37.2	—	—	13.1
1955	36,772	65.3	7.6	10.1	—	17.1
1956	35,261	60.0	30.0	10.0	—	—
1957	33,960	69.2	13.2	9.7	—	11.9
1958	36,498	68.1	11.4	12.3	—	—
1959	28,547	80.6	6.9	10.2	—	2.3
1960	48,994	59.4	11.5	14.9	—	15.2
1961*	—	—	—	—	—	—
1962	96,020	50.0	38.5	—	—	11.5
1963	181,185†	21.9	45.8	—	20.7	11.6
1964	141,697	26.4	44.7	—	32.1	5.8
1965	161,558	28.1	42.3	—	18.3	11.3
1966	164,644	30.5	45.0	—	17.9	6.6
1967	196,597	29.1	43.2	—	27.7	—
1968	179,793	27.3	43.7	—	24.0	5.0
1969‡	218,000	—	39.0	—	45.0	16.0

* Not available. Figures for 1962 cover the period Sept. 1, 1961 to August 10, 1962.

† 1963 covers a 16 month period ending Dec. 31, 1963.

‡ 1969 is an estimate provided by Clifford Scotton, NDP Secretary; national and sustaining membership fees were not separated as both are forwarded from the provincial to the federal offices; membership arrears are included under sundry for 1969.

Sources: CCF Records, Vols. 1, 2 and 3, 1958, 1959 and 1960; Report of 16th National Convention CCF, 1961; Reports of NDP Annual Conventions, 1962, 1963 and 1964; NDP Financial Statements 1966, 1967, 1968.

movement, most notably the Ontario Federation of Labour's Political Action Committee, the United Packinghouse Workers, the United Automobile Workers and the United Steelworkers.[33]

Two conflicting trends are displayed in the postwar financial history of the CCF. The forward thrust maintained during the war years faltered after 1945. Failure to displace the Conservatives as the leading Opposition Party provoked both a political and financial decline. However, while its financial resources were falling to their lowest point since the thirties, the financial base of the party had begun to shift. In the long-run this shift from dependence on individual donors to dependence on the trade unions has been more significant to the future of the party than the postwar decline in revenues. In 1961 the party changed its form and name, the labour movement emerged as the prime source of NDP funds, thus ending the chronic shortage suffered by its predecessor.

THE NEW DEMOCRATIC PARTY 1961-1968[34]

Soon after the NDP Founding Convention, the party's financial relationships with the trade union movement were formalized. The federal office has ceased to depend on quotas raised from the provincial parties. Since 1961 regular trade union contributions have been received in the form of affiliation fees raised by a fixed check-off of five cents per month from the wages of workers belonging to trade unions affiliated to the party. Such affiliation fees now provide approximately 40 percent of the party's regular income. The former reliance on individual membership dues has lessened, the sums realized from this source being only slightly higher than the special gifts of more affluent members raised through the sustaining membership. The consequent change in the party's financial situation is reflected in the receipts for ongoing expenses shown in Table 3-III, page 55.

The availability of assured resources on a regular and continuing basis has permitted the preparation of realistic and sound budgets for organizational purposes at the national level. With these revenues, ongoing expenditures at an annual rate of approximately $200,000 are being made as demonstrated in Table 3-IV.

Deficits are still incurred but given the assurance of a regular source of income these can easily be borne. However, a clear and more important index of the party's financial strength since 1961 has been the sharp rise in election expenditures, particularly at the national level. Here, too, the key element has been the availability of trade union support.

An accord with the provincial parties gives the federal office sole access to the national offices of the party's trade union affiliates for funds in support of federal election campaigns.[35] Prior to the election the federal executive meets with trade union representatives to learn the amounts

Table 3 - IV
NDP NATIONAL OFFICE EXPENDITURES 1965-68
(campaign expenses excluded)

Item	1965	1966	1967	1968
	$	$	$	$
Federal Office Administration	54,139	61,383	65,708	76,290
Federal Council and Executive*	6,836	11,411	11,649	17,374
Leadership Account	6,661	6,849	10,381	22,965
Organization†	48,216	55,958	58,069	42,931
Research	15,033	15,736	5,420	3,293
Publicity and Printed Literature	5,192	2,802	6,151	5,075
Women's Activities	14,059	14,557	10,160	9,607
Youth Section	6,132	8,538	9,032	9,600
Convention (deficit)	281	—	7,871	—
Election (deficit)	7,573	—	—	20,116
Totals	164,122	177,234	184,441	207,251

* Includes remittances of slightly more than $3,000 annually to the Socialist International.
† Includes regular assistance to the Quebec and Nova Scotia provincial party organizations.
Source: NDP Financial Statements for 1965, 1966, 1967 and 1968.

which may be expected from the labour affiliates. An estimate is prepared by the unions involved based on per capita contributions. This figure provides the basis for the preparation of a minimum and maximum budget in line with lower and upper estimates of anticipated income. The budget is elaborated by the publicity sub-committee of the federal executive and coordinated by the federal secretary, a full-time employee who is responsible for the final details. Similar procedures are applied by the "finance committees" of the provincial executives for each of the provincial parties and campaigns.

Table 3-V demonstrates the results of this new-found affluence.

Only the close proximity of the 1962 and 1963 elections, producing a need for two appeals in a short period of time, interrupted the steady rise in party expenditures based on funds derived in increasing measure from labour sources. Furthermore, the renewed impetus which this evolution brought to the party led to large increases in the numbers of individual members, a factor which benefited provincial and constituency party organizations.[36]

Monies spent in British Columbia, Saskatchewan, Ontario and Manitoba are raised in those provinces, which in addition make sums available for transfer through the federal office to the weak party organizations in

Table 3 - V
NDP FEDERAL ELECTION EXPENDITURES 1962-1968

Spending Level	1962	1963	1965	1968
	$	$	$	$
Total Estimated Costs	700,000	450,000	1,000,000	1,250,000
Federal Office Expenditures	117,000	71,000	207,000	216,100
Declared Expenditures by				
Reporting Candidates*	391,000	288,000	516,000	681,000
Provincial Offices' Expenditures	180,000	100,000	232,000	250,000

* The numbers of reporting NDP candidates in each election were 177, 164, 175 and 162 in 1962, 1963, 1965 and 1968 respectively.

Sources: Information provided by Terrence Grier and Clifford Scotton, past and present Federal Secretaries of the New Democratic Party; Report of the Committee on Election Expenses, The Queen's Printer, Ottawa, 1966, pp. 265-266; Paltiel, Noble and Whitaker, "The Finances of the Cooperative Commonwealth Federation and the New Democratic Party, 1933-1965," in Paltiel et al., Studies in Canadian Party Finance, Committee on Election Expenses, The Queen's Printer, Ottawa, 1966, pp. 347-386.

Alberta, the Atlantic Provinces and Quebec.[37] The scarcity of funds in 1963 "instigated a Canada-wide drive to raise funds from constituency associations for the campaign in Quebec."[38] That province also benefits from a regular annual subsidy for its NDP party organization from the federal budget; and again in the 1968 campaign the federal office provided $35,000 for Quebec "assistance."[39]

Trade union funds also flow into the provincial offices, notably in British Columbia and Ontario. Elsewhere, as in Alberta and Nova Scotia,[40] trade unions provide services or pay the salaries of full-time organizers during federal election campaigns. Little is known about the size of trade union contributions in British Columbia, owing to the inhibitions imposed by law on trade union contributions to political parties in that province;[41] party officials tend to be close-mouthed on the subject. But labour support for the party on the Pacific Coast is known to be substantial.[42] On the other hand, information regarding the party's relationship with labour in Ontario is available and may serve to illustrate similar links between the NDP and the unions elsewhere in Canada.

Initially it had been agreed that in the 1962 campaign union funds would be allocated directly in support of the federal office and local constituency organizations; the Ontario office was to benefit by a rebate of 20 percent of the funds earmarked for constituency campaigns. An indifferent response brought a revision whereby trade union support was to be shared on a one-third/two-thirds basis between the provincial and local organizations; some union locals, however, continued to adhere to the original scheme.[43] In 1962 over 70 locals, boards and labour councils contributed to the campaign of the Ontario NDP; one estimate attributes half the sum of $200,000 spent by the party in the province to trade union sources.[44] The Ontario Federation of Labour also supported the party by indirect expenditures on a public relations office, advertising in the ethnic press and assistance to riding associations.[45] A similar pattern was followed in the 1963 election with the United Steelworkers and other unions contributing heavily in areas of union strength through local area councils.[46] In 1965 contributions from labour sources, including the Canadian Labour Congress, provided between 60 to 80 percent of the $330,000 spent by the NDP in Ontario.[47] Union-giving in 1968 was on the same generous scale.

At the federal level trade union support was no less forthcoming. Practically all the sums spent by the federal office on the 1962 and 1963 campaigns came from labour sources.[48] In 1965 approximately $150,000 or 72 percent of the expenditures of the federal party was covered by trade unions, notably the United Steelworkers and the United Packinghouse Workers;[49] the money was collected by voluntary contributions of 50 cents per member from the unions involved. Similarly, more than two-thirds of the sum spent on the last federal general election in 1968, $145,000, was donated to the federal office of the New Democratic Party through the Trade Union Committee on Political Education; only $34,000, less than one-sixth of the amount spent at the national level, was raised from individual party members.[50]

This expansion was not without its strains. The federal office ended the 1968 campaign with a deficit of more than $25,000, which necessitated cut-backs in continuing expenditures such as the temporary suspension of publication of the party's national newspaper, the New Democratic News, termination of a $9,600 grant to its youth section, and reductions in the grants to the Nova Scotia and Quebec groups.[51] More serious, however, were the cuts made in the course of the campaign to the party's expenditures on the broadcast media. Spending at the national level on television, which had been $56,670 or 27 percent of the campaign budget in 1965, fell by more than half to $23,750 or 11 percent of the 1968 campaign budget; smaller cuts were made in radio and newspaper publicity which fell from $17,538 and $36,188 to $14,400 and $35,200 respectively.[52] These cuts in mass media expenditures reduced the amount of public exposure received by the party, a problem compounded by the reduction in the amount of free broadcasting time made available by the CBC in 1968.[53] Clearly there were limits to the party's new-found affluence.

THE WEAKNESS OF "GRASS-ROOTS" FINANCING

Money raised at the national or federal, the provincial, and the local association levels has always come from individual or affiliated membership fees and donations for both the CCF and the NDP. Sustaining memberships which evolved from the "Ontario 500 Club" in the nineteen fifties have been effective only in areas of established party strength. Affiliate membership fees have not been as productive as originally hoped for. Theoretically, such fees could have been received from many types of organizations, such as farm, women's and cooperative groups. Practically the only source of such revenues has been the trade union affiliates. Formally affiliated members join as individuals, a concept central to the party's ideology of individual giving. But the foregoing pages attest to the fact that individuals contribute sums adequate for sustained political activity only when they are part of a cohesive, well-disciplined group-giving structure. Only in Saskatchewan were there conditions suitable for successful financing at the grass-roots.

Structurally, grass-roots financing produced a very decentralized party. Each provincial party was expected to find the money needed for inter-election periods and campaign expenses from provincial sources. The CCF national office depended on allocations from the provincial organizations, each of which was committed to provide an amount commensurate with the size of its membership. In reality only Saskatchewan, British Columbia and Ontario could be depended upon. The CCF national office also acted as the transfer point for channelling funds to the weaker provincial organizations. Until 1961, Saskatchewan was the financial mainstay of the party at all levels; a timely cheque from this province's organization avoided repeated financial crises.

A mass membership was recruited in Saskatchewan at the constituency level who participated in the formulation of party policy. These local associations were coordinated and directed by an efficient and vigorous provincial office and were very effective in soliciting funds. Yet this apparently successful embodiment of the original CCF ideology is not without a certain ambiguity. The highly structured and group-oriented nature of the membership and the financial drives clearly suggest that the Saskatchewan member participates in a group-giving system, losing his individual identity as donor within a larger group, albeit retaining his influence over policy. In contrast to the rural environment of Saskatchewan, the urban and rural environment of Ontario has proved to be barren ground for grass-roots financing. Ontario, like British Columbia, has depended increasingly on financial support from the disciplined trade unions and the sustaining memberships of affluent supporters.

The history of the NDP has been marked by the increased availability of funds for general and campaign purposes. The bulk of this money has come from the labour movement, where the cohesive nature of the union structure has permitted the NDP to collect relatively large sums *en bloc.* The result has been a financial stability which always escaped its predecessor. But the financial structure of the party remains paradoxical. The NDP is now a major electoral rival of the two older parties but the financial means necessary to bring about this development has undermined the original CCF ideology of mass fund-raising. Trade unions are the financial foundations of the NDP. While such contributions differ qualitatively from the contributions of business corporations, it is also true that such donations are unlike the voluntary gifts of individual citizens.

FOOTNOTES

[1] Much of the historical detail in this chapter is drawn from Khayyam Z. Paltiel, Howat P. Noble and Reginald A. Whitaker, "The Finances of the Cooperative Commonwealth Federation and the New Democratic Party, 1933-1965," in Paltiel et al., *Studies in Canadian Party Finance,* Committee on Election Expenses, The Queen's Printer, Ottawa, 1966, pp. 317-404; and Study No. 6, section IV, *Report of the Committee on Election Expenses,* The Queen's Printer, Ottawa, 1966, pp. 257-266.

[2] For the history and background of the CCF, see the following: D. E. McHenry, *The Third Force in Canada: The Cooperative Commonwealth Federation, 1932-1948,* University of California Press, Berkeley and Los Angeles, 1950; Seymour Martin Lipset, *Agrarian Socialism: The Cooperative Commonwealth Federation in Saskatchewan,* University of California Press, Berkeley and Los Angeles, 1950; and Kenneth McNaught, *A Prophet in Politics, A Biography of J. S. Woodsworth,* University of Toronto Press, Toronto, 1951.

[3] McHenry, *op. cit.,* pp. 62-63.

[4] Paltiel, Noble and Whitaker, *op. cit.,* pp. 319-325.

[5] McHenry, *op. cit.,* pp. 43-44.

[6] Interview with the Hon. M. J. Coldwell, P.C., January 20, 1966.

[7] Lipset, *op. cit.,* p. 119.

[8] *Ibid.*

[9] *CCF Records,* vols. 2 and 3, Public Archives of Canada. Membership figures were presented annually to the CCF National Council.

[10] After 1942, CCF Clubs ceased to be an important source of members. Cf. Leo A. Zakuta, *A Protest Movement Becalmed — A Study of Change in the CCF,* University of Toronto Press, Toronto, 1964, pp. 43-44.

[11] McHenry, *op. cit.,* p. 47. The Canadian Congress of Labour (CCL) dubbed the party "the political arm of labour" in 1942, but this meant little in terms of contributions.

[12] Lipset, *op. cit.,* pp. 199-208.

[13] On the CCF and NDP in Quebec, see David H. Sherwood, "The New Democratic Party and French Canada 1961-1965," unpublished M.A. thesis, McGill University, Montreal 1966, *passim.*

[14] McHenry, *op. cit.*, p. 90.

[15] *Ibid.*, pp. 57-58.

[16] *CCF Records*, vol. 1, Public Archives of Canada, *Minutes of National Council Meetings*, meeting of September 5-6, 1943.

[17] Interviews with Hon. M. J. Coldwell, December 1965 - March, 1966.

[18] Report of the 1946 CCF Convention, p. 14ff.

[19] See footnote 9 above.

[20] *Report of the Committee on Election Expenses, op. cit.*, p. 260.

[21] *CCF Records*, Vol. 2, Public Archives of Canada, Meeting of the National Executive, November 27, 1948, p. 3.

[22] *Ibid.*, April 30-May 1, 1949, p. 1.

[23] *Ibid.*, Audited statement presented to Meeting of the National Executive, July 29, 1950.

[24] Paltiel, Noble and Whitaker, *op. cit.*, pp. 333-335.

[25] *CCF Records, op. cit.*, Memorandum on the National Three-Year Expansion Programme, n.d.

[26] Paltiel, Noble and Whitaker, *op. cit.*, pp. 335-337.

[27] See Table 3-III, p. 55.

[28] Paltiel, Noble and Whitaker, *op. cit.*, p. 338.

[29] Collections were $24,051 and expenditures $22,462. See Report of the 13th National Convention of the CCF, July 28-30, 1954, p. 17.

[30] CCF National Office Financial Report for year ending June 30, 1957, p. 17; presented to the 15th National Convention of the CCF, 1958.

[31] *CCF Records*, Vol. 53, Public Archives of Canada, Report on the Conduct of the 1957 Federal Election Campaign in Ontario, pp. 4-14.

[32] Report of the 15th National Convention of the CCF, 1958, p. 20.

[33] Most of the information on Ontario is drawn from *CCF Records*, Vol. 58, Public Archives of Canada, Report on the Conduct of the 1958 Federal Election Campaign in Ontario, May 8, 1958; see also, Paltiel, Noble and Whitaker, *op. cit.*, pp. 339-342.

[34] The author wishes to acknowledge the assistance and information provided by Clifford A. Scotton, Federal Secretary of the NDP, concerning the years 1966-1968 and the 1968 federal general election. Similar material was made available to the author and his staff on the Committee on Election Expenses for the years 1961-1965 by Terrence Grier, the previous Federal Secretary.

[35] Information provided by Morden Lazarus, director Ontario Federation of Labour, January 6, 1966 and by Mr. Grier.

[36] Information provided by T. Grier, December 8, 1965.

[37] *Ibid.*, and interviews with Mr. G. Notley, Alberta NDP Provincial Secretary, January 17, 1966 and Mr. M. Boulard, Quebec NDP Secretary, January 19, 1966.

[38] Sherwood, *op. cit.*, p. 128.

[39] See Financial Statements of the NDP 1966-68.

[40] Paltiel, Noble and Whitaker, *op. cit.*, pp. 355, 358, 367, 369, 383-384 and 386.

[41] The B.C. *Labour Relations Act* of 1961 which makes it illegal to use "check-off" funds for political purposes is discussed in Chapter 7.

[42] For details see Paltiel, Noble and Whitaker, *op. cit.*, pp. 387-390.

[43] *Ibid.*, pp. 349-350.

[44] Interview with J. Bury, Ontario NDP Secretary, December 15, 1965.

[45] Report of the Election Campaign Committee to the 1962 Ontario New Democratic Party Convention.

[46] Letter to Research Staff of the Committee on Election Expenses from Mr. J. Bury, January 28, 1966.

[47] See footnotes 45 and 46 above, and Executive Committee Report to the Ontario NDP Provincial Council Meeting November 27-28, 1965.

[48] *Report of the Committee on Election Expenses, op. cit.,* p. 261.

[49] Letter from T. Grier, December 13, 1965.

[50] Letter from Clifford A. Scotton, NDP Federal Secretary, September 22, 1969.

[51] Statement by Clifford Scotton, NDP Federal Secretary, reported by the Canadian Press, January 14, 1969.

[52] See footnotes 50 and 51.

[53] See Chapter 5, pp. 87-88.

FOUR

DEVOTEES AND THE LITTLE MAN: FUND-RAISING FOR THE SOCIAL CREDIT MOVEMENT AND THE RALLIEMENT DES CRÉDITISTES[1]

The utter eclipse of the Social Credit Movement in the federal general election in 1968 appears to have spelled the end of any national ambitions which its leadership may have once entertained. Although in decline since the Diefenbaker landslide of 1958, the national party's last phase appears to have been signalled by the final abandonment of Social Credit doctrine by the long-time former Premier of Alberta, Ernest Manning, shortly before the 1968 election when he called for the agglomeration of all right-wing conservative forces in Canada under the banner of Social Conservatism. In closely linked developments the national leader, Robert N. Thompson, abandoned the party and successfully sought the nomination as Progressive-Conservative candidate in his constituency of Red Deer, Alberta; another veteran member, H. A. "Bud" Olson of Medicine Hat, Alberta, joined the Liberals and became the federal Minister of Agriculture. Deprived of leadership and the support of their provincial stronghold in Alberta, the fate of the remaining 30 federal standard-bearers in 1968 was sealed. Only 62,956 votes were cast in favour of the Social Credit rump and none of its candidates succeeded in retaining or gaining a seat in the House of Commons.

The financial and parliamentary fortunes of Social Credit and its erstwhile allies, the Ralliement des Créditistes, are traced in Tables 4-I and 4-II.

Analysis of the above tables makes it evident that the parliamentary fortunes of the national Social Credit movement — apart from the brief interlude with the Ralliement des Créditistes — were directly linked to the votes and support received in the far western provinecs. Although clearly

Table 4 - I
SOCIAL CREDIT CANDIDATES AND MEMBERS OF THE HOUSE OF COMMONS
1949-1968

Year	British Columbia Candidates	M.P.s	Alberta Candidates	M.P.s	Quebec Candidates	M.P.s	Canada Candidates	M.P.s
1949	2	—	17	10	—	—	28	10
1953	22	4	17	11	—	—	73	15
1957	21	6	17	13	4	—	113	19
1958	22	—	17	—	15	—	82	—
1962	22	2	17	2	75	26	230	30
1963	22	2	17	2	75	20	224	24
1965	22	3	17	2	—†	—†	86*	5*
1968	19	—	3	—	—†	—†	30*	—*

* Ralliement des Créditistes members and candidates were not included in Social Credit totals after 1963. Two Créditiste candidates ran in Ontario and New Brunswick in 1965 and in the latter and Manitoba in 1968.
† In 1965 the Créditistes presented 75 candidates in Quebec electing 9 M.P.s, while in 1968 they presented 70 electing 14 to the House of Commons.

Table 4 - II
EXPENDITURES DECLARED BY SOCIAL CREDIT CANDIDATES
CANADA AND SELECTED PROVINCES 1949-1968

Year	British Columbia Amount $'000s	Reporting Candidates	Alberta Amount $'000s	Reporting Candidates	Quebec Amount $'000s	Reporting Candidates	Canada Amount $'000s	Reporting Candidates
1949	*	2	20	17	—	—	24	24
1953	32	20	32	17	—	—	81	64
1957	62	21	39	17	—	—	141	95
1958	22	20	37	16	1	3	70	56
1962	40	19	65	17	96	40	269	155
1963	30	17	57	15	82	44	227	149
1965	43	16	82	15	—‡	—‡	143†	60†
1968	35	15	9	3	—‡	—‡	47†	23†

* Less than $1,000.
† After August 1963, the Ralliement des Créditistes was no longer linked with the National Social Credit Association therefore the totals for Canada do not include the Quebec figures.
‡ In 1965, 37 reporting Créditiste candidates declared expenditures of $60,000 and in 1968, 32 candidates declared expenditures of $56,000.
Source: Appendix A, p. 000.

an emanation of the provincial parties, particularly that of Alberta, whose financial assistance was vital to the continued existence of the national movement, the relationship from the outset was ambiguous and ambivalent. A brief examination of the financial history of the national party reveals that when aid was available it was never truly sufficient to make a real breakthrough possible at the federal level; to the very end it remained a mere appendage of the provincial parties.[2]

SOCIAL CREDIT FINANCES 1935-1968

The striking victory of William Aberhart and his followers in the Alberta provincial election of 1935 was followed almost immediately by their appearance on the federal stage. Benefiting from Aberhart's ability to exploit the radio medium and the network of study groups established to spread the Douglasite doctrines across the foothills province, the Social Credit movement was able to enlist the support of devotees prepared to give their personal and monetary assistance to the electoral ambitions of their leaders and party.[3] Sweeping forward on the coattails of the provincial victors, 17 Social Credit members were elected in the federal election of October 1935; 15 from Alberta and 2 from Saskatchewan. In 1940 the federal Social Credit Party threw in its lot with New Democracy, a splinter party created and led by the Hon. W. D. Herridge, brother-in-law of the former Conservative Prime Minister, R. B. Bennett. Building on the same foundations and the grass-roots assistance of small merchants, farmers and local professional men who formed the nucleus of the party, the New Democracy Party elected 10 members to the federal House of Commons in 1940. The name "New Democracy" soon faded, however, and the party reverted to being known as Social Credit.

The moderation of the movement's doctrines brought the party new sources of support. Judicial review and federal disallowance had struck down much of its early legislation; the death of Aberhart and the purge of the extreme Douglasite faction by his successor Ernest Manning had stilled the fears of the orthodox. Economic conditions had changed for the better with the discovery of oil and the recovery of markets with the wartime boom. Business and industry, formerly alienated by its economic doctrines, now found in Social Credit a welcome antidote and bulwark to the CCF and social democracy which had won power in Saskatchewan in 1944.

In 1944 the National Social Credit Association was established in an effort to build the party in provinces other than Alberta. Supported by commercial and industrial interests close to the Alberta movement,[4] the National Association succeeded in electing 13 Members of Parliament from Alberta. But the election left the party's national office with a deficit of $3,000 which it had difficulty in liquidating.

The Minutes of the National Council, the Reports to the National Conventions and the publications of the National Social Credit Association, as well as the personal letters of its leaders, are replete with information concerning the dire and stringent financial circumstances facing the party. One motive offered for attempting to extend the party beyond the prairies into Ontario was the lusher resources assumed to be available in that province.[5] Yet despite appeals in the *Canadian Social Creditor* for sustaining funds under various names and guises such as the "On to Ottawa Fund" or the "Victory Fund," the financial results were extremely meagre.[6] A financial statement for the period July 1, 1946 to October 31, 1947 reveals that Association income in that sixteen-month period was only slightly more than $6,500. But of greater significance is the fact that more than two-thirds of the income came from the Alberta Social Credit League; the Ontario League which was the next largest contributor donated less than 15 percent of the sum raised.[7]

Such modest sums could permit only the very minimum of essential expenditures. Thus the National Secretary was paid a mere $1,254.91 and the Acting National Organizer, later the President of the Alberta Social Credit League, only $1,200 in the above-mentioned sixteen months; the National Leader was allocated a mere $450 for his expenses.[8]

Faced with such financial constraints, the National Association could do little to help its allies in Quebec like Réal Caouette who in 1946 ran in a by-election in Pontiac under the banner of the Union des Électeurs. The impecuniosity of the Association was demonstrated in the following letter from the National Leader at that time, Solon Low, to the National Secretary Treasurer:

> . . . for the past 10 days, we have concentrated in Southern Pontiac . . . Mr. Even and his crowd haven't done anything at all yet. They have left the advertising to me. I have got some bills for which we will have to pay I guess. Therefore I am sending you a cheque which I would like you to sign and send back as quickly as you possibly can so that the printers won't feel that we are neglecting them. The Members [i.e. the Social Credit M.P.'s] here have contributed to a fund of our own to take care of the expenses of the M.P.'s in their meetings in the North [in Pontiac for Réal Caouette's campaign]. Therefore there won't be any bills to pay in that direction.
>
> The National Organization owes Radio Station CJCA in Edmonton a matter of $330.47 representing the balance of rather a large broadcasting order in the last election. I would appreciate it if you would sign the enclosed cheque and return it to me so that I can sign it and mail it directly to them.
>
> . . . I am sending along a cheque for your signature payable to the Bell Telephone Company for $7.60. I would appreciate it if you would sign the same and return it for mailing.
>
> Sincerely,
>
> (Signed)   SOLON E. LOW, M.P.[9]

After the Union des Électeurs broke with the Social Credit Association of Canada early in 1948, the National Leader, Solon Low, decided to accept a splinter group as the national party's spokesman in Quebec. But once again correspondence, this time between the President of "La Ligue du Crédit Social" and Mr. Low in 1952, demonstrates how financial difficulties continued to inhibit the development of the federal party. The Quebec group formally appealed to the national party in the following terms:

> Whereas Social Credit has a solid foothold in the Province of Alberta and whereas progress towards the establishment of a Social Credit Government at Ottawa cannot be hoped for until every province supplies Social Credit deputies, and whereas Louis Even's movement will not offer any more candidates, the undersigned believe it is time to lay a solid basis for a Democratic Social Credit Movement in the Province of Quebec. We believe that you can help us to find $5,000.00 to start our association and keep it operating for one year with a full time secretary, with an office and an electrical sign in the busiest square in Quebec. After that year we are assured that sufficient funds will be available to allow us to spread to other cities. We base our present proposition on your statement at the Palais Montcalm about four years ago that you knew a number of people in this province who could advance that kind of money for a really democratic organization.[10]

The reply of Mr. Low to the proposal of the Quebec Social Credit League is equally revealing:

> My dear Mr. Bouchard:
> Mr. Hansell and I have had only a few minutes together since he arrived back in the city, but that seems fairly enough time to get the financial picture clearly. Unfortunately, our Movement seems always to have to get along with little or no money. Somehow or other we do seem to be able to rake up enough to face an election campaign, that is, enough to help us to win. But, the amount we spend is frightfully small as compared with the other parties. For example, our Party Headquarters in Vancouver spent no more than $10,000 all told in the B.C. Campaign, to elect nineteen Members. Over and above this of course, each individual candidate did spend some money, but the amount would not be in excess of four or five hundred dollars each.
> These figures must seem to you to be infinitesimal. They are. We have learned to campaign effectively without spending great sums of money. We don't pay big amounts for assistance of any kind. About the only thing that we have been able to spend on is advertising and radio costs. The nickels, dimes and quarters of the people's contributions take care of the rest.
> There is nothing we can do for you in a financial way except to suggest that you form a committee for the purpose and have them make a canvass amongst the people of your Province who might be prepared to contribute to your campaign. That is the way we had to do it in all provinces thus far and I suppose that if money is raised in Quebec, that is the way it will have to be.[11]

No Social Credit candidates presented themselves in Quebec in the 1953 federal general election campaign. However, following its provincial success in British Columbia in 1953, the federal party made a breakthrough in British Columbia sending four members to Ottawa in that year. From that time the incumbent provincial British Columbia party became one of the two mainstays of the national movement providing approximately half the sums at the disposal of the Social Credit Party in federal election campaigns.[12] Enjoying the advantages of incumbency and posing as the champion of free-enterprise and sworn opponent of socialism, the British Columbia provincial party has consistently employed the fund-raising tactics and reaped the financial benefits available to parties in power. Business and industry operating in the province have provided the bulk of its support.[13] The party made some gains in British Columbia and Alberta in the 1957 federal election but its representation at Ottawa was completely wiped out in the 1958 Diefenbaker victory.

Since 1958, the history of the moribund federal party is largely the story of its faltering and ultimately unsuccessful efforts to reach some *modus vivendi* with the Ralliement des Créditistes. In the early nineteen sixties the British Columbia and Alberta parties despatched organizers to other parts of Canada in an attempt to resurrect the national movement. As a result of these efforts the Ralliement des Créditistes was represented at a National Social Credit Convention held in Ottawa in July 1960.[14] Under the redrafted party constitution, provincial associations were granted complete autonomy; but promised little support from the national party, the provincial groups were left to their own financial resources. The Ralliement, as will be seen below, built its own financial organization which enabled it to make an easy transition to independent existence when the final split with the national party came in 1963.

The national Social Credit party enjoyed a temporary revival in the elections of 1962, 1963 and 1965. But outside of Quebec it elected only four members in 1962 and 1963 and five in 1965; in 1968 even this token representation was lost. The financial side of the story of those years is quickly told. Funds, as usual, were largely supplied by the Alberta and British Columbia movements. In 1965, 60 of the 86 Social Credit candidates submitted reports revealing average expenditures of $2,380 per reporting candidate; while in 1968, 23 of the 30 candidates made declarations showing average spending of $2,065. Expenditures on the mass media dropped more drastically. Print media expenditures in the 1965 campaign amounted to $87,115; but in contrast to other parties, the bulk of spending on press advertising (about 59 percent) was placed at the expense of the provincial associations, as usual those of Alberta and British Columbia; the National association spent less than nine percent of the total.[15] Even more indicative of the party's decline was the sharp two-thirds drop in spending on broadcasting from 1965 to 1968. The purchase of broadcast time on radio fell from $23,583.93 to $7,777.50; and on television the fall was from $25,070.20 to $8,222,51.[16]

CRÉDITISTE FINANCE 1958-1968

In contrast to Social Credit in Alberta which found its social base in the heart of a fairly homogeneous society of agriculturalists producing for a world market,[17] the movement in Quebec struck roots on the margins and fringes of a subsistence farming and forest economy amongst the *déclassé* victims of the twin pressures of industrialization and urbanization. First represented in Quebec by the *Ligue du Crédit Social* (1936-1939), Social Credit was propounded for almost two decades by the Union des Électeurs, a group which has now faded into sectarian obscurity and the religious enthusiasms of the "bérets blancs." Although the Union des Électeurs has abjured electoral activities since 1949, it retains a certain historical importance in that its organizational and fund-raising structures served as a model for its electoral successor, the Ralliement des Créditistes.

The Union des Électeurs was a "devotee" party[18] organized on cellular lines with a hierarchy of members and activities bearing such titles as "voltigeurs" or "pèlerins," "défricheurs," "animateurs," "conquérants," and full-time "missionaires." Discipline was maintained through an Institute of Political Action consisting of the most militant activists in each county. The Institute in turn was controlled by a seven-man directorate appointed by and including the two founders, Mr. Louis Even and Mme. Gilberte Côté-Mercier. The movement's activities centred around its bimonthly periodical *Vers Demain*. Subscribers formed cells to discuss and spread Social Credit doctrine and vied with one another in canvassing for, selling and distributing the journal; subscriptions to the latter constituted membership in the Union. "Most of the people who subscribed to *Vers Demain* were people of little means: farmers, urban workers, and above all small townspeople such as shopkeepers, tradesmen, and service personnel."[19] In 1948 gross annual revenue topped $100,000, derived from more than 50,000 regular subscribers. The proceeds were used to meet editorial and publishing costs, newspaper and radio propaganda, and organizational activities on the parish, regional and provincial levels; the greatest proportion, however, went to promote the campaigns of candidates in various federal and provincial elections during the nineteen forties. Disappointment with the failure of their electoral efforts in the provincial and federal elections of 1948 and 1949, and the heavy financial strains resulting from these campaigns, brought the ideological predilections of the two founders to the fore, and resulted in a decision by the Union des Électeurs to bar such activities in the future. In orthodox Douglasite terms, elections were corrupt in any case.[20] Almost a decade was to pass before Réal Caouette and ten other breakaway members decided to abandon this passive role and resume the electoral battle under the name of the Ralliement des Créditistes.

From the outset the Ralliement was oriented toward the electoral process. In contrast to the Union, ideology was the handmaid rather than the goal of the party's campaign efforts. As in the case of the movement's Alberta founder, success was built on an early appreciation of the electoral impact of the electronic media; television did for M. Caouette what radio had contributed to William Aberhart's success more than two decades earlier.

Shortly after the formal establishment of the Ralliement on April 11, 1958, the Caisse Populaire loaned $30,000 to its leader to finance a series of television broadcasts on the Rouyn-Noranda and Jonquière stations. Additional sums were borrowed in the autumn of 1959 to cover the costs of broadcasts in the Sherbrooke and Quebec City areas.[21] The reaction to these broadcasts enabled the leadership trio of Mr. Caouette, Laurent Legault and Gilles Grégoire to set about forming a mass party around the small nucleus of early followers consisting largely of defectors from the Union des Électeurs. Staff was engaged and headquarters established in Quebec City. Laurent Legault took charge of the party's organizing activities and Gilles Grégoire became editorial director of its new monthly paper *Regards*.

The Ralliement's initial grass-roots organization and finances were built on a singular scheme linking the growth of the television audience, newspaper subscriptions and party membership. Viewers were urged to join the Ralliement, special cards having been printed for that purpose; once in, the urge to deepen their knowledge of Social Credit would impel them to subscribe to *Regards,* and become canvassers for members and further subscribers. Increased income enabled the further extension of the broadcasts; if sufficient membership was achieved, a local station carried Mr. Caouette's broadcasts, whose demagogic appeal early met wide popular acceptance. These complementary devices enabled the Ralliement to boast of an active paid membership of 12,000 early in 1961.[22]

Although the Ralliement joined the National Social Credit Party in July 1961, this move brought it little accretion of strength and no financial support. A few days later at the party's provincial congress, Mr. Legault outlined the organizational strategy which was to lay the basis for a central campaign fund for the 1962 federal election.[23]

This plan centred on a $70,000 television campaign to be mounted from October 1961 in the Lower St. Lawrence, Gaspé, Trois-Rivières and Montreal areas in addition to those covered in 1958 and 1959. Expenditures were to be made at the rate of $2,000 per week and backed by an additional $20,000 to be spent on press and broadcast advertising. The necessary funds were to be raised in a manner not dissimilar to that used two decades earlier by the old Union des Électeurs; subscriptions to *Regards* and memberships in the Ralliement were to be sold jointly and paid for on a monthly basis. But in contrast to the older group, membership cards were to be issued from the provincial office, thus creating a central campaign fund. Organizers were to be appointed for every 10 polls or 1,000 voters in a constituency with assistants for every 100 voters; the object was to increase the original membership nucleus tenfold. Provision was made for a series of public meetings in each area culminating with a nominating convention to name the Ralliement's candidate.

Although not all features of the television campaign were carried out due to shortage of funds — Caouette and Legault had to draw on their personal funds and businesses during the campaign — the results were crowned with success. The Créditistes won more than 500,000 votes in 1962 and captured 26 of the 75 Quebec seats in the House of Commons on an estimated budget of less than $70,000;[24] the 40 declaring candidates reported total expenditures at the local level of $96,000 or average spending of $2,400 per seat.

The 1963 campaign followed the general plan and pattern set in 1962. However, efforts were made to increase party income by broadening the sources of funds, particularly to pay for the television broadcasts which appeared essential to the party's expansion. The provincial treasurer Fernand Ouellet[25] devised a scheme to raise additional money from small businessmen and entrepreneurs.[26] The "Club des Cents" (or club of 100 contributors) was formed to canvass donations from the more affluent members of the movement in the form of $100 contributions. Over $40,000 seems to have come into the party treasury in this fashion from about 200 contributors.[27] Other attempts to raise more money were less successful and the party entered the 1963 campaign with less than half the amount which had been available for the previous election. Despite the lack of help from the "national" party and severe shortage of funds which left it in considerable debt, the Ralliement lost only 6 seats in 1963, returning 20 members to the House of Commons. Of its 75 candidates, 44 reported total expenditures at the local level of $82,000; the average spending of $1,863 per constituency in 1963 represented a drop of 25 percent from the previous campaign.

The 1963 campaign was followed by considerable changes in the structure of the Ralliement. The always fragile links with the national Social Credit movement were finally broken in September 1963. A formal constitution was adopted defining the organizational structure of the party.[28] Shortly afterwards, in January 1964, the party's provincial council endorsed a mutual aid scheme as a device to encourage the recruitment of new members and to stimulate the raising of additional funds.

The Service d'Entraide Social (Mutual Social Aid Service) or S.E.S. enabled the leadership of the Ralliement to establish central control over all income and to keep a record of all active members.[29] A special secretariat was formed and located in Trois-Rivières under a director appointed by the party executive. On enrolment in the Ralliement, members were expected to fill out detailed application forms and pay a $12 membership fee. This fee was divided into two parts, half of the amount being reserved for organizational and publicity costs as well as the journal *Regards* with the other half going to the S.E.S. and its representatives in the constituency organizations for redistribution to the membership in the form of gifts and lottery prizes. Monthly drawings were held and prizes distributed; and condolence gifts were presented to bereaved families of members. But despite these devices membership fell, numbering no more than 8,000 prior to the 1965 election.[30]

Cleavages within the party and shortages of funds gravely hampered the 1965 campaign. Although $40,000 was budgeted for television broadcasts,[31] information provided by the Board of Broadcast Governors shows that the Ralliement spent only $22,000 on broadcasting in 1965, less than one-third the sum expended in 1962.[32] Only $2,500 was expended on print media advertising.[33] Official reports submitted to constituency returning officers indicate that expenditures of Ralliement candidates at the local level averaged a mere $1,600 per constituency. The results in 1965 were a near debâcle; total votes fell from over half-a-million to less than 350,000 and the party won only nine seats in the House of Commons.

Although the Créditistes made no information available concerning their finance in the 1968 federal general election, official statistics appear to confirm the previous trends. Party spending on television continued to fall, amounting to no more than $8,355 or 40 percent of the already tiny 1965 figure.[34] There was some increase in the purchase of radio time but this was outweighed by the drastic drop in free television time made available by the CBC which fell by half from 1965 to 1968.[35] Of the 72 Créditiste candidates in the Province of Quebec, 32 reported average expenditures of $1,754, a slight rise from 1965. One Créditiste, Henry Latulippe, M.P. for Compton, actually reported spending $11,475.75; without his outsize expenditures the Ralliement average would have dropped to under $1,400. In the event a better distribution of votes and an active volunteer group produced 358,327 votes in Quebec which helped to send an enlarged delegation of 14 Créditistes to Ottawa after the last federal election.

In contrast to its spiritual godfather, the Union des Électeurs, the structure of the Ralliement conforms more closely to the Canadian norm.[36]

The party has adopted the pattern of "mass" parties elsewhere, but is actually the personal instrument of Réal Caouette and his immediate group of followers. As such it is not unlike the "cadre" structure traditional to the Canadian party system. The failure of the Club des Cents and other approaches to the more affluent have helped to make necessity a virtue, and the party prides itself on its grass-roots fund-raising methods.

FOOTNOTES

1 This chapter draws heavily on sections V and VI of Study No. 6, Stein et al., "The Patterns of Canadian Party Finance," *Report of the Committee on Election Expenses,* The Queen's Printer, Ottawa, 1966, pp. 267-277; and Michael Stein, Study No. 6, "The Structure and Function of the Finances of the Ralliement des Créditistes," in Paltiel et al., *Studies in Canadian Party Finance,* Committee on Election Expenses, The Queen's Printer, Ottawa, 1966, pp. 405-457. Use has also been made of an unpublished study prepared by Professor Stein for the Committee on Election Expenses, entitled, "The Finances of the Ralliement des Créditistes" (typescript), January 1966.

2 Credit for information concerning the National Social Credit Association from 1945 to 1949 is due to Hugh Halliday, a former graduate student at Carleton University who drew much of his information from the papers of Solon Low, late leader of the party, deposited at the Glenbow Foundation, Calgary. See also H. A. Halliday, "Social Credit as a National Party in Canada," unpublished M.A. thesis, Carleton University, Ottawa, 1966 (typescript), 176 pp.

3 On the early history and doctrines of Social Credit, see John A. Irving, *The Social Credit Movement in Alberta,* University of Toronto Press, Toronto, 1959, *passim.* On financial matters see *ibid.,* p. 138, p. 193, p. 343. See also C. B. Macpherson, *Democracy in Alberta,* University of Toronto Press, Toronto, 1953, *passim.*

4 Stein, "The Finances of the Ralliement des Creditistes", (unpublished), *op. cit.,* p. 73.

5 Solon Low to S. J. Fisher, July 30, 1945 (Low Papers); *ibid.,* Appendix II, p. 1.

6 Minutes of Meeting of the National Council, Social Credit Association of Canada, September 10-11, 1945 (Low Papers); and Report on Second National Convention, Social Credit Association of Canada, April 4-6, 1946 (Low Papers); *ibid.,* Appendix II, pp. 1-2.

7 Minutes of National Council Meeting, Social Credit Association of Canada, November 29-30, 1947 (Low Papers); *ibid.,* Appendix II, p. 3.

8 *Ibid.*

9 Solon Low to the National Secretary Treasurer, August 21, 1946 (Low Papers); *ibid.,* Appendix II, pp. 3-4.

10 Extracts from the Minutes of the Quebec Social Credit League, June 27, 1952; *ibid.,* Appendix II, p. 5.

11 Solon Low to J. E. Bouchard (President of La Ligue du Crédit Social), November 25, 1952 (Low Papers); *ibid.,* Appendix II, p. 6.

12 Halliday, *op. cit.,* pp. 115-116.

[13] For the evidence of its chief fund-raiser, Einar M. Gunderson, see *Minutes of Proceedings and Evidence No. 16,* House of Commons Standing Committee on Finance, Trade and Economic Affairs, October 18, 1966, pp. 694-696.

[14] For details see Michael Stein, "Social Credit in Quebec: Political Attitudes and Party Dynamics," unpublished Ph.D. dissertation, Princeton University, Princeton, N.J., 1966, *passim.*

[15] Cee Chapter 5, Tables 5-VI and 5-VII, pp. 84-85.

[16] See Chapter 5, Table 5-XI, p. 90.

[17] For a detailed discussion of the roots of Social Credit in Alberta in Marxian terms, see Macpherson, *op. cit., passim.*

[18] This category was employed by Maurice Duverger in his classic study *Political Parties,* Methuen & Co. Ltd., London, 1954, pp. 27-36; it has been applied to the Union des Électeurs in Michael Stein, "The Structure and Function of the Finances of the Ralliement des Créditistes," in Paltiel et al., *op. cit.,* pp. 405-425.

[19] *Ibid.,* p. 412.

[20] *Ibid.,* p. 422.

[21] *Ibid.,* p. 426.

[22] Study No. 6, *Report of the Committee on Election Expenses, op. cit.,* p. 273.

[23] Laurent Legault, "Plan d'Organization pour l'Année 1961-62" cited in Stein, *op. cit.,* pp. 431-432.

[24] *Ibid.*

[25] *Ibid.,* p. 433. Ouellet who later became the eastern organizer for the "national" party was expelled from the Ralliement after the 1963 election in the events which led to the split with the National Social Credit Association.

[26] Some large contributions were allegedly received from such corporations as Quebec Power, St. Laurent Cement and Shawinigan Light, Heat and Power Co., *ibid.,* p. 448.

[27] Bilan du 30 août 1963 du Ralliement des Créditistes du Québec, Granby 1963, cited *ibid.,* p. 449.

[28] This provided for a provincial executive, provincial council, general assembly, constituency associations and an "active membership" category. Constitution du Ralliement des Créditistes adopted Granby Quebec, September 1, 1963.

[29] The name was changed later to Service Économique et Social (Economic and Social Service). For details see *Regards* December 1964, p. 7 and Stein *op cit.,* pp. 437-440.

[30] *Report of the Committee on Election Expenses, op. cit.,* p. 277 citing Stein's unpublished study.

[31] *Ibid.*

[32] Table 15, *ibid.,* p. 401.

[33] See Chapter 5, Table 5-VIII, p. 86.

[34] See Chapter 5, Table 5-XI, p. 90.

[35] See Chapter 5, Table 5-XI, p. 90.

[36] For a detailed discussion of the structure of the Ralliement des Créditistes see Stein, *op. cit.,* pp. 440-452. A more systematic treatment is contained in Professor Stein's dissertation. See footnote 14 above.

FIVE
THE HIGH COST OF THE MASS MEDIA

The art of democratic politics and the evolution of the communications media have always been closely linked. If the organization, mobilization and entertainment of voters was the characteristic electioneering technique of the immediate post-Confederation period, political leaders were not long in realizing that some more continuous means of maintaining contact with and retaining the support of their followers were required. In the nineteenth century, the inevitable choice was a newspaper which could be relied upon to convey the party's programs and policies, attack the opposition and rally the faithful during the periodic electoral battles. If self-supporting newspapers were in friendly hands, parties and political leaders enjoyed the benefits of relatively cost-free partisanship; if this was not so, they were faced with the heavy burden of establishing and maintaining their own organs of opinion.

Thus at the very outset of the Dominion, Sir John A. Macdonald felt impelled in 1869 to stimulate the foundation of a friendly paper in Toronto (*The Mail*)[1] and was periodically called upon to come to its assistance.[2] A generation later, a group of Liberals put up the funds to purchase the *Toronto Evening Star*.[3] *Le Soleil,* its predecessor *L'Electeur,* and *Le Cultivateur* were subsidized while *Le Soir* was established with Liberal party funds.[4] Money from party sources kept the *Globe* in the Liberal camp in the eighteen eighties[5] and won control of *La Patrie* in 1897.[6] Early in the century a well-informed contemporary observer calculated that "within the last five years between three hundred and four hundred thousand dollars of party money, or what amounts to party money, has been put into Liberal papers in Canada."[7]

Patronage in the form of generous advertising and job printing contracts was available to the journalistic supporters of the party in power.[8] Moreover the press generally benefited, and continued to do so until recently, from a host of hidden postal, telegraphic and fiscal subsidies.[9] As Laurier's official biographer put it: "Some newspapers gave free and independent support; others had to be sustained by government printing or advertising; others were maintained directly out of party funds."[10]

Newspaper publishers and editors loomed large in the calculations of parties and their leaders. Liberal and Conservative spokesmen and policy-makers had to reckon with the views and likes and dislikes of the Siftons, Joseph Atkinson of the *Toronto Star,* and Hugh Graham, later Lord Atholstan, of the *Montreal Star* who reputedly organized a literary bureau and spent a quarter-of-a-million dollars on behalf of the Conservatives in the general election of 1911;[11] Graham's dislike of Meighen[12] and Manion[13] certainly contributed to the difficulties of the Conservative party during their respective terms of leadership.

However, a changing social context has served to reduce the power of aspiring king-makers among the newspaper community; albeit some Toronto publishers are still said to aspire to the role. Changing technology and increasing dependence on advertising income have led newspapers to seek enlarged mass circulations. The partisan journal of opinion has had to give way perforce to "a bland, uncontroversial news-organ that offers objective, impartial news stories, and takes a public-service approach to policy."[14] This process has been encouraged by the growing trend to newspaper consolidation and the predominance of the single-newspaper community. The emergence of the broadcasting media and television in particular has effected, in conjunction with the trend outlined above, a fundamental change in the process of political communications in Canada. The advertising agency and the public relations consultant have taken the editor's place in the counsels of the parties.[15] The rise to party prominence of such advertising men as Senator Keith Davey the former national Liberal organizer, Senator Allister Grosart who performed a similar function for the Conservatives during Mr. Diefenbaker's rise to power, and Mr. Dalton Camp who precipitated the latter's undoing, bear witness to this process.

During the nineteen forties both the Liberals and the Conservatives began to employ advertising agencies to help plan their campaign activities. In 1943 the Conservatives engaged McConnell, Eastman and Company to prepare the publicity for the abortive Popular Finance Campaign.[16] In the same decade Cockfield, Brown of Montreal began to play an intimate role in Liberal Party election planning. As one close observer of the Liberals has observed:

Often, Ministers would by-pass the Central Office and deal directly with the agency . . . during election campaigns. . . . There are many within the party who claim that Cockfield, Brown was the central office of the party, particularly around election time. . . .[17]

. . . By late 1956 and early 1957, four members of the agency Cockfield, Brown sat in on the Federation Liaison Committee in order to prepare for the coming election.[18]

At the present time MacLaren's enjoys no less close a relationship with the Liberal Party, and agency men are fixtures of the Prime Minister's office, paid partially out of public and partially out of party funds. The role of the agencies is not limited to merely technical functions, such as the placing of advertisements, the preparation of materials and so forth, but is increasingly involved in the choice and selection of issues and the projection and elaboration of party and leadership images.[19] The rewards for these services lie in a preponderant share of government advertising contracts, should the agency's "client" be successful at the polls.[20] About $25 million a year is spent by the government on assignments to agencies who are chosen on a patronage basis. In the words of a research report prepared in 1969 for the Task Force on Government Information:

Patronage is the main basis of selecting advertising agencies to work for government departments and agencies. . . . It is based on returning a favour for a favour. Advertising agencies help a political party and some of the leading figures during election time. If the party is returned to office, the agencies concerned are given a share of the advertising business of the government. Some of the advertising agencies which have large government accounts do not quite approve of this system, preferring to be chosen on a merit basis rather than getting the business via the proverbial pork barrel. For the winds of favouritism are fickle. . . ."[20a]

Needless to say the employment of such services and techniques have assumed an ever increasing place in modern electioneering, which in turn is reflected in the growing budgets allocated for expenditures on the mass media. Studies conducted after the 1965 and 1968 general elections provide some data which may illuminate these trends. Clearly the largest sums are spent at the central and regional party levels, but candidate-spending cumulatively is also significant and some information at this level can be derived through an examination of candidate reports when these are available for inspection. Candidates in the 1965 general election were asked to indicate their spending on radio, television and newspaper advertising. Out of 1110 candidates who reported spending an average of $6,842.37 in that election, 454 made some response to this questionnaire.[21] This information is summarized in Tables 5-I, 5-II, 5-III, and 5-IV below.

Less than one-eighth of the responding candidates spent more than one thousand dollars on radio advertising in their local campaigns; eleven percent spent between five hundred and one thousand dollars; three-eighths spent less than five hundred dollars; and more than one-third of the respondents ignored radio advertising altogether.

Table 5 - I
CANDIDATE-SPENDING FOR RADIO ADVERTISING 1965
(constituency campaign only)

Amount Declared	Number	%	Grouped %
Over $3,000	1	0.2 ⎤	
$2,000 - $2,999	13	3 ⎪	12.2
$1,500 - $1,999	11	2 ⎬	
$1,000 - $1,499	31	7 ⎦	
$ 500 - $ 999	50	11	11
Below $500	166	37	37
Nil	160	35	35
Not Answered	22	4.8	4.8
Total	454	100	100

Source: Report of the Committee on Election Expenses, The Queen's Printer, Ottawa, 1966, p. 412.

Table 5-II demonstrates that less than one-sixth of the responding candidates spent over one thousand dollars on television in their constituency campaigns, but a somewhat larger percentage spent this amount on the visual in preference to the sound medium. Moreover, in the case of television there are reports of some candidates spending in the neighbourhood of nine thousand dollars in the 1965 campaign. But on the other hand almost half the candidates do not appear to have purchased any television advertising time; somewhat over one-fifth of the respondents spent less than five hundred dollars, and an additional twelve percent under one thousand dollars.

Cost and accessibility appear to affect the use of the more expensive visual as compared to the sound medium. Furthermore, the availability of free time on CBC and private radio and television stations as well as the possibility of sharing in party-sponsored broadcasts may well reduce the amount of time which candidates might otherwise feel compelled to purchase.

Candidates' responses indicate that expenditures on newspaper advertising are the most widespread and popular form of paid publicity at the local level. Almost one-third of the reporting candidates stated that they

Table 5 - II
CANDIDATE-SPENDING FOR TELEVISION ADVERTISING 1965
(constituency campaign only)

Amount Declared	Number	%	Grouped %
Over $4,000	5	1	
$3,000 - $3,999	5	1	
$2,000 - $2,999	17	4	15
$1,500 - $1,999	9	2	
$1,000 - $1,499	33	7	
$ 500 - $ 999	54	12	12
Below $500	100	22	22
Nil	210	46	46
Not answered	21	5	5
Total	454	100	100

Source: Report of the Committee on Election Expenses, The Queen's Printer, Ottawa, 1966, p. 412.

had spent more than one thousand dollars on newspaper advertising. Only slightly more than one-tenth declared that they had made no expenditures on newspaper advertising in the 1965 campaign. The range of such expenses is summarized in Table 5-III.

Table 5 - III
CANDIDATE-SPENDING FOR NEWSPAPER ADVERTISING 1965
(constituency campaign only)

Amount Declared	Number	%	Grouped %
Over $4,000	9	2	
$3,000 - $3,999	14	3	
$2,000 - $2,999	31	7	29
$1,500 - $1,999	37	8	
$1,000 - $1,499	41	9	
$ 500 - $ 999	72	16	16
Below $500	177	39	39
Nil	52	11	11
Not answered	21	5	5
Total	454	100	100

Source: Report of the Committee on Election Expenses, The Queen's Printer, Ottawa, 1966, p. 413.

Table 5-IV provides a percentage comparison in various ranges of the expenditures of candidates on the mass media in the 1965 campaign. Clearly, local newspapers continue to attract a substantial share of the candidates' campaign spending.

Table 5 - IV
COMPARATIVE SPENDING ON THE MASS MEDIA 1965
(Percentage of local candidates only)

Spending Range	Radio %	Television %	Newspapers %
Over $1,000	12.2	15	29
$500 - $999	11	12	16
Below $500	37	22	39
Nil	35	46	11
Not answered	4.8	5	5
Total (454 respondents)	100	100	100

Source: **Report of the Committee on Election Expenses,** The Queen's Printer, Ottawa, 1966, p. 414.

Clues to the actual dollar amounts expended by constituency, provincial and national party organizations on the mass media must be sought elsewhere than in the responses of candidates to questionnaires. With respect to the print media, a study prepared for the Committee on Election Expenses[22] permits a careful estimate of such expenditures in the 1963 campaign and a detailed analysis of newspaper and periodical advertising by all levels of party organization on a national and provincial basis for the 1965 federal general election.

Using a sample of 40 newspapers representing 68.9 percent of the circulation of Canadian daily newspapers in 1963, an estimate may be made that Canadian parties and candidates expended about three-quarters-of-a-million dollars on paid political advertising in the 1963 federal general election campaign.[23] Although it is clear that over 80 percent of these expenditures were made by the two major parties, the lack of sufficient data precludes a further breakdown of these figures.

On the other hand, extremely accurate information is available with respect to the 1965 election. This information was obtained by a complete census and actual measurement of the political advertising lineage which appeared in 108 dailies, 684 weeklies and 9 magazines, trade and other publications. (In actual fact 923 publications were checked throughout the campaign and in only four cases were the files incomplete.)[24] The

Table 5 - V

TOTAL PRINT MEDIA ELECTION EXPENDITURES AND LINEAGE
September 8 - November 8, 1965
By Province

	Daily Newspapers			Weekly Newspapers			Magazines, Trade and Other Publications			Provincial Total in Dollars
	No. of Papers	$	No. of Lines	No. of Papers	$	No. of Lines	Number	$	No. of Lines	
Newfoundland	3	4,253	36,730	4	397	4,055	—	—	—	4,650
Prince Edward Island	2	13,062	108,540	—	—	—	—	—	—	13,062
Nova Scotia	5	65,802	285,522	19	19,689	237,811	—	—	—	85,491
New Brunswick	5	32,964	183,421	15	9,734	132,107	—	—	—	42,698
Quebec	14	68,647	180,412	127	87,166	685,660	1	1,651	870	157,464
Ontario	46	338,940	1,649,878	218	83,918	1,175,364	—	—	—	422,858
Manitoba	7	31,147	135,765	65	24,018	265,581	1	104	424	55,269
Saskatchewan	4	23,034	135,200	76	23,791	323,990	—	—	—	46,825
Alberta	7	57,782	239,380	72	34,937	460,657	3	845	4,845	93,564
British Columbia	15	208,096	440,225	85	54,219	551,295	4	891	3,625	263,206
Yukon and Northwest Territories	—	—	—	3	2,788	42,300	—	—	—	2,788
Canada Total	108	843,727	3,395,073	684	340,657	3,878,820	9	3,491	9,764	1,187,875

Canada Wide Total

Source: **Report of the Committee on Election Expenses**, The Queen's Printer, Ottawa, 1966, p. 336.

value of this advertising was calculated by assigning to each advertisement the "standard flat or transient black and white rate for each publication as set out in the November-December 1965 issue of *Canadian Advertising*."[25] This method of evaluation was used, despite the possibility of actual discounts or surcharges, because it reflected more accurately the real value of such advertising in standard commercial terms.

Print media expenditures in the 1965 campaign amounted to $1,187,875 divided among the provinces as in Table 5-V.

It is clear that spending was concentrated in the provinces of Ontario, British Columbia, Quebec, Alberta and Nova Scotia in descending order. In Ontario, the primary spenders were Progressive Conservative candidates and that party's national Association.[26] Between them they spent over 60 percent of the sum expended on the print media in that province. In British Columbia, on the other hand, local Liberal candidates were the biggest spenders followed closely by the provincial Social Credit Association and the national Progressive Conservative Association.[27] The national, local and provincial Liberal Associations spent almost two-thirds of the amount expended on newspaper advertising in Quebec, with the Quebec wing of the federal party being the biggest single spender.[28] In Alberta, local Conservative candidates and their national Association expended one-third the total spent in that province, but there again the provincial Social Credit Association was a most significant factor.[29] Half the total sum spent on the print media in Nova Scotia in 1965 was spent by local, provincial and National Conservative Associations; here, provincial incumbency made the provincial Conservative association the biggest single spender.[30] The relative importance of each level of spending is indicated in Table 5-VI.

Broken down by party, political advertising in the print media in the 1965 federal general election by level of sponsorship within each party is given in Table 5-VII. An examination of this table reveals that in all cases except for Social Credit, the primary spending level was the Local Association or candidates, followed by the National Party Associations. In the case of Social Credit, however, which lacked any Canada-wide body of consequence, this role was filled by the British Columbia and Alberta provincial associations which were effectively the senior party organs.

When the total sum spent on the print media is allocated amongst the parties, it becomes apparent that the Liberal party was the biggest overall spender. However, the Conservatives were a very close second in this aspect of election expenditures in 1965, and in fact were slightly ahead in the daily newspaper category. This discrepancy between the major parties may be explained by the particularly small number of newspapers in Quebec, the area of greatest Liberal strength; on the other hand, Liberals spent more on weeklies which include a considerable number of organs of

Table 5 - VI

TOTAL PRINT MEDIA ELECTION EXPENDITURES AND LINEAGE
September 8 - November 8, 1965
By Type of Sponsor

Sponsor of Advertising	Daily Newspapers		Weekly Newspapers		Magazines, Trade and other Publications	
	$	No. of Lines	$	No. of Lines	$	No. of Lines
National Party Association ..	285,964	872,978	55,254	504,567	1,811	1,870
Provincial Party Association	116,364	331,415	30,557	291,185	104	424
Local Constituency Candidates or Local Constituency Association	441,399	2,190,680	254,846	3,083,068	1,576	7,470

Source: **Report of the Committee on Election Expenses,** The Queen's Printer, Ottawa, 1966, p. 337.

ethnic groups, a category of traditional Liberal strength. Table 5-VIII also demonstrates that the New Democrats were able to muster at best only one-third the showing of the major parties in this form of expenditure on political advertising.

Comparable information is not available for the 1968 campaign but data made available by national officers of the three leading parties indicate that there was little significant change in the dimensions of spending on the print media in the 1968 general election.[31] However, the relative weight of such advertising in the overall budgets of the parties seems to have dropped in favour of spending on the broadcasting media.

Canadian broadcasting has been subject to legislative and administrative controls for more than four decades. Technological and physical constraints as well as international considerations made close regulation of the media necessary. Cultural considerations and the imperatives of a far-flung, sparsely settled country dictated that the public interest could best be served through the establishment of a powerful and preponderant public sector accompanied by private stations with their strictly commercial orientations. From the outset Royal Commissions, Parliament and the political parties were agreed that the conditions for the use and sale of broadcasting time for political and election campaign purposes ought to be subject to stringent restraints.[32] Controls were imposed with respect to the sponsorship, dramatization and allocation of time for such programs. To

Table 5 - VII

TOTAL PRINT MEDIA ELECTION EXPENDITURES AND LINEAGE
September 8 - November 8, 1965
By Type of Sponsor and Party Affiliation

	Daily Newspapers		Weekly Newspapers		Magazines, Trade and other Publications	
	$	No. of Lines	$	No. of Lines	$	No. of Lines
National Liberal Association ..	104,146	256,635	36,675	296,805	916	450
National P.C. Association	132,357	478,450	6,205	50,442	735	420
National N.D.P. Association ..	46,779	122,773	6,115	81,215	—	—
National S.C. Association	1,532	11,690	6,123	73,575	160	1,000
National Créditiste Association	213	555	49	1,245	—	—
Other National Associations ..	937	2,875	87	1,285	—	—
Provincial Liberal Association	43,818	116,380	12,243	109,750	26	106
Provincial P.C. Association	25,462	112,740	3,117	18,630	26	106
Provincial N.D.P. Association	9,225	19,100	1,042	9,935	26	106
Provincial S.C. Association	37,199	82,545	13,851	152,575	26	106
Provincial Créditiste Association	12	110	—	—	—	—
Other Provincial Associations	648	540	35	435	—	—
Local Liberal Constituency Candidates	182,747	915,633	108,557	1,308,940	514	2,985
Local P.C. Constituency Candidates	186,353	930,423	94,819	1,196,936	35	220
Local N.D.P. Constituency Candidates	52,413	249,034	30,499	346,030	190	1,590
Local S.C. Constituency Candidates	14,086	69,955	13,461	158,207	677	2,785
Local Créditiste Constituency Candidates	—	—	2,132	16,070	—	—
Other Local Constituency Candidates	5,767	25,635	5,378	56,885	160	110

Source: Report of the Committee on Election Expenses, The Queen's Printer, Ottawa, 1966, p. 338.

Table 5 - VIII
TOTAL PRINT MEDIA ELECTION EXPENDITURES AND LINEAGE
September 8 - November 8, 1965
By Political Party*

	Daily Newspapers		Weekly Newspapers		Magazines, Trade and other Publications		Party Totals in Dollars
	$	No. of Lines	$	No. of Lines	$	No. of Lines	
Liberal	330,710	1,288,648	157,475	1,715,495	1,456	3,541	489,641
Progress Conservative	344,172	1,521,613	104,410	1,265,868	796	746	449,378
New Democratic Party	108,417	390,907	37,656	437,180	216	1,476	146,289
Social Credit	52,817	164,190	33,435	384,357	863	3,891	87,115
Créditiste	258	665	2,181	17,315	—	—	2,439
Independent and Others	7,353	29,050	5,500	58,605	160	110	13,013
Totals	843,727	3,395,073	340,657	3,878,820	3,491	9,764	
			Canada Wide Total (All Parties)				1,187,875

* Includes all expenditures, i.e., National, Provincial and Local Associations and Candidates.
Source: Report of the Committee on Election Expenses, The Queen's Printer, Ottawa, 1966, p. 337.

carry out their concomitant control functions, the successive regulatory bodies — the Board of Governors of the Canadian Broadcasting Corporation, the Board of Broadcast Governors and the present Canadian Radio-Television Commission — have been endowed with authority to compel the production of records and statistics concerning programs in general and political broadcasts in particular.[33]

Aggregate data made available from these sources indicate a slow but steady rise in the relative weight of paid political broadcasts on radio and television, purchased commercially from stations in the private sector. Although no public or private network or station is compelled to provide free broadcasting time for "party politicals" during election campaigns, the publicly owned Canadian Broadcasting Corporation has traditionally made such time available to "bona fide national parties" which fulfill the following conditions:

i. Have policies on a wide range of national issues.
ii. Have a recognized national leader.

iii. Have a nation-wide organization established as a result of a national conference or convention.
iv. Have representation in the House of Commons.
 v. Seek the election of candidates in at least three of the provinces and put into the field at least one candidate for every four constituencies.[34]

The last requirement was dropped in the nineteen forties when regional parties emerged. The total time available is allocated equally between the Government and Opposition if only two parties qualify; but if there are more than two, the Government party is allocated about 35 to 40 percent and the Official Opposition and smaller parties divide the other 60 to 65 percent on a roughly proportional basis. In the last six federal general elections the time made available on the CBC radio and television networks was allocated as indicated in Table 5-IX.

Table 5 - IX
PERCENTAGE OF FREE TIME ALLOCATED TO POLITICAL PARTIES ON CBC ENGLISH AND FRENCH NETWORKS IN SIX FEDERAL ELECTION CAMPAIGNS — 1957-1968

Party		1957	1958	1962	1963	1965	1968
		%	%	%	%	%	%
				Radio			
Liberal		31.3	30.6	29.2	30.0	34.1	37.5
Prog.-Cons.		29.2	33.3	37.5	35.0	29.5	31.25
CCF/NDP		20.8	19.4	20.8	17.5	18.2	18.75
Soc. Cred.		18.8	16.7	12.5	17.5	9.1	6.25
Créditistes		—	—	—	—	9.1	6.25
TOTAL	%	100	100	100	100	100	100
	Hours	12:00	9:00	6:00	5:00	3:40	2:40
				Television			
Liberal		33.3	29.2	29.2	30.0	34.1	37.5
Prog.-Cons.		29.2	33.3	37.5	35.0	29.5	31.25
CCF/NDP		20.8	20.8	20.8	17.5	18.2	18.75
Soc. Cred.		16.7	16.7	12.5	17.5	9.1	6.25
Créditistes		—	—	—	—	9.1	6.25
TOTAL	%	100	100	100	100	100	100
	Hours	6:00	6:00	6:00	5:00	5:30	4:00

Source: Reports on the Federal Election Campaign: 1957, 1958, 1962, 1963, 1965, 1968. CBC Station Relations, Ottawa.

It is clear that while radio broadcasting has a declining appeal for party leaders and spokesmen, the public network has generally maintained the total amount of visual exposure allocated to the parties. The sharp drop recorded for the 1968 campaign was compensated by the presentation of a two-hour debate among the leaders of the Liberals, the Conservatives, the NDP and the Créditistes; in this confrontation approximate equity was achieved by granting exposure throughout the program to Mr. Trudeau and Mr. Stanfield, Mr. Douglas being cut in somewhat later with M. Caouette presented last. It should be noted, too, that the Government party has generally received somewhat less than the 40 percent norm, in part because of the rigid 15-minute basic time period employed by the CBC in its calculations.

The network and station-time value of the free time provided on CBC networks in 1965 may be estimated at approximately $177,000.[35] Using a similar method of computation, the lesser amount of time provided free in 1968 may be put at about $125,000.[36] In addition to network time, the public sector provides time on local radio and television stations. Allocated on roughly the same basis as the network time discussed above, the overall value of local free time provided by the CBC in the 1965 and 1968 elections amounted to $38,042 and $40,775 respectively.[37]

Additional exposure is given to parties and candidates on so-called national and local public affairs programs. The nature of these broadcasts, which are initiated by the broadcasters who control their format, vary from interviews, debates, documentaries and other forms of discussion. In 1965 the imputed value of such broadcasts was placed at $79,609.[38] While no comparable figures were available for the 1968 election, it is clear that in addition to the above-noted two-hour debate among the party leaders, the Canadian Broadcasting Corporation considerably expanded its coverage of election issues and personalities, going so far as to prepare a series providing in-depth analyses of the campaign in various regions of Canada. Taking all these special programs into account, it would probably be no exaggeration to place the value of public affairs programing at not less than $350,000 for the 1968 federal general election campaign.

Although CBC policy forbids the sale of time for electioneering purposes on the publicly owned networks and stations, private commercial broadcasters not only sell time but provide large amounts of free time on radio and television to political parties and candidates. However, the trend in the private sector differs somewhat from that displayed on the CBC. In contrast to the public sector, the private stations appear to have provided more free time on radio in 1968 than the amount supplied to competitors in the 1965 election; but they seem to have given somewhat less television time during 1968 than in the previous election. This drop was most noticeable with respect to free announcements, i.e., the short

Table 5 - X

TOTAL PAID POLITICAL BROADCASTS, SOLD LOCALLY BY ALL STATIONS — 1957-1968

Election Year	Number of Stations	Liberal		P.C.		CCF/NDP		S.C.*		Others		Totals	
		Talks Hours	Ann. Number	Talks Hours	Ann. Number	Talks Hours	Ann. Number	Talks Hours	Ann. Number	Talks Hours	Ann. Number	Talks Hours	Ann. Number
Radio													
1957	168	424:06	18,154	291:54	7,357	60:00	1,476	46:18	7,407	49:32	561	871:50	34,955
1962	202	232:24	19,789	270:53	22,753	78:20	2,685	84:48	4,190	3:20	38	669:45	49,455
1963	214	163:37	14,462	262:40	19,549	59:19	2,018	56:30	2,447	17:09	208	599:15	38,684
1965	226	166:07	28,460	158:00	18,697	52:26	5,703	36:09	2,222	24:24	585	437:06	55,667
1968	260	196:54	34,732	170:13	30,116	48:55	5,778	64:26	1,496	6:33	547	487:01	72,667
Television													
1957	31	70:30	1,267	44:12	827	17:45	61	5:38	208	6:35	16	144:40	2,379
1962	59	131:55	3,460	234:44	4,919	90:22	542	62:30	649	3:15	—	522:46	9,570
1963	60	199:35	3,130	116:18	2,822	61:56	221	75:19	216	9:10	2	462:18	6,391
1965	58	106:42	2,913	94:12	1,808	36:10	842	13:14	256	33:35	175	284:03	5,994
1968	59	161:55	2,582	91:12	2,915	20:10	736	18:35	107	1:35	38	293:27	6,378

* S.C. includes the Créditistes.

Source: 1957 data from CBC Report on Federal Election Compaigns, 1957; 1962 and 1963 data from BBG returns. Complete information on the 1958 election is not available from either CBC or BBG records. 1965 data from BBG records. Numbers of stations involve only those that actually sold time, (including FM stations); the above sources indicate three FM stations in 1962 and 7 in 1963 that sold time. 1968 information was supplied by The Canadian Radio-Television Commission.

"spot" announcements designed to create the largest number of listener or viewer "impacts" (even on radio there was a drop in the total amount of time devoted to announcements although the total number of free radio "spots" seems to have risen on the private sector).[39] In 1965 the Board of Broadcast Governors placed a value of $407,921 on the free-time broadcasts provided by the private sector to political parties and candidates.[40] Although the CRTC did not enquire about the value of such broadcasts in the 1968 election, one can estimate on the basis of a calculation similar to that in 1965 that the value of free-time broadcasts provided by the private sector to all parties in 1968 was not more than $250,000.

The sharp drop in the amount and value of free radio and television time provided by the public and private sectors in the 1968 campaign was

Table 5 - XI
BROADCAST TIME PURCHASED BY POLITICAL PARTIES
FROM PRIVATE STATIONS IN THE 1965 AND 1968 ELECTIONS

Party	1965	1968
Radio		
Liberal	$288,521.73	$338,885.33
Prog.-Cons.	177,485.01	281,661.39
NDP	60,551.46	63,531.00
Soc. Cred.	23,583.93	7,777.50
Créditistes	1,996.05	3,516.25
Other	5,660.00	5,350.45
Total	$557,798.18	$700,721.92
Television		
Liberal	$292,369.40	$318,495.77
Prog.-Cons.	206,075.52	327,935.38
NDP	85,280.26	56,763.62
Soc. Cred.	25,070.20	8,222.51
Créditistes	20,173.50	8,355.10
Total	$628,968.88*	$719,772.33
TOTAL (Radio and TV)	$1,186,767.06*	$1,420,494.25

* To the 1965 sum must be added the sum of $63,160 for 37 announcements sold by the private CTV network to the Liberal, Conservative and New Democratic Parties.
Source: Khayyam Z. Paltiel and Larry G. Kjosa, **The Structure and Dimensions of Election Broadcasting in Canada,** paper prepared for delivery to the 1969 Annual Meeting of the Canadian Political Science Association, York University, Toronto, June 4, 1969, Table XIII.

made up by a spectacular increase in the amount of time sold by private stations. The trend over the past six elections is traced in Table 5-X.

The value of these paid broadcasts as reported by the station operators to the Board of Broadcast Governors in 1965 and to the Canadian Radio-Television Commission in 1968, is summarized in Table 5-XI. Total commercial revenues from political parties amounted to almost $1.5 million in the last federal election, a rise of about one-sixth from 1965, with the largest increase coming from the Conservative Party followed by the Liberals; the NDP in fact appears to have spent one-third less on television in the last election.

It is clear that the cutback in the provision of free broadcast time has a differential effect on the political parties. If their resources are large enough, as they appear to have been in the case of the two old major parties, the gap can be made up by purchase of time on the private stations. However, the smaller parties apparently found difficulty in taking this step in the last election, the net effect being a drop in their exposure via the sound and visual media.

The costs listed above are the minimal charges associated with the broadcast media. In addition to the time charges there are production costs which are a further burden on party treasuries. In at least one case known to the author, one major party set aside twenty percent of its television budget for these "production costs."

The staff of the Committee on Election Expenses estimated the "total value of political broadcasting from all sources for the 1965 campaign . . . [at] almost $2,000,000."[41] A like method of calculation would produce an estimate of $2.5 million for similar costs and expenditures in the 1968 federal general election.

FOOTNOTES

[1] *Correspondence of Sir John A. Macdonald*, selected by Sir Joseph Pope, Doubleday, Page and Co., Toronto, 1921, pp. 89-90.

[2] *Ibid.*, p. 235.

[3] John Porter, *The Vertical Mosaic*, University of Toronto Press, Toronto, 1965, p. 536.

[4] Lucien Pacaud, ed., *Sir Wilfrid Laurier: Letters to My Father and Mother*, The Ryerson Press, Toronto, 1935, p. 18 and p. 101; Laurier Joseph Lucien Lapierre, "Politics, Race and Religion in French Canada: Joseph Israel Tarte," unpublished Ph.D. dissertation, University of Toronto, Toronto, 1962, p. 311.

[5] W. T. R. Preston, *My Generation of Politics and Politicians*, Rose Publishing Co., Toronto, 1927, pp. 134-135.

[6] H. Blair Neatby, "Laurier and a Liberal Quebec: A Study in Political Man-

agement," unpublished Ph.D. dissertation, University of Toronto, Toronto, 1956, p. 226.

[7] Quoted in A. H. U. Colquhoun, *Press, Politics and People: The Life and Letters of Sir John Willison*, Macmillan Co. of Canada, Toronto, 1935, pp. 98-99.

[8] See Norman A. Ward, "The Press and the Patronage: An Exploratory Operation," in *The Political Process in Canada — Essays in Honour of R. MacGregor Dawson*, J. H. Aitchison, ed., University of Toronto Press, Toronto, 1963, pp. 3-16.

[9] Edwin R. Black, "Canadian Public Policy and the Mass Media," paper delivered to the 38th Annual Meeting of the Canadian Political Science Association, Sherbrooke, Quebec, June 1966.

[10] Oscar Douglas Skelton, *Life and Letters of Sir Wilfrid Laurier*, Vol. II, Oxford University Press, Toronto, 1921, p. 269.

[11] Mason Wade, *The French Canadians, 1760-1945*, The Macmillan Co. of Canada Ltd., Toronto, 1955, p. 602.

[12] Roger Graham, *Arthur Meighen*, Vol. II, Clarke, Irwin & Company Ltd., Toronto, 1963, *passim*.

[13] J. L. Granatstein, "Conservative Party Finances, 1939-1945," in Paltiel et al., *Studies in Canadian Party Finance*, Committee on Election Expenses, The Queen's Printer, Ottawa, 1966, p. 265.

[14] Wilfred H. Kesterton, "A Short History of the Press of Canada," *Gazette: International Journal of Mass Communication Studies*, Amsterdam, Vol. XV, No. 2, 1969, p. 90; see also Wilfred H. Kesterton, *A History of Journalism in Canada*, Carleton Library series, McClelland and Stewart Ltd., Toronto, 1967, *passim*.

[15] See the discussion on commercial politicians in Alexander Heard, *The Costs of Democracy*, The University of North Carolina Press, Chapel Hill, 1960, c. 15, "The Organization and Function of Campaigns," pp. 413-423.

[16] Granatstein, *op. cit.*, p. 299.

[17] Samuel Peter Regenstreif, "The Liberal Party of Canada; A Political Analysis," unpublished Ph.D. dissertation, Cornell University, 1963, p. 197.

[18] *Ibid.*, p. 234.

[19] See Richard Gwyn, "Ad-Men and Scientists Run this Election", *Financial Post*, LVI, No. 17, April 28, 1962. Reprinted in Hugh G. Thorburn, ed., *Party Politics in Canada*, Prentice-Hall of Canada Ltd., Toronto, 1963, pp. 70-72.

[20] Khayyam Z. Paltiel and Jean B. Van Loon, "Financing the Liberal Party," in Paltiel et al., *Studies in Canadian Party Finance*, Committee on Election Expenses, The Queen's Printer, Ottawa, 1966, p. 170.

[20a] Cited in *To Know and Be Known, The Report of the Task Force on Government Information*, The Queen's Printer for Canada, Ottawa, 1969, Vol. I, p. 28; see also Vol. II, pp. 324-325.

[21] For details see Study No. 11, "Candidate Spending Patterns and Attitudes," *Report of the Committee on Election Expenses*, The Queen's Printer, Ottawa, 1966, pp. 407-427.

[22] See Study No. 9, "Newspaper Advertising Expenditure and Lineage of the 1965 and 1963 Federal Elections," *Report of the Committee on Election Expenses, op. cit.*, pp. 331-358. This study is an excerpt from a far larger report prepared for the Committee by McDonald Research Limited, Toronto, in consultation with the Committee's research staff and the author, who was research director.

[23] *Ibid.*, pp. 352-353. The raw data concerning the 1963 campaign was collected

by the Committee's research staff; the estimate was then calculated using the 1965 information as a bench mark. Re methodology applied for the 1963 calculations, see *Ibid.*, pp. 350-358.

24 *Ibid.*, p. 332.
25 *Ibid.*, p. 333.
26 Table 10, *Ibid.*, p. 344.
27 Table 14, *Ibid.*, p. 348.
28 Table 9, *Ibid.*, p. 343.
29 Table 13, *Ibid.*, p. 347.
30 Table 7, *Ibid.*, p. 341.
31 Confidential communications from Liberal, Progressive Conservative and New Democratic Party sources, dated April 15, 1969, October 2, 1969 and September 22, 1969 respectively.
32 For details concerning Canadian political and election broadcasting, see Khayyam Z. Paltiel and Larry G. Kjosa, *The Structure and Dimensions of Election Broadcasting in Canada*, paper prepared for delivery to the 1969 Annual Meeting of the Canadian Political Science Association, York University, Toronto, June 4, 1969; publication forthcoming in *Jahrbuch des Öffentlichen Rechts der Gegenwart*, Neue Folge/Band 19, Tübingen. See also Study No. 10, "Political Broadcasting in Canada," *Report of the Committee on Election Expenses, op. cit.*, pp. 359-406.
33 Data regarding election broadcasts for the private sector are compiled by the Log Examination section of the Canadian Radio-Television Commission following the practice established by its predecessor the BBG; the CBC Department of Station Relations publishes regular Reports on Federal Election Campaigns.
34 *CBC White Paper* (Program Policy No. 65-1, *Political and Controversial Broadcasting*, Jan. 19, 1965), p. 5. This White Paper is currently undergoing revision. This could well result in different conditions being applied by the CBC in future election campaigns and new ground rules for party political broadcasts.
35 Table 6, *Report of the Committee on Election Expenses, op. cit.*, p. 389.
36 House of Commons, *Debates*, Vol. 113, No. 79, 1st Session, 28th Parliament, p. 4818.
37 *Ibid.*, and Table 8, *Report of the Committee on Election Expenses, op. cit.*, p. 392.
38 Table 9, *Ibid.*, p. 394.
39 Table 12, *Ibid.*, p. 399; and material provided by the Canadian Radio-Television Commission for the 1968 campaign.
40 Table 12, *Report of the Committee on Election Expenses, op. cit.*, p. 399.
41 *Ibid.*, p. 403.

PART III
THE CONTROL OF CAMPAIGN FUNDS

SIX

PUBLIC ATTITUDES AND CANDIDATES' REACTIONS: SURVEY FINDINGS*

The explanation for the almost exclusive dependence of Canadian parties on corporate financial or trade union sources for the wherewithal to carry out their activities lies not only in their history and structure but in the social context in which they have their being. Canadian scholars have only recently begun to explore in detail the nature and background of their party system and as yet the literature is extremely scanty.[1] Furthermore, it is only in the last few years that the extremely productive devices of survey research have been applied to the examination of Canadian political attitudes and behaviour.[2] In the face of such gaps the student who seeks to understand the financial practices of Canadian parties in terms of Canada's overall political culture and regional subcultures must perforce turn to the practices of her politicians and legislators as reflected in the legislative history of the attempts to control and regulate political and party finance. Variations in these control mechanisms may provide clues to Canada's political culture and are considered in subsequent chapters. Some survey research on the question of political finance is available and the light it casts on Canadian political behaviour will be considered here.

The reactions of Canadians to requests for party funds, and information concerning the methods used to solicit such donations, may be gleaned from a survey carried out on behalf of the Committee on Election Expenses following the federal general election of November 1965.[3] This

---

*Some of the material used in this chapter first appeared in Khayyam Z. Paltiel, "Contrasts Among the Several Canadian Political Finance Cultures," published as chapter 5 of Arnold J. Heidenheimer, ed., *Comparative Political Finance*, D. C. Heath and Co., Lexington, Mass., 1970, pp. 107-134.

study made no attempt to isolate contributors and the sample figures concerning the behaviour of the latter are very low. Nevertheless, with this *caveat* in mind, some meaningful information on this aspect of Canadian political activity does emerge.

The fundamental and determining finding is that only five percent of the Canadian respondents or their families had been asked to donate funds for the 1965 campaign and that only four percent of the sample actually did so.[4] This startling observation is supported by data which indicates that only slightly more than five percent of Canadians can be considered in any way to be party activists. Nor does the distribution of these activists, who helped a party in some way, vary greatly between the ten provinces or the two language groups. What may be significant, however, is the party distribution of activists which demonstrates that support for the social democratically oriented New Democratic Party was "considerably higher among the activists than among the sample as a whole."[5]

Table 6 - I
DISTRIBUTION OF ACTIVISTS BY PARTY — in Percentages

PARTY (self-identifiers)	Helped a Party	Did Not Help a Party	Residual	Total Number in Row
All Activists—1965	5.1%	94.5%	0.3%	2610
Liberal	6.0	93.9	0.1	985
Conservative	4.1	95.3	0.6	661
New Democratic	11.1	88.9	0.0	265
Social Credit	2.0	97.0	1.0	99
Créditiste	10.6	89.4	0.0	47
Union Nationale	14.3	85.7	0.0	14
Other	0.0	100.0	0.0	4
No Party	1.5	98.0	0.5	442
Refusal	2.6	97.4	0.0	77
Residual	0.0	100.0	0.0	17

Source: Adapted from Table 5 and Table A-3 in John Meisel and Richard Van Loon, "Canadian Attitudes to Election Expenses 1965-6," published in Paltiel et al., **Studies in Canadian Party Finance,** Committee on Election Expenses, The Queen's Printer, Ottawa, 1966, p. 43 and p. 136.

Questions with respect to opinion leadership, founded on the assumption that activism is related to awareness, apparently indicate that as one moves westward in Canada political awareness appears to increase. The per-

centage of respondents willing to persuade others how to vote moves from
8.3% in Newfoundland, to 20.4% in Quebec, 24.1% in Ontario, and as
high as 27.7% in Saskatchewan, which had been for long the bastion of
the CCF/NDP.[6] It should occasion no surprise, however, that only 4.3%
of all Canadians at the time immediately following the 1965 general election indicated that they were members of political parties.[7]

With respect to fund-raising, Table 6-II demonstrates that only one-fifth
of Canadians seem to have heard of such activities, with awareness rising
in relation to the usual East to West pattern.

Table 6 - II
AWARENESS OF FUND-RAISING BY PROVINCE

Province	Heard of Fund-Raising		Did Not Hear		Don't Remember		Residuals		Total	
	N	%	N	%	N	%	N	%	N	%
Canada	521	20.0	1675	64.2	409	15.7	5	0.2	2610	100.1*
P.E.I.	1	4.2	18	75.0	5	20.8	0	0	24	100.0
N.S.	8	10.7	54	72.0	13	17.3	0	0	75	100.0
N.B.	10	9.3	84	77.8	14	13.0	0	0	108	100.1*
Nfld.	1	4.2	20	83.3	3	12.5	0	0	24	100.0
Quebec	132	16.5	562	70.2	105	13.1	1	0.1	800	99.9
Ontario	218	20.7	651	61.6	184	17.5	3	0.3	1056	100.1*
Man.	36	27.7	81	62.3	13	10.0	0	0	130	100.0
Sask.	45	47.9	33	35.1	15	16.0	1	1.1	94	100.1*
Alberta	33	19.3	98	57.3	40	23.4	0	0	171	100.0
B.C.	37	28.9	74	57.8	17	13.3	0	0	128	100.0

*Due to rounding.
Source: Adapted from Tables 9 and 10 in John Meisel and Richard Van Loon, "Canadian Atti-
tudes to Election Expenses 1965-6," published in Paltiel et al., **Studies in Canadian Party
Finance**, Committee on Election Expenses, The Queen's Printer, Ottawa, 1966, p. 47.

This distribution is underlined by the finding that English-speaking respondents were more cognizant of fund-raising activities than French-
speaking respondents in a proportion of about 4 to 3.[8] Nor was this awareness any higher among Créditiste supporters in Quebec despite the party's
attempts to develop a mass-based popular fund-raising system.[9]

An attempt to isolate the fund-raisers from among the activists only
serves to confirm the observation made in Chapter 1 that fund-raisers constitute a tiny specialized body of persons. Only about one-sixth of the
already small (5.1%) group of activists admitted to canvassing for money

on behalf of a political party. Meisel and Van Loon conclude that "only a minute proportion of Canadians are likely to act as fund raisers."[10]

Attention must be concentrated on the five percent of the 2610 sample population which stated that it had been canvassed. Of these respondents, 79.1 percent actually contributed. Some of the details of this group of contributors are to be found in Tables 6-III and 6-IV.

Table 6 - III
PARTY IDENTITY IN FUND-RAISING
(Respondent only)

PARTY	Requests Made	% of Total Requests	Contri- butions Gained	Success Ratio
Liberal	27	29.7	14	0.52
Conservative	17	18.7	15	0.88
New Democratic	39	42.8	28	0.72
Social Credit & Créditiste	7	7.7	6	0.86
Other	1	1.1	1	1.0
Refusals & Residuals	0	0	8	—
TOTAL	91	100.0	72	—

Source: Table 13 in John Meisel and Richard Van Loon, "Canadian Attitudes to Election Expenses 1965-6," published in Paltiel et al., Studies in Canadian Party Finance, Committee on Election Expenses, The Queen's Printer, Ottawa, 1966, p. 51.

Table 6 - IV
TOTAL NUMBER OF DONATIONS TO PARTIES
(Respondent and family)

PARTY	LIB.	CON.	NDP	Créditiste & Social Credit	Others	Refusals and Residuals	TOTAL
Total Donations	33	25	44	9	3	12	126
% of Totals	26.2	19.8	34.9	7.1	2.4	9.5	99.9

Source: Table 14 in John Meisel and Richard Van Loon, "Canadian Attitudes to Election Expenses 1965-6," published in Paltiel et al., Studies in Canadian Party Finance, Committee on Election Expenses, The Queen's Printer, Ottawa, 1966, p. 52.

The above tables indicate that fund-raising on a mass basis is not seriously undertaken by Canadian political parties. The New Democratic Party alone appears to be truly active in this field; this is even more marked when considered in relation to its share of the popular vote. An examination of requests for donations by family income level lead Meisel and Van Loon to the conclusion that "Parties make almost no attempt to get at the 'little man' to finance their activities."[11] Data regarding the distribution of reported party giving by income categories indicate that the Liberals were the most successful with the highest income group, those with incomes of more than $15,000 per annum; that 60 percent of Conservative contributors earned below $8,000; and that NDP financial support was the most widely distributed although more than half of its contributors were from under the $8,000 bracket.[12] Surprisingly, of almost one-quarter of the total number of the survey respondents who were members of trade unions, only a miniscule number were either asked to contribute or contributed as individuals to the New Democratic Party which is dubbed the "political arm of labour"; clearly little effort is made to gain such financial support except at the organizational level.

Because of the regional-economic and regional-ethnic cleavages underlying the Canadian political system, some attention must be given to the provincial and linguistic distribution of party contributions. These are summarized in Tables 6-V and 6-VI.

Table 6 - V
PARTY GIVING BY PROVINCE (Number)

PARTY	LIB.	CON.	NDP	Créditiste & Social Credit	Others	Total
Province						
P.E.I.	0	0	0	0	0	0
N.S.	0	0	0	0	0	0
N.B.	0	0	1	0	0	1
Nfld.	0	0	0	0	0	0
Quebec	6	4	3	3	1	17
Ontario	5	7	13	0	0	25
Manitoba	1	0	1	0	0	2
Sask.	1	2	7	1	0	11
Alberta	0	1	0	2	0	3
B.C.	1	1	3	1	0	6
TOTAL	14	15	28	7	1	65

Source: Adapted from Table 17 in John Meisel and Richard Van Loon, "Canadian Attitudes to Election Expenses, 1965-6," published in Paltiel et al., **Studies in Canadian Party Finance**, Committee on Election Expenses, The Queen's Printer, Ottawa, 1966, p. 56.
In addition to the 65 identified donations, 4 in Ontario and 1 respondent in Alberta refused to identify the destination of their giving.

The fact that only one respondent in the Atlantic Provinces out of a regional sample of 230 contributed to a political party in the 1965 campaign would appear to confirm the claim in Chapter 1 that the Maritimes are on the receiving end of inter-regional transfers of campaign funds. It is also evident that Quebec and Ontario are the centres of fund-raising activity and that popular response to soliciting funds is greatest in Central Canada. The New Democratic Party has the widest distribution of financial support and, due largely to its efforts, Saskatchewan and to a lesser extent British Columbia are important areas of party giving.

Despite the smallness of the numbers involved some indication of ethnic financial support for parties of their choice may be gathered from the mother-tongues of responding givers.

Table 6 - VI
DONATIONS BY PARTY AND LANGUAGE OF RESPONDENT
(in percentages)

PARTY	LIB.	CON.	NDP	Créditiste and Social Credit
Language	%	%	%	%
English	50.0	100.0	85.6	42.8
French	42.8	0.0	10.7	57.2
Other	7.2	0.0	3.6	0.0
Total	100.0	100.0	99.9	100.0

Source: Derived from Table 18 in John Meisel and Richard Van Loon, "Canadian Attitudes to Election Expenses 1965-6," published in Paltiel et al., **Studies in Canadian Party Finance,** Committee on Election Expenses, The Queen's Printer, Ottawa, 1966, p. 57.

Clearly French-speaking Canadians give their support overwhelmingly to the Liberals and the Créditistes. The Conservatives gained no monetary aid whatsoever amongst French-speaking respondents. The NDP found a modicum of help among francophones but were essentially beneficiaries of English-speakers. Only the Liberals could claim a reasonable balance of monetary aid from the two main language groups.

Although it would be dangerous to draw conclusions on the basis of figures whose smallness may be statistically insignificant, one may be permitted to infer with Meisel and Van Loon that:

> The distribution of party giving by region reveals a concentration of contributions emanating from Quebec and Ontario and to a lesser extent from the West with virtually no attempt being made to raise funds, at least among the public, in the Maritimes. The Liberals and Conservatives concentrate their activities most

strongly in Ontario and the NDP also shows a higher reading in Ontario than else-where with another high reading in Saskatchewan. Social Credit, not unnaturally, concentrates its efforts in Alberta while the Créditistes, of course, must rely on Quebec. . . .

Some differences in Canada's major language groups [may be] noted. The English appear to have given somewhat more frequently than the French and have more often heard of fund-raising activities. The French do not seem to shower the Con-servatives with donations and contribute only rarely to the NDP while the English may be slightly more likely to donate to the Conservatives than to the Liberals. The NDP again takes a numerically greater share of the English donations than does any other party.[13]

Information made available by respondents regarding the methods of approach used in soliciting funds reveals that the styles are fairly uniform across Canada and from party to party.[14] It is clear that the personal approach is the one preferred with emphasis placed on canvassing by friends, fellow workers or business colleagues. Organized fund-raising methods on a mass scale using sophisticated means of persuasion are eschewed by and large by Canadian parties. Indeed, it is only recently that the fund-raising dinner beloved of American parties has appeared on the Canadian scene, the infrequency of its occurrence being perhaps a com-ment on its limited success.

Canadians in general do not participate in the financing of the electoral process, nor are they aware of the methods adopted to meet the monetary needs of their parties. Canadian parties have done little to change this situation and indeed are not equipped to do so. Reform, if any, will evi-dently not issue from the party level.

Questions concerning alternative means of financing campaign activities produced a different regional and geographic distribution of attitudes than those displayed above. Quebec voters and candidates for public office[15] are more receptive to the idea of outright state subsidization of election expenses than their counterparts elsewhere in Canada. Meisel and Van Loon report that while about two-thirds of all respondents favoured full or partial subsidization of election campaigns, more than 70 percent of Quebec respondents were so inclined and that one-third more residents of Ontario than Quebecers were opposed to any subsidization.[16]

Moreover, although Maritimers were favourably inclined to the notion, as one moved westward support fell and opposition grew to publicly sub-sidized election costs. Similarly, almost 50 percent more English- than French-speaking Canadians were opposed to subsidies of any kind. A study of élite attitudes demonstrated by candidates in the 1965 federal general election reveals that 87 percent of the Quebec respondents favoured direct state subsidization of election campaigns with a mere 9 percent opposed. However, only 65 percent of responding candidates in

Ontario and 70 percent of all Canadian respondents were favourable, with 28 percent and 23 percent respectively opposed to such measures. These attitudes are summarized in Table 6-VII.

Table 6 - VII

CANDIDATES' ATTITUDES TO DIRECT SUBSIDIZATION OF CAMPAIGNS

(By Region)

Response	Western Provinces N=129	Ontario N=124	Quebec N=158	Atlantic Provinces N=43	Canada N=454
	%	%	%	%	%
In Favour	54	65	87	63	70
Opposed	35	28	9	23	23
Don't Know	11	7	4	14	7
Total	100	100	100	100	100

Sources: Khayyam Z. Paltiel, Jill McCalla Vickers and Raoul P. Barbe, "Candidate Attitudes Toward the Control of Election Expenses," in Paltiel et al., **Studies in Canadian Party Finance**, Committee on Election Expenses, The Queen's Printer, Ottawa, 1966, p. 488; and **Report of the Committee on Election Expenses**, The Queen's Printer, Ottawa, 1966, p. 418.

Similar disparities amongst regional and cultural groups, be they of an élite or mass character, may be noted with respect to partial subsidies such as free mailing privileges, which interestingly enough appear to be more popular elsewhere in Canada than in Quebec.[17] Despite these variations in attitude it is clear that there does exist "unmistakable enthusiasm for government subsidies"[18] in Canada. However, when survey teams questioned respondents about current methods of financing parties and campaigns, it appeared that Canadians . . .

> are not alarmed about the financing of parties through private initiative and almost 50 per cent . . . appear to be unmoved by the often-heard warnings that the financing of parties by private sources . . . may pervert the ideal process in which the definition of the national interest takes place through a free and equal struggle among the parties.[19]

Faced with contradictory attitudes toward alternative control measures and the regional, ethnic and cultural cleavages which lie behind them, practical, pragmatic advisory committees and legislators may well stop short of drastic change and settle for compromise.

Asked whether they would have given to their favourite party if requested, only 18.5 percent of the sample of Canadians indicated that they would have been prepared to do so.[20] West of the Ottawa River more than one-fifth of the population were ready to give, rising to one-third of the respondents in Saskatchewan; east of the National Capital, less than 11 percent were prepared to lend their financial support; only in Nova Scotia did one-quarter of the respondents indicate such preparedness. There is also a marked disparity between English- and French-speaking Canadians with respect to willingness to give money to the parties of their choice; 22.6 percent of English-speakers would have done so compared to only 8.5 percent of French Canadians.[21] Moreover, whereas only slightly more than half the anglophones would definitely refuse their financial help, more than three-quarters of the French would definitely not give. Breakdowns by income and religion indicate that as income rises so does the propensity to give. Of the major religious denominations, Roman Catholics are the least inclined to donate. (This may well be related to the fact that the overwhelming majority of Roman Catholics in the sample were French-speaking.) Between 21 and 25 percent of the members of the United Church, Presbyterians, Jews and Anglicans are likely to give, the Greek Orthodox being the most favourably inclined. Not surprisingly, attitudes to giving by party identification show the NDP and the Créditistes most eager, the Liberals hovering above the average and the Union Nationale supporters the least responsive.

Questioned with respect to their willingness to give time or money, Canadians appear far more ready to work for, rather than to donate to, the parties of their choice.[22] This zeal is most marked among NDP self-identifiers but is significant for all parties since only slightly more than one-quarter of the respondents stated that they would do neither. Protestants and Jews are far more receptive than Roman Catholics, and the English far more so than the French, almost 40 percent of whom said they would neither help nor donate to their parties. The usual East-West pattern is maintained in this instance as well. Of some significance is the finding that:

> People who do not belong to any association seem far less willing to give time or money to a party than do association members. Of those belonging to associations, members of professional associations show the greatest willingness to give money and labour union members the least. Labour union members are more willing to give time than anyone else while trade association members are most likely to give both.[23]

A tentative conclusion which may be drawn is that there exists an untapped potential amongst the Canadian population. Apparently the number of contributors might be quadrupled and the army of volunteers expanded enormously. A question remains, however, whether Canadian parties have the organizational techniques and resources to exploit these possibilities; in any case, it is certain that the task would be easier and far more productive amongst English-speaking Canadians, especially west of the Ottawa River, than amongst French-speaking Quebecers or Maritimers.

Most Canadians appear to think alike with respect to the sources of campaign contributions. Questions posed regarding the legitimacy of business corporation and trade union giving indicate that over 50 percent of respondents were opposed to such donations but that in general they did not fundamentally object to them.[24] Breakdowns by language, religion, voluntary organization membership, and income show few variations in viewpoint. Even half of the trade union members and NDP self-identifiers also objected to trade union as well as corporate giving.

Élite attitudes as revealed in candidate responses would appear to support these findings. Candidates were asked after the 1965 campaign whether "large contributors" would tend to corrupt a political party.[25] Large contributors are generally viewed with suspicion by candidates whether the latter are examined by political affiliation, region, rural/urban area of residence, past membership in the House of Commons, success or failure in the campaign.[26] Minor party candidates are far more suspicious of large contributors than either the Liberals or the Conservatives; Maritimers and Quebecers and rural candidates are more fearful than Ontario, Western or urban respondents. Incumbents and elected candidates are less worried about big donors than non-members or defeated candidates.

Canadians obviously do not anticipate nor are they very anxious about fundamental changes with respect to election finance. Meisel and Van Loon sum up the attitudes prevailing in the winter of 1965-1966 as follows:

The most appropriate catchword to characterize the voters' mood is **laissez-faire.** The public's predisposition to leave things as they are and not to interfere with present arrangements is apparent in the way in which members of our sample responded to the five proposals or reforms submitted to them in our questionnaire ...

1. That tax deductions be allowed on contributions to parties or candidates.
2. That parties publish their expenses.
3. That parties disclose the names of their contributors.
4. That the amounts given by each contributor be published.
5. That the government pay all or some of the costs of election campaigns.

... trying to fit the responses into simple "yes" or "no" clusters we can summarize as follows:

1. No (65 percent to 30 percent).
2. Yes (69 percent to 20 percent).
3. No (48 percent to 42 percent).
4. No (50 percent to 40 percent).
5. Yes (67 percent to 24 percent).[27]

Table 6 - VIII
SHOULD POLITICAL CONTRIBUTIONS BE TAX DEDUCTIBLE?
(Candidates' Attitudes)

Response	LIB. N=136	CON. N=85	NDP N=126	S.C. N=37	Créd. N=42	Ind. & Other N=28
	%	%	%	%	%	%
Yes	78	80	47	51	55	50
No	16	12	48	46	40	43
Don't Know	6	8	5	3	5	7

Source: Khayyam Z. Paltiel, Jill McCalla Vickers and Raoul P. Barbe, "Candidate Attitudes Toward the Control of Election Expenses," in Paltiel et al., **Studies in Canadian Party Finance,** Committee on Election Expenses, The Queen's Printer, Ottawa, 1966, p. 480.

It is interesting that tax deductions are least popular among the "major" party supporters, the higher income groups and the Eastern Provinces, and more popular in Ontario, the West and among the English-speaking.[28] Élite attitudes as represented amongst the candidates contrast sharply, however, with mass views; tax deductions are generally endorsed, particularly in the Conservative and Liberal parties, as shown in Table 6-VIII.

It is with respect to disclosure that Canadians show a contradictory but in effect stand-pat posture. The present practice of publishing election costs at the candidate level is generally endorsed without any major social or regional variations in response,[28] but there is marked reluctance to approve the disclosure of the names of donors[29] or the amounts given to parties.[30] The urge to protect the privacy of individuals was breached only in the case of Prince Edward Island with British Columbia and Quebec revealing a plurality but not a majority in favour of disclosure of donors' names. This is borne out by the finding that a plurality of French- in contrast to English-Canadian respondents would endorse such disclosure but a substantial number of "undecided" reveal marked hesitancy on the matter. Only the New Democrats and the Union Nationale show a majority in favour of the disclosure of donors' names and they are joined by the Créditistes with respect to the amounts given to parties. Other than Prince Edward Island, only in the province of Quebec is there a plurality of respondents favouring disclosure of amounts given to parties, but here too the "don't knows" reveal great hesitancy.

Similarly élite attitudes as expressed in the responses of candidates shift sharply when the respondents were asked to add the disclosure of sources of candidate and party funds to the reports of candidate income and expenses.[31]

The New Democratic and Créditiste respondents were strongly in favour of the publication of candidate reports: 94 and 93 per cent respectively. Liberal and Conservative respondents were much less strongly in favour, [with] majorities of 54 and 58 per cent respectively ... [and] ... Social Credit respondents ... 76 per cent in favour. ...

[This] was modified still further when the publication of party reports stating ... sources was considered. Liberals and Conservatives generally disapproved of the scheme with only 38 and 35 per cent respectively in favour. At the other end of the scale, 96 per cent of the New Democrats were enthusiastic. Between these two extremes ... were the Social Credit respondents with 70 per cent and ... the Créditiste respondents . . . with 86 per cent reporting in favour of such a measure. ... [32]

It may well be that an awareness of the hesitancies and lukewarm attitudes of the Canadian electorate and party activists with respect to drastic reform, as well as a fear of disturbing established fund-raising patterns, lies at the root of the failure to enact or propose vigorous measures to disclose the sources and amounts of party income. The steps taken in this direction are analyzed in the next three chapters.

FOOTNOTES

[1] Two useful compendia have been published in recent years: Hugh G. Thorburn, ed., *Party Politics in Canada,* 2nd ed., Prentice-Hall of Canada Ltd., Toronto, Ontario, 1967; and John C. Courtney, ed., *Voting in Canada,* Prentice-Hall of Canada Ltd., Toronto, Ontario, 1967. See also F. C. Engelmann and M. A. Schwartz, *Political Parties and the Canadian Social Structure,* Prentice-Hall of Canada Ltd., Toronto, Ontario, 1967.

[2] One example is the study based on secondary analyses of Gallup Poll material by Mildred A. Schwartz, *Public Opinion and Canadian Identity,* University of California Press, Berkeley and Los Angeles, 1967.

[3] This formed part of a larger study based on the Michigan Survey Research Centre post-election surveys, the results of which have not as yet been published. The main study was designed by Philip E. Converse of the University of Michigan, Maurice Pinard of McGill University, Peter Regenstreif of the University of Rochester, Mildred Schwartz of the National Opinion Research Centre of Chicago, and John Meisel of Queen's University. The author, as Research Director of the Committee on Election Expenses, participated in the design of questions added re party finance and the control of election expenses.

The findings referred to in this chapter appear in John Meisel and Richard Van Loon, "Canadian Attitudes to Election Expenses 1965-6," published in Paltiel et al., *Studies in Canadian Party Finance,* Committee on Election Expenses, The Queen's Printer, Ottawa, 1966, pp. 23-146.

[4] *Ibid.,* p. 50.

[5] *Ibid.,* p. 44.

6 *Ibid.*, p. 45.
7 *Ibid.*, p. 46.
8 *Ibid.*, p. 48.
9 *Ibid.*, p. 49.
10 *Ibid.*, p. 50.
11 *Ibid.*, pp. 53-54.
12 *Ibid.*, pp. 54-55.
13 *Ibid.*, pp. 62-63.
14 *Ibid.*, pp. 58-60.
15 A detailed survey of candidate attitudes and behaviour in the 1965 campaign is found in Khayyam Z. Paltiel, Jill McCalla Vickers and Raoul P. Barbe, "Candidate Attitudes Toward the Control of Election Expenses," *Ibid.*, pp. 459-594; a summary entitled "Candidate Spending Patterns and Attitudes" has been published as Study 11, *Report of the Committee on Election Expenses*, The Queen's Printer, Ottawa, 1966, pp. 407-427.
16 Meisel and Van Loon, *op. cit.*, p. 115 ff.
17 *Ibid.*, 114-116; and Paltiel, Vickers and Barbe, *op. cit.*, p. 489.
18 Meisel and Van Loon, *op. cit.*, p. 127.
19 *Ibid.*, p. 125.
20 Based on *Ibid.* Tables 22-26 and pp. 63-69.
21 *Ibid.*, Appendix II, Table A-7, p. 137.
22 *Ibid.*, Tables 27-33, pp. 70-78.
23 *Ibid.*, p. 77.
24 *Ibid.*, Tables 34-38, pp. 78-87.
25 *Report of the Committee on Election Expenses, op. cit.*, Table 13, p. 417.
26 Paltiel, Vickers and Barbe, *op. cit.*, Tables 9, 13, 17, 21, 22, 29; pp. 478, 487, 490, 493, 495, 502.
27 Meisel and Van Loon, *op. cit.*, pp. 126-127.
28 *Ibid.*, Tables 44-47, pp. 93-100.
29 *Ibid.*, Tables 48-53, pp. 100-107.
30 *Ibid.*, Tables 54-59, pp. 107-114.
31 Paltiel, Vickers and Barbe, *op. cit.*, Tables 45-50, pp. 522-530.
32 Condensed from *Ibid.*, p. 522 and p. 526.

SEVEN
FEDERAL AND PROVINCIAL LEGISLATION: A CRITICAL APPRAISAL[1]

Laissez-Faire has been the dominant characteristic of the federal and provincial approach to the twin problems of party finance and campaign funds in Canada. The laws do not stem from a recognition that money presents a special problem in the conduct of modern election campaigns but have been adopted in response to repeated scandals. Demonstrations of public interest in reform have usually faded away with the memories of the scandals which roused the attention of reluctant legislators. The laws which have been enacted have been directed at the behaviour and expenditures of individual candidates at the constituency level; the existence of parties and their central role in the campaign process have been all but ignored. One useful device which has been adopted generally in Canada is the doctrine of agency whereby legal responsibility for the use of money has been placed on a single agent. The one other significant development has been to oblige the candidate and his agent to make a declaration of their campaign income and expenditures and to detail how the funds were spent. Only the Province of Quebec* has recognized and assumed a more far-reaching public responsibility with regard to the costs of campaigns; the background and structure of this radical departure from the Canadian norm are discussed in the next chapter.

---

*Since this chapter was written, the Province of Nova Scotia has adopted an election expense law based on the Quebec subsidy system discussed in Chapter 8. The Nova Scotia legislation has not as yet been put to the test of an election campaign, therefore its efficacy cannot as yet be judged. Cf. *The Elections Act*, Revised Statutes of Nova Scotia, 1967, chap. 83 as amended by 1969, chap. 40, 18 Eliz. II.

N.B. For the principle of the system see note at the end of this chapter, p. 121.

THE EVOLUTION OF FEDERAL LEGISLATION

At the outset, Canadian law paid little attention to the question of election funds. At Confederation only certain corrupt practices such as the offering and acceptance of bribes, treating — notably with intoxicating liquors— and the conveyance of voters to the polling stations in particular circumstances, were considered to be illegal. The law completely ignored the possibility of corruption arising out of the obligations of candidates to those who had contributed to their campaigns. Nor was there any recognition of the effects of the uneven distribution of funds amongst parties and candidates. The first serious consideration given to these problems followed the revelation of the earliest of Canada's major railway scandals in 1872.

The steps which Parliament took under the leadership of the Reform Government of Alexander Mackenzie have guided Canadian thinking on the subject to the present day. The Pacific Scandal precipitated in 1874 the first legislative attempt to use publicity as a means of controlling the misuse of election funds.[2] A candidate was to be required to appoint an agent who would be accountable legally for the use of money; both were made responsible for an official declaration of how funds were expended. The doctrine of agency was a useful device; its introduction permitted the establishment and fixing of responsibility for the spending of funds. However, the means by which monies were raised was ignored, it apparently being felt that the electorate itself would be the appropriate judge of this process. Publicity was to be applied to spending and the objects of expenditure but the sources of money and its main channels were disregarded and have remained free from publicity ever since; the nub of the issue which prompted Parliament to act was deliberately overlooked.

The original Canadian statute and subsequent amending legislation were inadequate in other respects. The law totally ignored the existence of parties and that the central party organizations raised most of the funds and were the principal providers of the wherewithal for constituency campaigns as well. Party leaders and fund-raisers could be held accountable for reporting funds raised and spent only in constituencies where they themselves were candidates. Another crucial weakness, even in terms of the philosophy which purportedly has guided Canadian legislators, was the failure to provide any effective enforcement machinery; initiative in the laying of charges against alleged violators of the law was left to the public at large, and that in effect has meant nobody. No provision was made for establishing the accuracy of the declarations made and no official was charged with the duty of prosecuting candidates and/or their agents who had transgressed the stipulations of the law. Nor was any arrangement made for the collection, tabulation and central publication of the reports made by the candidates. In the absence of adequate enforcement, the candidates and their agents have failed to take their legal obligations seriously, as witnessed by the rising tide of delinquencies in submitting the sketchy election expense returns, which the Committee on Election Expenses ruefully described as being largely "incomplete and misleading."[3] After the federal election in June 1968 no fewer than 27.6 percent of the candidates failed to file the reports required by law.

Analysis of the eight elections since the end of the Second World War presents the following picture:

Table 7-I
REPORTING OF CANDIDATE EXPENDITURES IN EIGHT
CANADIAN FEDERAL ELECTIONS, 1949-1968

Election Year	Total Number of Candidates	Number Failing to Report	Percentage not Reporting
1949	849	144	17.0%
1953	901	133	14.8
1957	868	121	13.9
1958	836	163	19.5
1962	1017	198	19.5
1963	1028	248	24.1
1965	1013	255	25.2
1968	967	267	27.6

Sources: Report of the Committee on Election Expenses, The Queen's Printer, Ottawa, 1966, p. 138, and Canada, House of Commons, Sessional Paper, November 7, 1968.

For the past six elections the proportion of defaulters has been increasing. From the statistics presented in Table 7-II it would appear that the candidates of the victorious party tend to file their declarations, probably to protect their seats; while those who are unsuccessful at the polls are not as apt to make a return. However, here again regional political cultures modify behaviour. After the 1968 election, one-quarter of the Progressive-Conservative candidates, over one-third of the New Democrats, one-fifth of the Social Crediters, and more than half the candidates of the Ralliement des Créditistes and "others" neglected to comply with the provisions of the law.

Clearly the belief that the electors themselves would act as watchdogs or that the parties would check each other by mutual vigilance has not been fulfilled.

Further scandals simply led to minor or ill-conceived amendments to the *Act* of 1874. Revelations concerning McGreevy's collection of kick-

Table 7 - II
PERCENTAGE OF CANDIDATES NOT SUBMITTING EXPENDITURE DECLARATIONS IN EIGHT CANADIAN FEDERAL ELECTIONS, 1949-1968: BY PARTY

Political Affiliation	1949	1953	1957	1958	1962	1963	1965	1968
	%	%	%	%	%	%	%	%
Liberal	1.9	3.0	7.5	23.4	9.8	12.5	12.5	6.8
Progressive-Conservative	14.0	14.9	7.8	2.3	13.9	19.2	18.5	25.1
CCF/NDP	15.6	21.2	16.7	23.7	18.8	29.3	31.4	38.4
Social Credit	14.3	12.3	15.9	31.7	32.6	33.5	30.2	23.3
Ralliement des Créditistes	—	—	—	—	—	—	51.9	55.6
LPP/Communists	17.6	23.0	30.0	27.7	16.6	18.1	33.3	21.4
Others	60.5	45.5	50.0	52.7	48.7	50.0	41.5	52.5

Sources: **Report of the Committee on Election Expenses,** The Queen's Printer, Ottawa, 1966, p. 139, and Canada, House of Commons, **Sessional Paper,** November 7, 1968.

backs on government contracts led to an amendment which made it a corrupt practice for anyone to assist a candidate in return for a "valuable consideration" or for the assurance of "any office, place or employment."[4] However, prosecutions were left in the hands of the Crown whose enthusiasm for pursuing the party in power might be questioned, not to gainsay the problem of providing substantive proof of such charges. Another series of ineffectual reforms was enacted when blatant patronage, electoral and administrative corruption provoked renewed public interest in the first decade of this century.[5] Foreigners were prohibited from aiding in Canadian elections, principally in order to ban the participation of ex-Canadians who were customarily brought to vote at great cost from the United States. The doctrine of agency was fortified by making it an indictable offence to make any contribution apart from personal expenses to a candidate except through his official agent; but parties still went unrecognized and undefined. A third amendment which prohibited corporations from contributing to candidates and parties proved in the event to be one of the most ridiculous chapters in this melancholy story of ineffective legislation.

A typical product of the "progressive" era, this ban on corporate giving did not constitute an obstacle to contributions from business interests. On the other hand, it prevented the financial participation of trade unions in the electoral process, for an amendment enacted in 1920 made the clause applicable to all companies and associations whether incorporated or not.[6] After a decade of agitation by trade union and socialist members of parliament, the clause which prohibited campaign gifts by trade unions as well as corporations was repealed[7] on the very eve of the disclosure of the Beauharnois Affair.

The 1920 *Act* had attempted, along with certain clarifying provisions, to broaden the scope of existing legislation by requiring the disclosure of the sums received and the names of contributors in candidates' expense declarations;[8] but the existence of parties continued to be ignored. Enforcement procedures remained lamentably weak. The only Member of Parliament to be disqualified under a provision of this *Act* was a Progressive candidate who lost his seat in 1922 on the technicality of having failed to report the cost of hiring a band — the result of concerted efforts of the major parties who initiated the action against him.[9] But the Beauharnois Scandal, the most notorious Canadian election fund scandal of modern times, was based on the contribution of a huge sum of money by a private hydro-electric power company to the Liberal Party (some said to the Conservatives as well), allegedly in return for a valuable government concession. The fact that no prosecutions were ever undertaken despite the evidence of the company's gift to party collectors demonstrated the bankruptcy of the legislation.

Summing up its review of federal election expense legislation, the Committee on Election Expenses concluded:

> The [Beauharnois] scandal demonstrated the irrelevance of reporting laws which failed to recognize parties in that all the money in question had been given to party collectors, not to candidates. It was in many ways one of the worst scandals in Canadian history, and one which arose directly out of campaign fund corruption; yet on this occasion not even another platitude was called in to mollify public opinion.
>
> Indeed, after 1920, whatever innovating spirit Parliament had once possessed concerning election expenses seemed to disappear altogether. Not a single new law of any significance has been brought down since that time. Campaign funds have been the subject of a good deal of public comment; newspapers and magazines have, often enough, contained articles on the matter, usually accompanied by pleas for reform. Parliament itself, in committees and discussion of private members' bills, has considered a number of ideas; the Provincial Legislatures have, on occasion, passed far-reaching and even radical legislation. Yet for almost a half-century nothing of significance to election expenses has changed in the federal statutes.[10]

THE PRESENT FEDERAL LAW

The existing legislative controls of election expenses are spelled out in the *Canada Elections Act*.[11] Candidates must name an official agent through whom all expenditures must be made, with few minor exceptions such as personal expenses paid by the candidate himself up to an amount of $2,000. Contributions to help meet a candidate's costs must also be made through the official agent. The act forbids private expenditures by supporters of a candidate but he and his agent cannot be held responsible for such assistance if it can be shown that all reasonable means were used to prevent them. Financial claims arising from the campaign must be presented for payment within one month following the date of the election and must be paid by the agent within fifty days of the poll. The payment of bills after this date requires the approval of a judge and the agent must make a special report concerning such liabilities.

A sworn detailed statement of a candidate's election finances must be submitted to the constituency returning officer by his agent within two months following the election, and must be supported within ten weeks by the candidate's own sworn statement. This declaration *(form 61)* must record all payments made by the agent supported by bills and receipts, the candidate's personal expenses, disputed claims, unpaid claims, and all monies or their equivalent given or promised to the agent showing the contributor and the amount and form of this support. The constituency returning officer is obliged to publish a summary of the candidate's return in a newspaper in the constituency where the election was held within 10 days of its receipt at the candidate's cost. The declaration together with the supporting documents must be available for public inspection for six months thereafter at a nominal charge of 20 cents, following which these may be returned to the candidate or destroyed.

Legal sanctions may be applied for failure to submit a report, including a fine not exceeding $500 or imprisonment up to one year or both. A penalty of $500 for every day in which he sits or votes in the House of Commons may also be imposed on a successful candidate who has not submitted a report. Falsification with intent of a candidate's declaration is an indictable offence subject to a fine of $2,000 and/or imprisonment up to two years; failure to pay this fine could lead to an additional prison term of three months.[12] The election of a successful candidate may be nullified, and he may be disqualified from being elected to or sitting in the House of Commons for seven years for a corrupt act, and five years for an illegal act, whether he be personally guilty, or has knowingly allowed his agent to commit such offences.[13] However, the initiative for launching court proceedings has been left to private citizens or rival candidates or their representatives.

Canadian law imposes no ceilings on contributions or expenditures. The only existing limitation applies to civil servants who are expressly forbidden to participate in federal or provincial politics or to contribute to political parties. Aimed at preserving the impartiality of the public official, the law categorically states that:

(1) No deputy head or employee shall
(a) engage in partisan work in connection with any election for the election of a member of the House of Commons, a member of the legislature of a province or a member of the Council of the Yukon Territory or the Northwest Territories; or
(b) contribute, receive or in any way deal with any money for the funds of any political party.
(2) Every person who violates subsection (1) is liable to be dismissed.[14]

Contemporary thinking on the subject is probably best represented by the following exchange in the House of Commons.

MR. PETERS: What is wrong with a [civil servant] belonging to a political party? Is that not democracy? . . . I fail to see how this could be objectionable.
MR. McILRAITH: If a civil servant pays membership [dues] in a political party then he is indicating his partisan interest, and he is putting himself in a position where his interest may conflict with his duty as a civil servant. His duty as a civil servant is to carry out administrative processes along the lines laid down by the government of the day, and if he becomes a dues-paying member of a political party then he is putting himself in a position where his interest may be opposed to his duty as a civil servant.[15]

Clearly, many provincial governments have not been so fastidious. There are also unresolved questions concerning the rights of civil servants arising out of the sheer growth of the public service, and the implications of the introduction of party politics at the municipal level, where civil servants have traditionally been permitted to participate. However, these questions are beyond the scope of this chapter and will not be pursued here.[16] Some relaxation of these stringent restrictions is apparent in the provisions of the *Public Service Employment Act* (Statutes of Canada, 1966-67, chap. 71, sec. 32) which permits employees in the public service to present themselves as candidates for election.

The weaknesses of existing federal legislation arise out of the narrowness of the reporting requirements, the failure to accept the implications of the existence of political parties, and the lack of any enforcement machinery worthy of the name. Since the candidate's declaration combines small local donations with lump sums received from party associations and fundraisers at various levels, who are not required to report the source of their funds, these reports are not only useless but deceptive. The large amounts of money which pass through national and provincial party organizations are ignored. The identity of important contributors is not disclosed. Nor are parties required to reveal their national or provincial expenditures on nation-wide advertising campaigns through the mass media, the costly cross-country tours of party leaders, the salaries of party organizers and other administrative expenses. The present act completely overlooks the role of the party in the modern electoral process and the fact that individual candidates are simply the local manifestation of the party.

Moreover, no attempt has been made to limit or control expenditures or the size and volume of donations, other than the stillborn effort in 1908 to ban corporate giving. Practically no assistance has been given to parties and candidates by way of direct subsidies, apart from the absorption by the state of such costs as the enumeration of electors and the payment of certain poll workers. Tax advantages for contributions to parties and candidates are nonexistent.

There are also considerable gaps in the reporting procedures required by federal law.[17] Since candidates are not required to file reports prior to the election, information is not available to the electorate in time to affect its decision; publication 70 days after the vote cannot be expected to affect the outcome of even subsequent elections. Nor is the form of publication such as to excite the interest of journalists and other students of politics. Furthermore, no permanent record of declarations is made by constituency returning officers, nor does the Chief Electoral Officer attempt to summarize this information. It should be stated that an informal system has been in operation since 1949. A Member of Parliament, usually from the CCF or NDP, has customarily submitted a question after each federal election asking for these returns and the names of candidates who have failed to submit reports. The answer then appears as a Sessional Paper of the House of Commons which serves in lieu of a permanent record. However, the value of a reporting system which clearly depends on full and adequate disclosure is vitiated by a lacuna which prevents the Chief Electoral Officer from insisting that constituency returning officers demand the production of financial statements by candidates. Linked to this is the neglect in providing for the formal auditing of such reports and the general lack of enforcement. Full and adequate reporting is a necessity if candidates are to be protected from the importunate requests of contributors. Statutory income and expense limits or self-regulating normative systems of control depend ultimately on the honesty of such reports. The weaknesses of the one aspect of Canadian election expense statutes which might be effective make a mockery of its purported aim.

PROVINCIAL LEGISLATION

Provincial provisions for the control of election expenses generally follow the pattern set by federal legislation. The election acts of two provinces, New Brunswick and Prince Edward Island, however, contain no clauses on the subject, but leave the definition of legitimate or lawful expenditures to the wording of the clauses which define corrupt practices.[18] Therefore, this section is limited to the statutes of seven provinces; Quebec is dealt with for comparative purposes only, since its law is considered separately in the next chapter.

Most provinces have adopted the federal doctrine of agency. The laws of the four Western Provinces,[19] Nova Scotia,[20] and Quebec stipulate that all payments on behalf of a candidate apart from personal expenses must be made through the official agent; Ontario sets an upper limit for any payments which may be made by persons other than the candidate's official agent.[21] Quebec also requires that a party name an official agent in order to be "recognized" and permitted to incur election expenditures. Not required in New Brunswick, the appointment of an agent in Newfoundland is simply permissive.[22] Alberta, British Columbia, Manitoba, Newfoundland, Nova Scotia, Ontario, Quebec and Saskatchewan require that all financial claims concerning elections must be sent to the candidate's agent.[23] The various Acts define the nature of lawful and unlawful payments, the periods in which expenses can be incurred and paid and what constitutes corrupt or illegal practices. The latter sections of provincial election acts in effect prohibit certain types of expenditures but only British Columbia enumerates what constitutes lawful expenses.[24] Most provinces limit the "personal expenditures" which may be made by a candidate and prohibit all others. Bribery is universally forbidden and in addition various restrictions apply to the transport, treating and entertaining of voters; but what may be legal in one province may be unlawful in another. Thus the conveyance of voters to the polls is tolerated in British Columbia but banned in Manitoba.

All but two of the provinces, New Brunswick and Prince Edward Island, require declarations from each candidate concerning their expenditures accompanied by supporting documents, although here again the form and the details demanded vary among the provinces.[25] There are also differences with respect to the length of time such records are preserved and the form in which these reports are published within the constituencies. British Columbia has a *de facto* form of central publication of candidate declarations,[26] while the *Quebec Act* requires the Chief Returning Officer to publish such a report within four to six months after the election day. Failure to submit such reports is punishable variously by fines and/or imprisonment. Although no province other than Quebec has provided for the mandatory publication of the expenses of central party organizations, Manitoba[27] and British Columbia[28] require that such statements be submitted to their respective Chief Electoral Officers.

Manitoba is the only province to attempt to place ceilings on election expenditures by legislation. Stimulated no doubt by the anti-party tradition dating back to the days of Progressive Party influence on that province's political scene,[29] the Manitoba *Election Act* limits the spending of central party organizations in the following terms:

The total electoral expenses incurred by the central or general committee of any political party, or by or through any officer or member thereof, in connection with a general election for the Legislative Assembly, shall in no case exceed the sum of **twenty-five thousand dollars;** and no such expenses shall be incurred or authorized except for a central office, the holding of public meetings, radio broadcasting, the presentation of election literature, and the publication, issue, and distribution, thereof.[30]

The failure to enact parallel ceilings on the expenditures of candidates renders this provision somewhat meaningless; a fatuous gesture in the direction of tradition, it has had little effect on actual political behaviour. The related requirement that contributions to central party organizations be publicized,[31] is no more meaningful than the Ontario provision calling for publicity respecting donations to candidates above $50.[32]

Far more serious in its implications has been the attempt to block contributions to campaign funds from certain sources. Stemming from a distaste for the purported influence or political philosophy of particular social or economic groups, such legislation often represents an attempt to tip the scale for or against a particular political party. True to the Progressive tradition, Manitoba law appears to have been directed at the Eastern-dominated "interests" in its ban on election donations by business corporations. The British Columbia prohibition on the use of "check-off" funds for electoral purposes seems, on the other hand, to be aimed at weakening trade union support for the leading provincial opposition party, the New Democrats.[33] The Manitoba *Act* states that it is a corrupt practice:

(a) for any company or association having gain for its corporate object or one of its objects, or for any person directly or indirectly on behalf of such a company or association, to contribute, loan, advance, pay, or promise or offer to pay, any money or other thing of value to any person, corporation, or organization, for use for any political purpose in an election; or

(b) for any person or corporation, or the officials in charge of any organization, to ask for or receive any such money or thing of value from such company or association.[34]

There is little evidence that business groups have been unduly hampered in giving to the parties of their choice, nor do Manitoba parties appear to have suffered from a ban which applies merely to the official election period.

The British Columbia restrictions have been far more effective and controversial. The 1961 amendment to the provincial *Labour Relations Act*, known as Bill 42, states in part:

... No trade-union and no person acting on behalf of a trade-union shall directly or indirectly contribute to or expend on behalf of any political party or to or on behalf of any candidate for political office any moneys deducted from any employee's wages under subsection (1) or a collective agreement, or paid as a condition of membership in the trade union. ...

... Notwithstanding any other provisions of this Act or the provisions of any collective agreement, unless the trade-union delivers to the employer who is in receipt of an assignment under subsection (1) or who is party to a collective agreement, a statutory declaration, made by an officer duly authorized in that behalf, that the trade-union is complying and will continue to comply with clause (c) during the term of the assignment or during the term of the collective agreement, neither the employer nor a person acting on behalf of the employer shall make any deduction whatsover from the wages of any employee on behalf of the trade-union.[35]

In 1961, Imperial Oil Limited, an important employer, refused to continue the check-off on the wages it paid and gave the labour organizations an opportunity to challenge the constitutionality of the *Act*. The Attorney-General of British Columbia intervened with the result that the legislation was tested in three courts, including the Supreme Court of Canada.[36] The province's claim that the provisions were a valid exercise of provincial competence in the field of property and civil rights was upheld, and the charge that the amendment constituted an infringement of the right of voluntary political activity and was directed at a specific political party was rejected. The learned judges agreed that funds should not be taken from an employee to be spent on a political party or cause of which he may not approve.

Although the provincial Attorney-General denied that the law was meant to apply to federal elections or the activities of parent unions, a minority of the Supreme Court of Canada thought otherwise and the issue remains unresolved. The fact that there is a need to guard against provincial interference with the freedom of federal election campaigns is borne out by a more recent decision of the Supreme Court of Canada concerning a municipal bylaw limiting the display of election posters. As the majority of the Court stated:

The legislature has no power to enact [such] a prohibition... as [it]... would be a law in relation to proceedings at a federal election and not in relation to any subject matter within the provincial power ... The subject matter of elections to Parliament appears ... to be from its very nature one which cannot be regarded as coming within any of the clauses of subjects assigned to the legislatures of the provinces by section 92 [of the British North America Act].[37]

Despite this decision it is still not clear whether trade-union locals are prohibited under the British Columbia *Act* from contributing to the political funds of parent unions which are likely to be more interested in the federal rather than the provincial arena. This problem may become increasingly acute, since there are indications that political leaders in the Atlantic Provinces, Ontario and the Prairies are considering further restrictions of this type.

N.B. THE NEW NOVA SCOTIA ACT

In April, 1969, the Nova Scotia legislature adopted a system of candidate reimbursement based on the Quebec model in the form of an amendment to *The Elections Act* (Revised Statutes of Nova Scotia, 1967, chap. 83, as amended by 1969, chap. 40, 18 Eliz. II).

This system has not as yet been tested in a provincial general election. While setting out to improve upon certain features of the *Quebec Act,* it suffers from the same major disability. The existence of political parties is recognized and limitations are placed on their expenditures (a party's expenses during a general election may not exceed the aggregate of 40¢ multiplied by the total number of electors in the electoral districts in which the party has one or more official candidates). However, the *Act* does not provide any subventions for the expenditures of parties as such; central party organizations must still have recourse to their traditional sources to finance their activities.

Limitations have also been placed on the expenditures of candidates in their constituencies. A candidate may not expend more than $1 per elector in respect of the first 5,000 electors; 85¢ per elector in respect of the number of electors in a constituency which exceeds 5,000; and 75¢ per elector in respect of the number of electors in a district exceeding 10,000. E.g. in a constituency of 15,000 electors, a candidate would be permitted to expend a total sum of $13,000.

The principal feature of the new Nova Scotia system is the provision of a subvention in the form of the reimbursement of a candidate's election expenses to an amount not exceeding 25¢ for each elector whose name was on the official list of electors in a constituency. Thus, in a constituency of 15,000 voters a candidate's expenses could be reimbursed up to the sum of $3,750. All winning candidates or those who have received 15 percent of the valid votes cast and have complied with the provisions of the *Act,* including a detailed report of expenditures, would be entitled to such reimbursements.

FOOTNOTES

[1] For detailed reviews of Canadian federal and provincial legislation, See *Report of the Committee on Election Expenses,* The Queen's Printer, Ottawa, 1966, chapter 2, pp. 13-35 and Study 8, pp. 321-329. Cf. Norman A. Ward, *The Canadian House of Commons: Representation,* University of Toronto Press, Toronto, 1963, Chapters XIV-XV, pp. 240-269.

[2] *The Dominion Elections Act,* 1874, Statutes of Canada, 1874, 37 Vict. chap. 9, secs. 121-125.

[3] Stated by the Committee in arguing for a change in existing legislation; *Report of the Committee on Election Expenses, op. cit.,* p. 30.

4 An *Act* to amend *The Dominion Elections Act 1874,* Statutes of Canada, 1891, 54-55 Vict. chap. 19, sec. 14.

5 An *Act* to amend *The Dominion Elections Act, 1908,* Statutes of Canada, 1908, 7-8 Edw. VII, chap. 26, secs. 28, 33, 36.

6 *The Dominion Elections Act 1920,* Statutes of Canada, 1920, 10-11 George V, chap. 46, sec. 10.

7 An *Act* to amend *The Dominion Elections Act 1930,* Statutes of Canada, 1930, 20-21 George V, chap. 16.

8 *The Dominion Elections Act 1920,* chap. 46, secs. 13, 78 and 79.

9 *Re: Moose Jaw (Dom.) Johnson v. Yake et al.* [1923] S.C.R. 377, affirming [1922] 3 W.W. R., 328.

10 *Report of the Committee on Election Expenses, op. cit.,* p. 22.

11 *The Canada Elections Act, 1960,* Statutes of Canada, 8-9 Eliz. II, 1960, chap. 39 as amended; see secs. 62 and 63 in particular.

12 *Ibid.,* sections 77(2) and 78.

13 *Ibid.,* section 80.

14 *The Civil Service Act 1961,* Statutes of Canada, 9-10 Eliz. II, 1960-1961, chap. 57, sec. 61. Reproduced with the permission of the Queen's Printer for Canada.

15 Canada, House of Commons, Special Committee on the Civil Service Act, *Minutes of Proceedings and Evidence,* 1961, p. 437. Reproduced with the permission of the Queen's Printer for Canada.

16 For the discussion of the political rights of civil servants, see O. P. Dwivedi, "The Civil Servants of Canada: A Study of their Rights," unpublished M.A. thesis (typescript) Carleton University, Ottawa, 1964, chapter III, pp. 44-72. For a comparative study of this topic, see *Report of the Committee on Election Expenses, op. cit.,* Study No. 1, p. 87ff.

17 For an exhaustive study of Canadian and foreign reporting procedures, see *Report of the Committee on Election Expenses, op. cit.,* Study No. 2, pp. 113-141.

18 New Brunswick: *Elections Act, 1952,* R.S.N.B. 1952, chap. 70, sec. 91; and Prince Edward Island: *The Election Act, 1963,* chap. 11, sec. 144.

19 British Columbia: *Provincial Elections Act,* R.S.B.C. 1960, chap. 306, sec. 172; Alberta: *The Election Act,* S.A. 1956, chap. 15, sec. 162(1); Saskatchewan: *The Election Act,* R.S.S. 1965, chap. 4, sec. 48; Manitoba: *The Election Act,* R.S.M. 1954, chap. 68, sec. 167(1), as amended by 1961, chap. 14, sec. 40.

20 Nova Scotia: *Elections Act,* S.N.S. 1962, chap. 4, sec. 162. In 1969 Nova Scotia made a major break by adopting a subsidy system based on the Quebec model. Cf. *The Elections Act,* Revised Statutes of Nova Scotia, 1967, chap. 83, as amended by 1969, chap. 40, 18 Eliz. II.

21 Ontario: *The Election Act,* R.S.O. 1960, chap. 118, sec. 188(1).

22 Newfoundland: *The Election Act,* S.N. 1954, No. 79, sec. 119(1).

23 Alta. secs. 163-164; B.C. secs. 172-173; Man. secs. 169-170; Nfld. sec. 119 (4-8); N.S. secs. 160-161; Ont. secs. 189-190; Sask. sec. 205.

24 B.C. sec. 175.

25 B.C. sec. 174; Alta. sec. 165; Sask. sec. 206; Man. sec. 171; Ont. sec. 191; N.S. sec. 163; Nfld. sec. 119.

26 The B.C. Opposition follows a procedure similar to that used in the federal House of Commons to enable the tabling of the necessary documents.

27 Man. sec. 168(2, 3).

28 B.C. sec. 177(1).
29 On this point see W. L. Morton, *The Progressive Party in Canada,* University of Toronto Press, Toronto, 1950, *passim.*
30 Man. sec. 168(1), as amended by 1961, chap. 14, sec. 40; emphasis added. The original ceiling was $15,000.
31 *Ibid.,* sec. 163(2).
32 Ont. sec. 191.
33 On this see Walter D. Young, "The NDP: British Columbia's Labour Party" in John Meisel(ed.) *Papers on the 1962 Election,* University of Toronto Press, Toronto, 1964, p. 185.
34 Man. chap. 68, sec. 131 (originally enacted in 1931).
35 B.C. *Labour Relations Act,* R.S.B.C. 1960, chap. 205, sec. 9; as amended by 1961 chap. 31, sec. 5.
36 -*Oil, Chemical and Atomic Workers International Union, Local No. 16-601 v. Imperial Oil Ltd.,* 30 D.L.R. (2d) (1962), p. 667; 36 WWR (1961-1962) p. 385.
-38 WWR (1962), 583 at p. 537; 33 D.L.R. (1962), 732 at p. 735.
-[1963] S.C.R. 584.
37 *McKay, et al. v. The Queen* [1965] S.C.R. 798 at p. 806; 53 D.L.R. (2d) (1966), 533, at pp. 538-539 — appeals from *Regina v. McKay and McKay* 38 D.L.R. (2d) (1963) p. 668 and 43 D.L.R. (2d) (1964), p. 401. Reproduced with the permission of the Queen's Printer for Canada.

EIGHT

A DIFFERENT APPROACH:
THE QUEBEC SUBSIDY SYSTEM

The sharpest break with the British electoral tradition dominant in Canada and its provinces has occurred in the province of Quebec. The death of the long-time Premier, Maurice Duplessis, in 1959 and the fall from power of his notorious party machine, the Union Nationale, in 1960[1] set the scene for the introduction of what for Canada was a wholly new concept of election finance. Reacting against the abuses of the past and impelled by the innovating spirit of the "revolution tranquille," the Quebec Liberal Party made the recasting of election expense legislation a principal plank in its platform for the Quebec general election of June 22, 1960. After assuming office, the Quebec Liberals commissioned a study of electoral reform.[2] This report was discussed at a convention of the Quebec Liberal Federation which laid the groundwork for the introduction of a Bill in the Quebec Legislature in 1962.[3] On July 10, 1963 the new *Quebec Election Act* was adopted.[4] With this legislation Quebec joined those jurisdictions like Puerto Rico, the Federal Republic of Germany and more recently Sweden which subsidize competitors in the electoral process from the public purse.[5]

The *Act* formally acknowledges the existence of political parties.[6] Expenditure ceilings are imposed and the law requires the reporting, disclosure and publication of party and candidate spending during election campaigns. Some burdensome election-day costs are transferred to the provincial treasury, additional free services are supplied to parties and candidates, and cash subsidies are provided to candidates in the form of reimbursements for campaign expenses "incurred and paid" in conformity with the *Act*.

124

Only "recognized political parties"[7] are permitted to make campaign expenditures in their own name through official agents appointed for that purpose. Such parties enjoy the privilege of having their names appear on the ballot papers following those of their candidates. The *Act* defines "recognized" parties as the party of the provincial Prime Minister or of the Leader of the Opposition, or of a party which had at least 10 official candidates in the previous provincial election or the election in progress. These parties are entitled to spend up to 25 cents for each elector, in general elections, in the aggregate of electoral districts in which each presents official candidates.[8] A party which presented candidates in all 108 provincial constituencies in the election held June 5, 1966* would have been permitted to spend up to $797,757.25. Together, the four recognized parties could have spent almost three million dollars.

The official agent of the leader of a recognized party must submit a sworn report of party election expenses, together with the appropriate invoices and supporting documents, to the Chief Returning Officer of the province within 120 days of the election. The latter must in turn publish a summary of the return in the Quebec Official Gazette within 15 days of its receipt. These reports must be available for public inspection for six months, following which they may be destroyed or returned on request.[9] Failure to file a report may disqualify a party leader from sitting or voting in the Assemblée Nationale until it has been delivered and the delay excused by judicial order.[10] Penal sanctions face official party agents who violate the ceilings and the reporting provisions; party leaders are subject to similar penalties for corrupt practices plus the threat of disqualification and the annulment of their election if they have knowingly tolerated the offences.[11]

Candidates and their agents must keep detailed accounts of expenses with itemized invoices necessary to prove purchases of $10 and over.[12] A candidate's agent must file a return, together with supporting documents backed by an affidavit, within 60 days following the election. The constituency returning officer must publish a summary signed by the agent within 10 days of its receipt in a French and English newspaper in the constituency. Reports and documents must be open for public scrutiny for

---

*Although a more recent provincial general election was held in Quebec on April 29, 1970, official reports concerning the size of the subsidies to the competing candidates were not available at the time of publication and will not be available until December, 1970. However, the spending limits for parties and candidates were the same as in 1966, as was the scale of possible reimbursements. On the other hand, it appears that 299 candidates will be eligible for subventions in 1970 as compared to 226 in 1966, an increase of about one-third. One may therefore expect that the amount of candidate expenditures to be reimbursed in 1970 will rise to well over $2 million. A detailed description of the 1966 reimbursements may therefore serve as an accurate guide to the subsidies paid in 1970.

six months and are later forwarded to the Chief Returning Officer of the province who must retain them for one year, and for an even longer period of two years if the election is contested in the courts. Only then may the reports be disposed of by destruction or returned to the candidate.[13] Winning candidates, who sit or vote in the legislature without reporting their expenses and who are found guilty of a corrupt practice, are liable to fines of $500 per day and disqualification from sitting or voting in the Legislature for 6 years.[14] Fines and imprisonment face an agent who knowingly violates these provisions.

Quebec's legislation is unique in that it requires the reporting of the monetarily important party expenses and it encourages the reporting of candidates' expenses by making such returns a prerequisite for reimbursement of costs under the candidate subsidy provisions. However, in common with the rest of Canada, publicity requirements are minimal. Nor does the law make provision for the adequate reporting of contributions or their sources. Likewise, enforcement is left merely to the Chief Returning Officer who is already burdened with the establishment and operation of the election machinery. Furthermore, the *Act* does not create a separate body, such as a quasi-judicial commission which had been recommended originally, to oversee the proper observance of the limitations and reporting provisions of the *Act*.

The truly significant features of Quebec's legislation are the financial assistance which is made available to qualifying candidates and the accompanying limits imposed on their spending. Permissible spending is related to the number of electors and the geography of constituencies.[15] Each candidate may spend 60 cents for each of the first 10,000 electors in a constituency, 50 cents for each of the next 10,000, and 40 cents for each of the remaining electors. Thus a candidate in a constituency of 30,000 electors would be permitted to spend $6,000 plus $5,000 plus $4,000, or $15,000 *in toto*. In four remote and sprawling electoral districts an additional 10 cents per elector may be expended.

This flexible ceiling permitted individual candidate expenditures in the 1966 provincial general election ranging from $4,627.70 to $30,366.80;[16] because of variations in the number of candidates, allowable expenditures per constituency could vary between $9,225.40 and $138,556.80. For all 418 candidates the permissible limit approximated $6.5 million. A "recognized" party presenting 108 candidates in the 1966 campaign could have spent no less than $2,388,673.95, including $1,590,916.70 at the candidate level and the 25 cents per elector allowed by the provincial headquarters. Taking full advantage of ceilings permitted under the *Act,* a sum of $9.5 million might have been legally spent by all parties and candidates in that campaign; actual expenses as computed below were not that high.

To help meet these anticipated expenditures, the *Quebec Election Act* provides a public subsidy in the form of reimbursements for the proven expenditures of candidates who have gained at least 20 percent of the eligible votes cast, or who are the standard-bearers of a party whose candidate had achieved the greatest or the next-to-greatest number of votes in the previous election in that constituency.[17] A qualifying candidate is entitled to receive up to 15 cents per listed elector for election expenses actually made and vouched for by documentary evidence.[18] In addition, the Chief Returning Officer shall also reimburse an amount equal to one-fifth of expenses between 15 and 40 cents, plus all costs over 40 cents per listed elector up to the permitted expense ceiling.[19] Thus a candidate in a riding of 30,000 electors who has spent his full limit of $15,000 will be reimbursed to the amount of $9,000. In a riding of 15,000 with a ceiling of $8,500 per candidate, the latter may be subsidized to the extent of $5,500. The possible reimbursements in the 1966 campaign ranged from $3,305.50 to $16,683.40 per candidate, and because of the varying number of candidates from $6,611 to $47,640.60 per constituency.[20]

Total expenditures at the party and candidate level in the 1966 election amounted to $4,442,478.27 or about half the permitted amount.[21] Spending by the "recognized" parties totalled $1,309,575.35 with the Government and Opposition parties accounting for $1,276,954.04 and the two minor parties a mere $32,621.31. At the candidate level, total expenses were $3,132,902.92, of which $2,848,382.23 was spent by 216 Government and Opposition candidates, $174,535.64 by 163 candidates of the two minor "recognized" parties, and $109,985.05 by 39 assorted independent and other candidates.[22]

Out of 418 candidates, only 226 or slightly more than half qualified for the subsidy. Total reimbursements amounted to $1,691,537.95 and were distributed in sums ranging from a high of $16,165.50 to a low of $2,205.81. The allocation of these funds among the respective parties in comparison with party and candidate expenditures may be found in the following Table 8-1 on page 128.

An examination of the composition of the group of candidates which qualifies for reimbursement appears to justify the main objection to the Quebec system. The minor parties have had difficulty achieving the 20 percent of the vote required of qualifying candidates and have complained that the *Act* was designed to benefit the dominant Union Nationale and Liberal parties. The 226 candidates qualifying for reimbursement in 1966 included only 5 minor party and 5 independent candidates. All 108 Liberal candidates and all 108 Union Nationale candidates qualified, including 15 U.N. candidates who lost their deposits by failing to gain one-half the votes polled by the winners in their constituencies. Nine of

Table 8 - I
EXPENSES AND REIMBURSEMENTS BY RECOGNIZED PARTY
IN 1966 QUEBEC GENERAL ELECTION

Party	No. of Candidates	Total Reported Party Expenditures	Candidate Expenditures Total Reported	Portion Reimbursed
Union Nationale	108	$ 588,666.46	$1,408,661.39	$ 805,240.66
Liberal	108	688,287.58	1,439,720.84	822,623.49
Ralliement Nationale (R.N.)	90	15,513.24	98,010.22	21,022.34
Rassemblement pour L'Indépendance Nationale (R.I.N.) ..	73	17,108.07	76,525.42	6,110.12
Independents & Others	39	—	109,985.05	36,541.34
TOTAL	418	$1,309,575.35	$3,132,902.92	$1,691,537.95
Maximum Allowable For Party With Full Slate	108	$ 797,757.25	$1,590,916.70	$ 953,000.00

Source: Élections 1966, Report of the Chief Returning Officer, The Queen's Printer, Quebec, 1967, Appendix VIII, pp. 395-435.

the latter qualified under the 20 percent rule, but six, some of whom received fewer votes than those who did not qualify, were covered by the fact that their party's candidates had come first or second in their constituencies in the previous general election.[23] It is this virtual guarantee of reimbursement to the candidates of the two dominant parties which is viewed as most inequitable.

A similar bias is apparent in another measure of assistance provided to candidates under the new *Act*. In addition to the two polling station officials, the deputy returning officer and the poll-clerk, who are appointed on the recommendation of the Government party candidate and Opposition party candidate respectively,[24] provision has been made for the payment of agents, traditionally known as scrutineers, in each polling station. All candidates may appoint such agents but only two in each poll are paid by the province: one named by the winning candidate, or by the official candidate of the recognized party which gained the greatest number of votes in the previous election, and the agent of the recognized party which was the runner-up to the first in that constituency.[25] (The wording of the relevant clause permitted the payment of a third agent in the polls of a constituency won by an independent candidate in the previous election of 1962.) A small army was required to man the 16,424 regular and special polling stations opened for the election. The number of polls in a constituency ranged from 31 to 357 with an average of 152 per constituency. Presumably the agents recruited were drawn from among the party faithful who had rendered service on the hustings prior to polling day. The provincial treasury was thus required to pay for the services of 33,057 poll agents, 16,424 for each of the dominant Liberal and Union Nationale parties plus 207 named by the independent member for St. Anne's.[26] No other party or group of candidates benefited from this provision. These poll agents are remunerated at a rate fixed by the Lieutenant Governor-in-Council,[27] currently $19 for the regular polling day and $32 for the special advance polls.[28] The total paid to party and candidate poll agents amounted to $631,880, divided almost entirely between the Government and Opposition parties except for the miniscule sum of $3,946 paid to the agents of the one qualifying independent candidate.[29] The payment of these agents constitutes a substantial transfer to the state of a formerly burdensome party and candidate expense.

The new *Act* also provides a valuable free service to each candidate in the form of 20 copies of the constituency electoral lists.[30] These lists are prepared five weeks prior to each election at considerable public expense by enumerators specially appointed and paid for this purpose.[31] The cost of printing these lists at the rate of 17 cents for each name and each address may exceed $1 million. One informed and reliable observer has estimated that the average value of the 20 lists supplied to each candidate may be set at $1,500. This service may, therefore, be valued at $627,000.[32]

The only direct assistance to political parties derives from the allocation of free broadcasting time for campaign purposes on the federally owned radio and television networks. For the 1966 election the CBC allocated a total of 6 hours of radio and 7½ hours of television time on its English and French networks valued at $52,000, detailed in Table 8-11.

Although this service gave the parties direct access to the only network broadcasting facilities available in Quebec, time on private independent stations had still to be purchased, and the value of the free time was a mere pittance compared to the sum of $1,055,413.85 which the four recognized parties declared they had spent on advertising and publicity in 1966.[34]

Taking into account the reimbursements actually made, the payments to poll agents, the value of electoral lists and the free time allocated by the CBC networks, the subventions received by the four recognized parties

Table 8 - II
ALLOCATION AND VALUE OF CBC RADIO AND TELEVISION TIME IN 1966 QUEBEC ELECTION

Party	Radio		Television	
	Time	Value	Time	Value
Liberal	2 hours	$2,800	2½ hours	$14,600
Union Nationale	2 hours	2,800	2½ hours	14,600
R.N.	1 hour	1,400	1¼ hours	7,250
R.I.N.	1 hour	1,400	1¼ hours	7,250
TOTAL	6 hours	$8,400	7½ hours	$43,600

SOURCE: Canada, **House of Commons Debates**, November 30, 1966, p. 10549. Reproduced with the permission of the Queen's Printer for Canada.

and 418 candidates in the 1966 Quebec general election amounted to over $3 million as follows:[35]

Table 8 - III
SUBVENTIONS TO PARTIES AND CANDIDATES IN 1966 QUEBEC GENERAL ELECTION

Reimbursements to 226 Candidates	$1,691,537.95
Payment of 33,057 Poll Agents	631,880.00
Provision of Electoral Lists	627,000.00
Total from Quebec Treasury	$2,950,417.95
Value of CBC Broadcasts	52,000.00
Total Overall Subvention	$3,002,417.95

The provincial subsidies covered over half of the expenditures made by candidates and almost 40 percent of the combined expenses reported by parties and their local standard-bearers. While the reimbursements are weighted in favour of the dominant established parties, a circumstance which can be explained by the desire to discourage the consolidation of potential rivals, they come near to meeting the real financial needs of the competitors in the electoral process. Stimulated by the rising political self-consciousness of French Canada summed up in the slogan and the desire to be "maître chez nous," a serious beginning has been made to provide a much-needed alternative to the traditional sources of party and campaign funds. Ambivalence on this issue lingers on, however, and may explain the failure to extend public aid to political parties as such.[36] This is the fundamental weakness of an otherwise forward-looking approach. Candidates in Quebec have generally looked to central party organizations for assistance in meeting the great bulk of their financial needs. The subventions provided under the *Election Act* of 1963 do little to disturb this pattern of dependency. What has happened is the partial replacement of one source by transfer from the party to the public treasury. The sources of party funds for party purposes have been left untouched.

FOOTNOTES

[1] For a discussion of the Union Nationale Party and Duplessis, see Herbert F. Quinn, *The Union Nationale*, University of Toronto Press, Toronto, 1963; and, Pierre Laporte, *The True Face of Duplessis*, Richard Daignault (trans.), Harvest House Limited (French Canadian Renaissance Series), Montreal, 1960.

[2] Harold E. Angell, *Report on Electoral Reform of the Province of Quebec*, Quebec Liberal Federation, Montreal, October 1961 (mimeographed), 100 pp.

[3] For a study of these developments, see Harold E. Angell, "The Evolution and Application of Quebec Election Expense Legislation," *Report of the Committee on Election Expenses*, The Queen's Printer, Ottawa, 1966, pp. 279-319.

[4] *The Quebec Election Act*, 1963, Revised Statutes of Quebec, 1964, chap. 7; (as amended by 13-14 Eliz. II, 1965, chap. 12 and chap. 13, and 14-15 Eliz. II, 1966-Bill 3); The Queen's Printer, Quebec, 1966.

[5] For a comparative study of subsidy schemes including the author's on-the-spot study of the pioneering Puerto Rican system, see "Public Subsidization of Parties and Candidates," *Report of the Committee on Election Expenses*, *op. cit.*, pp. 203-223.

[6] The following analysis is based largely on an earlier paper by the author, Khayyam Z. Paltiel, "The Public Subvention of Election Expenses in Canada," delivered to the specialist Panel on Political Finance at the 7th World Congress of the International Political Science Association, Brussels, Belgium, September 18-23, 1967.

[7] *Quebec Election Act*, 1963, Art. 2, subsection 20; Arts. 147, 193, 375.

[8] *Ibid.* Art. 379(1).

[9] *Ibid.* Art. 383.

[10] *Ibid.* Art. 384.

[11] *Ibid.* Arts. 388, 389, and 390.

[12] *Ibid.* Art. 378(1).

[13] *Ibid.* Art. 382 as amended by 1965, chap. 12, sec. 39.

[14] *Ibid.* Arts. 388 and 390.

[15] *Ibid.* Art. 379.

[16] All figures relating to the Quebec general election of June 5, 1966 are drawn from *Élections 1966*, Report of the Chief Returning Officer, The Queen's Printer, Quebec, 1967, pp. 397-435.

[17] The *Quebec Election Act,* 1963, Arts. 380 and 219.

[18] "Election Expenses" are defined in *Ibid.,* Art. 372.

[19] An additional 25 cent expense per listed elector is permitted candidates in by-elections but cannot be considered for reimbursements. This additional expense is granted in lieu of party expenditures which are expressly forbidden in by-elections. *Ibid.,* Art. 379.

[20] For additional details see Angell "The Evolution and Application of Quebec Election Expense Legislation," *op. cit.* pp. 315-318.

[21] *Elections 1966, op. cit.* Appendix VIII, pp. 397-435.

[22] *Ibid.* The four "recognized" parties were the Liberals (Government), Union Nationale (Opposition), Ralliement Nationale (R.N.), and Rassemblement pour L'Indépendance Nationale (R.I.N.). The election was won by the Union Nationale which gained 56 seats to 50 for the Liberals. Independents won 2 seats.

In 1970 there were 436 candidates including 108 each for the Liberals, Union Nationale and Parti Québecois respectively. The Créditistes and the NDP ran 99 and 14 candidates respectively with 30 Independents. The Liberals won 72 seats, followed by the Union Nationale with 17, the Créditistes with 12 and the Parti Québecois with 7 seats.

[23] *The Quebec Election Act,* 1963, Arts. 380 and 219.

[24] *Ibid.,* Art. 171.

[25] *Ibid.,* Art. 219.

[26] For these and other relevant details my gratitude is due to M. François Drouin, Q.C., the Chief Returning Officer of the Province of Quebec, who in a lengthy letter dated April 19, 1967 clarified certain obscure points regarding the *Quebec Election Act* and is the authority for the figures given here.

[27] *The Quebec Election Act,* 1963, Arts. 219, 422, and 423.

[28] *Ibid.,* Sched. 2, par. 34 and 38. These honoraria were increased in 1970.

[29] For source see footnote 26 above.

[30] *The Quebec Election Act,* 1963, Art. 77 (1).

[31] The appointment of these enumerators also constitutes another hidden subsidy to the Government and Opposition parties which are granted the right to name such persons. *Ibid.,* Art. 49 (1).

[32] Angell, "The Evolution and Application of Quebec Election Expense Legislation," *op. cit.,* p. 318.

[33] In the 1962 election the CBC allocated 10 hours on radio and television to the parties valued at $29,255. Canada, *House of Commons Debates,* June 6, 1966, pp. 5979-5980.

[34] *Elections 1966, op. cit.,* p. 397.

[35] Using a similar method of calculation and taking into account the larger number of eligible candidates, increased payments to poll agents and increased printing costs, it may well be that subventions to parties and candidates in the 1970 election will approach $4 million.

[36] On this point see the speech by the former Liberal Premier of Quebec, Jean Lesage, on his party's financial structure, "Cartes sur Table," delivered in Quebec City, May 26, 1965, which indicated that the party's chief fund-raisers were a French-speaking banker and an English-speaking investment dealer; and that furthermore party accounts were to be kept secret.

NINE

THE RECOMMENDATIONS OF THE COMMITTEE ON ELECTION EXPENSES AND OTHER REFORM PROPOSALS*

Despite recurring election fund scandals and the ever present problem of financing campaign activities, remarkably little systematic thought had been given to reform in this delicate area until the present day. The prevalent approach, once adopted in the eighteen seventies, has undergone remarkably little change, as demonstrated in the historical review in Chapter 7. Some federal legislators have made proposals which would have considerably strengthened the control aspects of existing legislation. At the provincial level intermittent efforts have been made in a similar direction, but as noted previously it is the Quebec system of partial subsidies which has been the most dramatic legislative development. On the federal scene the most serious effort to prepare and rally public opinion on this issue, the *Report of the Committee on Election Expenses* has yet to be acted upon.

Stringent restrictions on campaign spending and the audit of election accounts by a public official had been proposed by Edward Blake in 1870.[1] The late Hon. C. G. Power, for long a prominent and key Liberal organizer in Quebec, made repeated attempts to have statutory ceilings imposed on campaign spending. In 1938 a detailed scheme was presented to the House of Commons.[2] Under this plan, a limit of 20 cents per elector, other than $1,000 for a candidate's personal expenses, would

---

*The discussion of the Recommendations of the Committee on Election Expenses presented here is based largely on a previous appraisal by the author; Khayyam Z. Paltiel, "The Proposed Reform of Canadian Election Finance: A Study and Critique," *Jahrbuch des Öffentlichen Rechts der Gegenwart*, Neue Folge/Band 16, J. C. B. Mohr (Paul Siebeck), Tübingen, 1967, pp. 379-409.

have been set on constituency spending. The powers of the Chief Electoral Officer would also have been strengthened by making him responsible for publicizing election accounts and authorizing him to launch an investigation on the basis of complaints by at least 10 electors (a returnable deposit would have been required to establish that the allegations were "well-founded"). When the Second World War intervened, the bill was dropped.[3] Re-introduced in modified form in 1949, it achieved second reading only to fail passage once again due to the dissolution of the House. In 1964 and 1966, Mr. Andrew Brewin, M.P. proposed spending ceilings for both candidates and parties, but as in the case of most private members' bills his efforts too were stillborn.

The establishment in 1964 of the Committee on Election Expenses was a response to growing public disquiet about the sources of party funds and, in part, followed the demand by some political leaders for reforms which would check the sharp rise in election costs and obviate the need for recourse to special and even questionable interests for financial support. The Quebec reforms and the burdens placed on party fund-raisers by the frequency of general elections appear to have prompted the Liberal Party of Canada to include the limitation of election expenses in its platform for the 1963 federal election campaign. Following the Liberal Party's return to office the formation of the Committee was presaged in the Speech from the Throne at the beginning of the 1964 session of Parliament which stated the Government's "intention to establish a committee of inquiry"[4] to advise on the best practicable way to set enforceable limits on expenditures in election campaigns. The House of Commons was informed of the appointment, composition and terms of reference of the Committee by the then Secretary of State, the Hon. Maurice Lamontagne, on October 27, 1964.[5]

The task assigned by the Minister to this "small group of men with practical experience and expert knowledge" was to "inquire into and report upon the desirable and practical measures to limit and control federal election expenditures."[6] The Secretary of State prefaced his declaration with the observation that this was "a complex problem which affects the very basis of our democratic system," one which had "become particularly important these last few years due to the increase of communication media, especially since the advent of television."[7] Amplifying his remarks he stated "these terms of reference are general, and we expect that the committee will give them a broad interpretation." Then, having announced the composition of the five-man committee, the Minister concluded his remarks by assuring the House of Commons that:

> When their report is completed it will, of course, be made public. It is the first time in our country that a study of this kind has been undertaken and that a government has declared its intention to take effective steps to limit election

expenditures. As a result of those steps we hope that our political life will be improved and will reflect more faithfully our democratic ideals.[8]

The Government's statement was welcomed by spokesmen for all parties in the House of Commons.[9] The Leader of the Opposition and former Conservative Prime Minister, the Right Hon. John G. Diefenbaker, stated that the Committee's object was one that would commend itself not only to members of the House and defeated candidates but also to the public as a whole. He too viewed the costs of television and radio as contributing to the rising trend of campaign expenditures which "renders it very difficult for an average Canadian to take his part in public life." The leader of the socialist New Democratic Party, T. C. Douglas, welcomed the formation of the Committee and hoped that it would recommend not only measures to curtail campaign expenses but "also disclosure of the sources of campaign funds." The Social Credit Party spokesman and the leader of the Ralliement des Créditistes, M. Réal Caouette, concurred with the Committee's establishment, although he was doubtful that the study would check the influence of the "finance barons" on the major parties.

Pressures stemming from the Province of Quebec were evident not only in the Committee's terms of reference but in its composition. At a press conference following his statement to the House of Commons, the Secretary of State indicated that the Committee's terms of reference would enable it to consider the payment of part of election campaign costs out of the federal treasury[10] in imitation of the Quebec model. Even more significant was the appointment of a former President of the Quebec Liberal Federation, M. François Nobert, a known advocate of electoral reform, as the original chairman of the Committee. Moreover, when he fell ill and died, he was replaced by M. Alphonse Barbeau, a Montreal lawyer who had been the chairman of the party commission which had recommended the reform espoused by the Quebec Liberals at their convention of 1961. (M. Barbeau has since been elevated to the Bench.)

The members of the five-man committee represented three political parties, the Liberal, the Conservative and the New Democratic Parties. It included two former Members of Parliament, a Conservative, Arthur R. Smith of Calgary, and the Hon. M. J. Coldwell, the respected former leader of the Cooperative Commonwealth Federation, the socialist predecessor of the New Democratic Party; two prominent political organizers, the chairman and Gordon R. Dryden, Q.C., a fellow Liberal lawyer, who held the post of Secretary-Treasurer of the Liberal Federation of Canada; and a noted author and student of Canadian government and politics, Professor Norman Ward.

Supplementing the Committee members was an administrative staff headed by English- and French-speaking Co-Secretaries, one a practising lawyer who had once been a candidate for federal office, and the other a professor in the Civil Law Faculty of the University of Ottawa. The author was engaged as Research Director and headed a research staff which consisted of 10 post-graduate students in law and political science. Contracts were also entered into with a private independent research organization and several university scholars who carried out a number of specific studies for the Committee.

The Committee took a broad view of its terms of reference from the outset and undertook a fundamental and far-reaching investigation of Canadian party finance. It accepted the view that the control of election expenses involved questions concerning the ways by which campaign funds were raised as well as the manner in which they were spent.[11] The investigations carried out by the Committee members and research staff had a three-fold aim: to establish the nature and extent of Canadian party finance and election expenses; to examine the efficacy of the legislative measures taken to limit and control and ease the burden of election expenses in Canada; and to provide information regarding proposals and steps taken in other jurisdictions to deal with the problems faced by Canadian parties and candidates which might be suggested for adoption by Canadian legislators. Since the Committee on Election Expenses was an advisory committee to the Secretary of State, it did not possess the extensive powers of a Royal Commission or a Departmental Commission of Inquiry. Lacking the power to *subpoena* witnesses or to compel the production of documents it depended on the goodwill of individuals and interested groups in order to gather the information required. This enhanced the role of the research staff.

The Committee's inquiry took the following course. Considerable factual information with respect to election finance and the control of campaign costs in Canada was compiled and analyzed. Extensive private conversations were held with politicians, party officials and campaign fund-raisers at both the federal and provincial levels. Financial records made available by candidates and parties were examined. Special research studies were carried out on the effect of the use of the mass media, especially radio and television broadcasting and newspapers, on the costs of Canadian election campaigns. Existing legislation and the history of attempts to regulate election expenses at federal and provincial levels were reviewed in detail.

The Committee's eagerness to learn from the experience of other countries with similar problems in comparable contexts "led to detailed comparative studies by the Committee's research staff and a series of visits by members of the Committee and its staff to seven foreign countries whose systems of control . . . might serve as models for Canada."[12] The opinions of foreign scholars, political leaders and party organizers were sought by means of interviews or correspondence.

The opinions and attitudes of electors and interested groups as well as those of politicians and party workers were solicited. The Public hearings were held across Canada and members of the public and interested organizations were encouraged to come forward and express their views to the Committee. The opinions of candidates, party officers and fund-raisers were elicited in more confidential settings. A questionnaire was also sent to every candidate in the 1965 federal general election soliciting information regarding his expenditures, income and attitudes towards controls. The attitudes of electors were tested by means of a carefully prepared series of questions included in a public opinion survey administered to a scientifically selected national sample of the Canadian people. Briefs and memoranda were requested from public bodies and organizations including the mass media.

The results of these inquiries were embodied in the chapters, studies and appendices of the massive 528-page three-part *Report of the Committee on Election Expenses.* Seven supplementary studies were included in the equally bulky 598-page volume entitled *Studies in Canadian Party Finance* published for the Committee.

The *Report,* containing a detailed proposal for the reform of Canadian party and campaign finance, was tabled in the House of Commons at Ottawa by the Hon. Judy LaMarsh, Secretary of State, two years after the establishment of the Committee, on October 11, 1966. The 45 recommendations, spread over 28 pages of Chapter 4,[13] were based on the following considerations:

i. Political parties should be legally recognized and, through the doctrine of agency, made legally responsible for their actions in raising and spending funds.

ii. A degree of financial equality should be established among candidates and among political parties, by the extension of certain services and subsidies to all who qualify.

iii. An effort should be made to increase public participation in politics, by broadening the base of political contributions through tax concessions to donors.

iv. Costs of election campaigns should be reduced, by shortening the campaign period, by placing limitations on expenditures on mass media by candidates and parties, and by prohibiting the payment of poll workers on election day.

v. Public confidence in political financing should be strengthened, by requiring candidates and parties to disclose their incomes and expenditures.

vi. A Registry under the supervision of a Registrar should be established to audit and publish the financial reports required, and to enforce the provisions of the proposed "Election and Political Finances Act."

vii. Miscellaneous amendments to broadcasting legislation should be enacted to improve the political communications field.[14]

An examination of these recommendations in detail makes it evident that the Committee attempted to find some method to reform Canadian election finance while accepting the current style of Canadian politics and campaigning. This twin attempt to reform and to preserve the context within which modern elections are conducted in Canada constitutes both the strength and weakness of the *Report*. On the one hand, the proposals appear to be realistic in terms of contemporary Canadian political life; on the other hand, these endeavours may be hampered by the continued acceptance of practices whose persistence would undermine the goals which the Committee set for itself.

THE COMMITTEE'S RECOMMENDATIONS

Recognition of Political Parties: The Committee's recommendations open with a frontal attack on the myth which has pervaded Canadian electoral law, namely that political parties do not exist. It points out that the general rule is evaded in the appointment of enumerators and the *Canadian Forces Voting Rules* and adds significantly that the *Senate and House of Commons Act* (R.S.C. 1952 c. 249) specifically speaks of party leaders and that the existence of parties is basic to the function of Parliament. The Committee, therefore, recommends that:

> Each national political party which intends to nominate candidates to contest future federal general elections or by-elections be required to register formally in the form prescribed by the Registry. . . . Each political party should be required to register the name of the recognized leader of the party, the members of the national executive, the party's exact name, the address of its offices where its records are maintained, and its official financial agent. The party agent should be required to file reports and information with the Registry, as provided by the enabling legislation and in accordance with its provisions. Failure of a party to register officially with the Registry should disqualify it from receiving any benefits recommended in this Report, and its candidates should be described on official ballots only as "independent."[15]

Surprisingly, however, the Committee failed to provide a definition of what constitues a national party, although precedent exists in the above mentioned *Senate and House of Commons Act,* the rules governing allocation of time to political parties on the publicly owned broadcasting network[16] or the previously cited legislation adopted in the Province of Quebec.

The Committee also proposed that the doctrine of agency now existing between agents and candidates should be fully applied to the relationship between agents and parties. Although this would probably result in certain changes in party structure, this step was suggested in order to establish the concept of responsibility for the public reporting, disclosure and limitation of party income and expenditures[17]. The Committee also recommended that, in contrast to current practice, the party affiliation of candidates should be included on the ballot following the candidate's name, address and occupation. A candidate would consequently be required to file a consent in writing of the registered leader of his party or of a party official designated by the latter at the time he submits his nomination papers to the local returning officer. Failure to submit this consent would result in the candidate being designated as an "independent" on the ballot.[18]

Subsidies to Candidates and Parties: The Committee accepted the need of candidates and parties for funds in order to conduct effective election campaigns. According to the Committee:

Considerable evidence was adduced suggesting that lack of finances eliminated many serious candidates from seeking election in the federal field. Modern election campaigning relies heavily on the use of the mass-media, which is extremely expensive to the politicians. The Committee therefore considers it desirable that certain basic necessities of a minimal election campaign receive public support, so that all serious candidates may be provided with an opportunity to present their views and policies to the electorate.

. . . [But] in sharp contrast to the system in some jurisdictions where funds are made available to candidates for whatever purposes they determine, the Committee . . . unanimously agreed that subventions should be made available only toward the basic requirements of communicating with the electorate . . . [and] that public funds should be used only to assist the serious candidate who has reasonable support in his constituency.[19]

Candidate Subsidies: All candidates who receive a minimum support of 15 percent of the valid votes cast in their constituencies would be compensated equally, with a sum equal to two cents for every elector on the official list of electors for their proven expenses in the purchase of time or space in the broadcasting or print media. Claims for reimbursement would have to be supported by vouchers and invoices to be submitted to the Registrar and payment would be made only after it had been indicated that a candidate had fully complied with the law. All candidates, no matter what their share of the popular vote, would benefit by being reimbursed for one free mailing to their constituents and the state would absorb the costs now borne by individual candidates of printing and mailing the customary notice mailed late in the campaign informing electors of the location of their local polling station.[20] The Committee did not attempt to recommend that broadcasters be ordered to provide free broadcast time to individual candidates because of the administrative difficulties involved.[21]

Subsidized Broadcasting for Parties: The only direct assistance proposed for political parties would be the allocation of free and subsidized broadcasting time on radio and television. Parties would be prohibited from purchasing time beyond the allocated amount; this recommendation constitutes the sole limit imposed on the expenditures of political parties as such. The Committee was satisfied that barring the imposition of controls and assistance in this area the costs of such activities would continue to rise. The Committee concluded that political parties should not assume the broadcasting costs for their national campaigns. This would relieve them of a substantial financial burden, and . . . limit the use of the media to reasonable proportions.[22]

The Committee recommended that a total of six hours of prime broadcasting time be made available in the four weeks preceding polling day for allocation among the registered national parties on each public and private network, network-affiliate, and independent station free of cost to the parties. The formula to be used in allocating this time would be arranged in negotiation with the publicly owned Canadian Broadcasting Corporation with an appeal lying to the Board of Broadcast Governors, now renamed the Canadian Radio-Television Commission, the regulatory body charged with supervising public and private broadcasting networks and stations in Canada. The allocation formula reached would be applied to all networks and stations.[23]

The Committee further proposed that the financial burden of this subvention be borne by the public and the broadcasters in the following manner.

> The broadcasters, as a condition of license, shall be expected to provide without compensation 50% of the broadcast time allocated to political parties.
>
> The broadcasters shall be permitted to charge the Registrar of Election and Political Finance for the remaining 50% of the commercial value of the six-hour requirement, and that such partial compensation be based on the published regular standard rate for the time involved, so that no special political rate is levied.
>
> No time beyond the six hours of broadcast time provided shall be purchased by the political parties. . . .[24]

Tax Credit for Contributions to Candidates and Parties: In lieu of the rejected notion of direct monetary subsidies to candidates and parties, the Committee recommended a tax incentive in order to broaden the base of political giving and "to promote greater participation by electors in the affairs of state." The advantages claimed by the Committee for its proposal which was aimed at individual but not corporate or non-resident taxpayers was that it would avoid the debilitating effect on party organization resulting from the distribution of public funds according to some impersonal formula.[25]

> A personal income tax credit be instituted for donations to candidates for a federal election in an election year or to a national party in any year.
>
> The donor be entitled to a credit against his actual tax payable as follows:

Contribution	Credit
$1 to $20	50% of the contribution
$21 to $100	40% of the contribution
$101 to $300	30% of the contribution.[26]

The Committee also specified the manner in which such donations would have to be made in order to prevent abuses and assure disclosure of contributions to the proposed Registry. To benefit, donations must be made to the official agents of the national (not the local or provincial) party organization annually and the agents of candidates in election years.

Limitations on Income and Expenditure: The Committee displayed marked reluctance to impose any overall or partial limitations on income or expenditures on the grounds that such devices are easily evaded and would make a mockery of the law encouraging a cynical attitude on the part of the electorate and those who are presumably subject to the controls.

No restrictions on Donors: The Committee rejected any attempt to limit the size or source of contributions to parties or candidates. "Any restrictions on legitimate sources of income . . . would simply increase the difficulties they now face. . . . The Committee concluded that existing abuses in the field of contributions can be curtailed if not eliminated by the cleansing effect of audit and disclosure."[27] Furthermore, the Committee suggested that future legislation should encourage, and protect the right of individuals, corporations and trade unions to donate to federal parties of their choice, free from possible interference by provincial legislation. This recommendation appears to have been a response to the above-mentioned British Columbia law which restricts the use of check-off funds by trade unions for electoral purposes.

Limitations on Expenditure: The Committee also rejected the notion of a total dollar limitation on overall expenditures as being unenforceable; it considered this type of control as "inviting by its simplicity but meaningless in practice."[28] Instead, it suggested restrictions on specific activities and expenditures which could be "traced and proved," particularly the "public media whose use can be policed."[29]

First, the Committee proposed that expenditures for advertising purposes be limited by a *shorter campaign period*. It recommended that:

> Parties and candidates be prohibited from campaigning on radio and television, and from using paid print media including newspapers, periodicals, direct mailing, billboards and posters, except during the last four weeks immediately preceding polling day.[30]

Parties and candidates would not be prohibited from holding organizational meetings or announcing nomination conventions nor was the suggestion meant to prevent the mass media from discussing public affairs.

Second, the Committee placed a *monetary ceiling on advertising* by candidates in a proposal that:

> A candidate should be prohibited from expending in excess of 10 cents per elector on the revised List of Electors in his constituency, on the print and broadcasting media which include television, radio, newspaper, periodical advertisements, direct mail, billboards, posters, and brochures.[31]

Third, the ceiling on candidate advertising expenditures was parallelled by a complete *ban on the purchase of broadcasting time by political parties.* The Committee recommended that:

> A political party be prohibited from purchasing or using any paid time on radio or television in addition to its share of the six hours of subsidized time recommended above.[32]

Fourth, these expenditure ceilings were to be supplemented by a *limitation on advertising rates* which publishers and commercial broadcasters would be permitted to charge. The Committee recommended that:

> The charging by a broadcaster or publisher, and the payment by a candidate, of more than the regular local rate as evidenced by the standard rate card for local advertising, be made an offence.
> Broadcasters and publishers be prohibited from giving advertising free, or at a reduced rate, to any candidate if the same offer is not similarly and equally made to all other candidates in the same constituency.
> The charging of more than the usual national rate for advertising by a political party in a newspaper or periodical be made an offence.
> Newspaper and periodical publishers be prohibited from extending any preferential rate to any political party, if the same rate is not similarly offered to all other parties.[33]

Fifth, *restrictions on the direct electoral activities of* non-party groups would be imposed in a recommendation that:

> No groups or bodies other than registered parties and nominated candidates be permitted to purchase radio and television time, or to use paid advertising in newspapers, periodicals, or direct mailing, posters or billboards, in support of, or opposition to, any party or candidate, from the date of the issuance of the election writ until the day after polling day.[34]

The Committee was aware that this could be interpreted as an interference with the freedom of political action but argued that to ignore such groups and their activities would "make limitation on expenditures an exercise in futility, and render meaningless the reporting of election expenses by parties and candidates."[35]

Sixth, the Committee made a highly controversial proposal to *limit the publication of public opinion polls.* It did not propose to ban their use for private purposes by parties and candidates, but it argued that such surveys were often urged upon candidates principally for their propaganda value and thus constituted an improper and unwarranted expense. It recommended that:

> The publication for public consumption of the results of any such poll, from the date of the issuance of the election writ to polling day, be prohibited. The prohibition of publication should include not only private polls arranged by

parties or candidates, but polls conducted by any other organization during the same period.[36]

Seventh, the Committee recommended that a greater effort be made to *enforce existing corrupt and illegal practices legislation*,[37] particularly concerning the giving of gifts at election time. Furthermore, it recommended that traditional practices of *payments to party workers for poll watching and transportation of voters be outlawed*.[38]

Finally, in order to lessen the financial burden on independent candidates and those from smaller groups, it suggested that *the conditions for the return of the deposit required of candidates be made less onerous*. The Committee recommended that:

> The requirement that, to qualify for return of his deposit, a candidate gain 50% of the vote obtained by the winner, be amended to permit the return of the deposit to any candidate who receives ⅛ or 12½% of the total valid votes cast in his constituency.[39]

Disclosure and Reporting: Having expressed its conviction that "the disclosure of funds and their sources seems ... to be indispensable if the electorate is to have confidence in the democratic system,"[40] the Committee made far reaching recommendations for the reporting, disclosure and publication of candidate and party income and expenditures as well as requiring reports from publishers and broadcasters concerning political advertising. However, it stopped short of the full disclosure and publication of the sources of party funds. This varying treatment of party and candidate activities probably constitutes the chief weakness of the recommendations.

Disclosure – Candidates: Candidates and their agents would be required to make complete reports regarding their expenditures, income and source of funds. The Committee recomended that:

> Each candidate should, within thirty days after the election, through the official agent designated by him at the time of his nomination, file with the Registrar of Election and Political Finance (with a copy to the local returning officer), in the form prescribed by the Registrar, a sworn report of his campaign income and expense showing:
> (a) The full name and address of each donor.
> (b) The amount of each contribution. If a donor is a local riding association, the names and addresses of all its donors should be listed together with the amount of each contribution received by it during a period of four months preceding election day, exempting only income from normal membership dues.
> (c) A list of the sources and amounts of loans made to the candidate or his agent.
> (d) Money or value promised but not received.

(e) The name and address of every recipient of money expended in the candidate's campaign, together with an identification and description of the exact goods or services received for such payment in such form as may be required by the Registrar; all expenditures in excess of $10 to be substantiated by a voucher filed with the Registrar at the time of filing the report.
(f) The name and address of every person, association or corporation from whom goods or services were required, and a description of those which remain unpaid or under dispute.
(g) A list of all donated goods and services, excluding time volunteered by the actual donor.[41]

Disclosure — Parties: In contrast to the full reports required of candidates, parties would not be required to disclose publicly the sources of their campaign funds. Accepting the argument that such disclosure would "alienate contributors" and lead to "drying up legitimate sources,"[42] the Committee stopped short and recommended that:

Every registered financial agent of a registered national party be required to file with the Registrar of the Election and Political Finance Registry, annually, and within 60 days following any election, a statement of the party's income, showing:
(a) The total number of dollars received from private individuals.
(b) The total number of dollars received from corporations.
(c) The total number of dollars received from trade unions and associations.
(d) The total number of dollars received from foreign sources.
(e) The total number of donors in each category.
(f) The total number of dollars received from all sources.
Similarly, a statement of disbursements be required to show:
(a) Total dollars given by the national party to each candidate to assist in his or her local campaign.
(b) Assistance given by the national party to provincial and regional party organizations for campaign purposes.
(c) The total amount expended by the national party in each of the mass media, divided between daily, weekly newspapers, printed brochures, etc.
(d) Total costs of the leader's tour or tours.
(e) Other transportation costs by party spokesmen and officials.
(f) Total costs of salaries and services.
(g) Total costs of administration and miscellaneous.
(h) Total expenditures for all purposes.
The parties' reports on receipts and expenditures should be audited by the Registrar . . . certified by him, tabled in Parliament, and published in the Canada Gazette.
Each party's annual statement of expenses should divide the expenditures into at least the following categories:
(a) Assistance given provincial or local party organizations.
(b) Travelling expenses.

(c) Costs of mass media.
(d) Salaries for administration.
(e) Salaries and expenses concerned with research.[43]

Disclosure – Fund-Raisers: The Committee also recommended that the names of canvassers and others who solicit funds for national parties be registered with the proposed Registry. A similar requirement however, would not be made of those who raise funds for candidates provided the funds so collected are deposited to the credit of the candidate's official agent and not transferred to other destinations in the party. Party fund-raisers would be required to report to the Registrar the amounts collected by them annually under the headings set out above.[44]

Disclosure – Mass Media Expenditures: The principle of reporting was extended to broadcasters and publishers; a suggestion which has aroused opposition from the interests concerned. Broadcasters would be required to file with the Registrar of Election and Political Finance a breakdown of the total free time given to parties and candidates showing the time, date, length and name of the party, candidate or spokesmen participating in each broadcast; the total subsidized time used by parties showing the time, date and length and rate charged for each broadcast; the total time sold to candidates showing the time, date, and length and rates charged for each candidate; and the name of any candidate remaining indebted to the broadcaster for time sold and the amount of each claim. Publishers of newspapers, magazines or periodicals which sell more than $25 of political advertising during the four weeks preceding each election would be required to file a report with the Registrar indicating the amount of advertising sold to each candidate and party, the date of insertion of each advertisement and the number of inches or lines and the rate charged for each advertisement.[45]

Control and Enforcement – the Registrar: The most far-reaching recommendation of the Committee on Election Expenses is its proposal for the establishment of a powerful Registry of Election and Political Finance whose Registrar would have "unchallengeable qualifications of impartiality and integrity, and [whose] appointment and removal should be the sole prerogative of the House of Commons."[46] ". . . the Registrar . . . would supervise the financial activities of the contending parties and candidates and their supporters as these bear on election campaigns."[47] He would be solely responsible for the enforcement of the legislation based on the Committee's recommendations and would be expected to assist in the enforcement of the *Canada Elections Act* and the *Dominion Controverted Elections Act*.

Duties – Reports and Audit: The Registrar would be given authority to prescribe the forms to be filed, fix dates for their submission by candidates and parties, determine the manner in which these reports would be published and disseminated and "make such other regulations as may be necessary to carry out the intent of the legislation."[48]

An audit of party records would be required annually, and following each general election, as well as at such other times as may be considered necessary by the Registrar. The audits of party records would be carried out on the premises of any political party or in such place as the parties keep their records. The Registrar would have the authority to examine the financial records, vouchers and receipts of the parties to assure the accuracy of the reports submitted. The Registrar would also have the responsibility of auditing the financial reports of all candidates following every general or by-election. Priority would be given to the audit of the records of those candidates where a public petition for audit had been submitted by 20 electors in any constituency. The Registrar would be empowered to demand the production of all records bearing on the finances of a party, candidate, official agents, donors to, and recipients, of funds from any party or candidate.

Publication – by Registrar: The financial reports of political parties and candidates would be published in summary form in the official *Canada Gazette* and tabled in the House of Commons. A summary of the financial returns of each candidate would be published in a newspaper of general circulation published in his constituency following each general or by-election. Responsibility for receiving, examining, tabulating, summarizing, publishing and preserving this data would be placed upon the Registrar. All reports would be available for public inspection and facilities for copying this data would be provided at cost to journalists and the public. These reports and data would be kept by the Registrar for a period of 10 years following which they would be deposited in the Public Archives. The Registrar would similarly be responsible for reporting delinquencies in complying with the Act.

Report to Parliament: The Registrar would be required to submit an annual report to Parliament through the Speaker of the House of Commons. This report would include summaries of the audited financial returns of the parties and candidates, a statement of infringements of the Act and regulations as well as a summary of the actions taken by the Registrar to enforce the Act. The accounts of the Registry, including any legal costs which may have been incurred, and the statutory subsidies paid to or in behalf of parties and candidates would also be included in the annual report.

Power to recommend Changes: The Registrar would similarly be charged with the responsibility of keeping the legislation under review in the light of changing conditions and would be empowered to make recommendations to the House of Commons concerning amendments to the Act including variations in the amounts of ceilings and subsidies in the light of changing economic conditions.

Registrar to pay Subsidies: The Registrar would be charged with the responsibility for the payment of the subsidies and financial reimbursements proposed in the Committee's report. On receipt of a certificate from the Chief Electoral Officer that a candidate had received the minimum of 15 percent of the valid votes cast, the Registrar would issue to each candidate who had filed a financial report an indication that he had complied with the legislation concerning disclosure. The interim certificate of the Registrar together with the certificate from the Chief Electoral Officer would entitle the candidate to payment of the subsidy. Candidates' deposits would not be refunded until the interim certificate had been issued. The Committee also recommended that the House of Commons consider that no candidate be sworn in as a member of the House of Commons until an interim certificate had been issued by the Registrar.

The Registrar would also be responsible for the payment to broadcasters for the share of paid time allocated to each registered national party in accordance with the provision for subsidized time in the broadcasting media. The Registrar would have the task of verifying the rates and charges made by each network and station. The Registrar would also prescribe the form and date for filing the reports required from the press media for political receipts in excess of $25. This data would be preserved, tabulated and published by the Registrar in the manner set out above.

Enforcement: The Committee pinned the responsibility for the prosecution of infractions on the Registrar. It found it unacceptable that such actions should be left to private citizens alone, on the grounds that there was danger "that malicious action by irresponsible individuals could be instituted on a minor infraction,"[49] and secondly, that to leave it to the public meant that "under such circumstances nobody takes action."[50] Therefore,

> the Registrar, on his initiative and discretion and at public expense, may on his own authority institute and maintain an action against the candidate, political party, or third persons involved in any breach of the requirements of the proposed Election and Political Finances Act.[51]

The Committee also recommended that the public interest and fairness to the accused demanded a simple, direct and expeditious procedure to speed up final determination of actions instituted under the proposed Act.[52]

Sanctions: Severe penalties are recommended for infractions of the proposed legislation,[53] since the whole purpose of the report would be defeated in the absence of rigorous enforcement procedures. Where a successful candidate and/or his agent had been convicted under the Act, the candidate would be unseated, the election declared void and the candidate disqualified from participating in a federal election for a period of seven years from the date of conviction. Such a candidate or agent would also be subject to fine and/or imprisonment in the same manner as unsuccessful candidates and/or agents where the seriousness of the offence so warranted. Unsuccessful candidates and/or their agents would be liable to a fine of from $100 to $1000 and imprisonment from one to twelve months and disqualification from seeking election for seven years.

Where a party leader and/or the party's agent had been convicted for a breach of the Act, the party would be subject to a fine of from $5000 to $50,000 and the party leader and/or agent would be subject to the same penalties as an offending candidate. Such fines would be recoverable by execution upon the property of the party. The persons constituting the executive of the party would be subject to civil action at the discretion of the court for failure on the part of the convicted party or association to pay fines levied against the latter. Convicted parties or associations would be prohibited from sharing in any election subsidies until such fines are fully paid. The Committee also recommended that:

> Heavy fines and imprisonments should be prescribed to enforce compliance by third persons, associations or incorporated bodies who fail to report their financial involvement and participation in an election, and for those who illegally carry on a campaign in support of, or opposition to, a candidate or party during the periods restricted by the Act.[54]

Flexibility in Broadcasting: Despite the proposed limits on the broadcasting media the Committee did recommend that greater flexibility be allowed in the use of mass media. Consultations between the public and private broadcasters and the regulatory bodies concerned were suggested with a view to future amendments to the *Broadcasting Act.* It found that a prohibition against "dramatized political broadcasting"[55] had been narrowly interpreted and did not take account of the possibilities for increasing public interest in the discussion of public affairs "while maintaining the integrity of the presentation."[56] Similarly, the Committee recommended that the government consider altering the 48-hour "black-out period" imposed in areas where municipal and provincial elections were being held in order to assure parties free use of the broadcasting media in federal election campaigns[57]. The Committee also recommended that the Broadcasting Act be amended to permit the political parties to appeal for funds through the broadcasting media, a practice which is now prohibited[58]. It also suggested that the ban against the use of foreign broadcasting media by candidates of their supporters be extended to political parties[59]. The *Broadcasting Act* of 1968 reduced the "black-out" period to 24 hours; and the CRTC relaxed the restrictions on "dramatization" during the 1968 campaign. Thus far these are the only steps taken to implement the Committee's recommendations.

By-Elections: The Committee also suggested that the controls, limitation, assistance, reporting, auditing and publishing procedures proposed for federal general election campaigns be applicable to by-elections as well; with the exception that national party organizations would be barred from using the mass media in order to influence directly the outcome of a particular by-election.[60]

AN EVALUATION OF THE COMMITTEE'S PROPOSALS

Comparison of the Committee's recommendations with the Quebec system of candidate subventions leads to the conclusion that the goal of both schemes has been to supplement the existing mode of party finance rather than to bring about its replacement. Although the two plans introduce features which are new to Canada, in large part they build on elements which have been present in provincial and federal law for a long time. The lack of innovative proposals appears to rest on an implicit desire to avoid disturbing the present political and party equilibrium which in recent years has shown signs of increasing instability.

Any attempt to arrive at the total value of the subsidies, transfers and services proposed by the federal committee depends on the number of candidates, electors, polling stations and votes cast in each constituency. In the 1968 federal general election, 967 candidates presented themselves for the 264 seats in the Canadian House of Commons, almost 4 candidates per seat. These candidates represented three nation-wide and two minor regional parties, as well as a number of tiny groupings and independents. Seventy-five percent of the 10,860,888 electors actually voted in 51,253 polling stations.[61]

If there is no return to the traditional two-party system, one can assume that in the present fragmented state of Canadian politics, three out of four candidates on the average will achieve 15 percent of the vote in their constituency. Therefore, on the basis of the 1968 electoral lists and party structure it may be estimated that the two-cent reimbursement per elector for media expenses could cost considerably more than $600,000. The first-class mailing subsidy that would be available to all candidates could approximate to $2.5 million. The saving on the mailing of "You Vote At" cards to the two old parties would be in the neighbourhood of $900,000 in postage charges and a similar amount in printing costs since both of these responsibilities would be assumed by the Chief Electoral Officer. Taking into account the share of the additional free broadcasting time on radio and television which would be made available to parties, half the cost being covered by the federal treasury, it would appear that the overall public subvention of parties and candidates might reach $6 million, distributed as shown in the following table:

Table 9-1
ESTIMATED COST TO FEDERAL TREASURY OF COMMITTEE PROPOSALS

Item	Value
A. Half of Cost of Additional Broadcasting Time Allocated to Parties	$1,000,000.00
B. Reimbursements to Qualifying Candidates	600,000.00
C. First Class Mailing for All Candidates	2,500,000.00
D. Transfer of Costs of "You Vote At" Cards	1,800,000.00
Total Estimated Subvention	$5,900,000.00

Although substantial, the amounts involved would appear to cover only one-quarter to one-third the estimated expenditures at all levels in the 1968 campaign. Candidates would continue to be heavily dependent on central party funds and their collectors.

No final judgment can be entered, however, until legislation is adopted. Statutory controls have been recommended; but other than the limits on traceable expenditures on the mass media, no attempt has been made to fix overall expense and income ceilings. The emphasis given to reporting, disclosure and publicity indicates that priority continues to be given to the force of public opinion and electoral attitudes, which in the past have not proved to be very effective controls. The requirement that constituency candidates obtain the endorsation of party leaders and the greater advantages offered to parties in the tax credit proposal could reinforce the trend to centralization. The net result may well be a further reduction of the relative weight of the parliamentary factions to the advantage of the leadership and a greater tendency towards the *institutionalization* of the existing party system.

The purity of the Canadian electoral process is clearly at the heart of the Committee's proposals. However, there is ground for concern at the failure to demand of parties the same degree of disclosure as would be required of candidates. This lacuna can scarcely contribute to greater equity, for in addition to promoting further centralization, it may lead to the concealment of the sources of the bulk of funds spent in campaigns. Equity in access to and use of the mass media at the candidate level would be encouraged, and smaller parties would have a proportionately greater share of the broadcasting media. Nevertheless the failure to fix limits on other forms of spending and party expenditures as a whole may result in a shift in the pattern of expenditures rather than in an overall reduction in costs.

Minor tax advantages would be made available for individual contributors to party and constituency campaign funds. The money must be raised, however; and the repeated failure of the traditional parties in the area of popular fund-raising gives scant grounds for hope that the dependence on the usual sources would be lessened. Significant changes may well depend on further development of the Quebec system along the lines of the West German, Swedish and Puerto Rican schemes.

The Committee's proposals, despite these strictures, are a significant step forward. The crucial role of parties has been recognized and the doctrine of agency has been strengthened. A far-reaching system assuring reasonably complete reporting, disclosure, publicity and enforcement has been laid before Parliament. The plethora of information that would be made available as a result of these measures could dispel much of the mystery surrounding the monetary aspects of Canadian politics. Information currently denied the public and Parliament would permit changes in the law based on well-founded and verified data. The vesting of responsibility for enforcement in a Registrar who would also be charged with the duty of recommending amendments to the proposals anticipates continuing development in this vital area. Much would rest on the Registrar's independence and the vigour with which he would pursue his appointed task. Because of the prevailing *laissez-faire* attitude, adoption of these suggestions alone would mark a great step forward.

FOOTNOTES

[1] Canada, *House of Commons and Senate Debates,* March 10, 1870, p. 363.
[2] Canada, House of Commons, Bill 90, *An Act Respecting Political Expenditures,* 3rd Sess., 18th Parliament, 1938.
[3] Canada, House of Commons, Special Committee on Electoral Matters, *Minutes of Evidence,* June 23, 1938-May 1, 1939. Session 1938-39. Typed copy in Office of Chief Electoral Officer. (See also, *House of Commons, Debates,* April 5, 1938, pp. 2036-2046.)
[4] Canada, *House of Commons Debates,* February 18, 1964, p. 2.
[5] This and the following references are to *Ibid.,* October 27, 1964, p. 9457.
[6] *Ibid.*
[7] *Ibid.*
[8] *Ibid.* Reproduced with the permission of the Queen's Printer for Canada.
[9] *Ibid.,* pp. 9457-9458.
[10] *Robert W. Needham* in the London (Ontario) Free Press, October 28, 1964.
[11] *Report of the Committee on Election Expenses,* The Queen's Printer, Ottawa, 1966, p. 6.
[12] *Report of the Committee on Election Expenses, op. cit.,* p. 7.
[13] *Ibid.,* pp. 37-65.
[14] *Ibid.,* p. 37.
[15] *Ibid.,* p. 39.
[16] . . . such parties would meet all the following requirements: i. Have policies on a wide range of national issues. ii. Have a recognized national leader. iii. Have a nation-wide organization established as the result of a national

conference or convention. iv. Have representation in the House of Commons.
v. Seek the election of candidates in at least three of the provinces and put
into the field at least one candidate for every four constituencies.

[17] *Ibid.*, p. 40.

[18] *Ibid.*

[19] *Ibid.*, pp. 40-41.

[20] *Ibid.*, pp. 41-42.

[21] However, it did recommend that where such time was voluntarily offered
it should be made available equally to all candidates in a constituency. In
multi-constituency metropolitan areas or in rural areas where one radio or
television outlet covers a number of constituencies it was suggested that
spokesmen for groups of opposing candidates ought to be given equal time
to present their views if stations did offer such free time. *Ibid.*, pp. 42-43.

[22] *Report of the Committee on Election Expenses, op. cit.*, p. 43.

[23] The guiding principal [traditionally adopted by the Canadian Broadcasting
Corporation] has been to allocate 40 percent of the available [free] time to
the Government Party, with 60% divided *equitably* (author's emphasis)
among the Official Opposition and the minor parties. Where only two parties
qualify, an equal division of periods is normally made.

[24] *Ibid.*, p. 45.

[25] *Ibid.*, p. 35.

[26] *Ibid.*, p. 47.

[27] *Ibid.*, p. 48.

[28] *Ibid.*, p. 49.

[29] *Ibid.*

[30] *Ibid.*

[31] *Ibid.*

[32] *Ibid.*, p. 53.

[33] *Ibid.*, p. 52.

[34] *Ibid.*, p. 50.

[35] *Ibid.*

[36] *Ibid.*, p. 51.

[37] *Ibid.*, p. 52.

[38] *Ibid.*, p. 51.

[39] *Ibid.*, p. 51.

[40] *Ibid.*, p. 35.

[41] *Ibid.*, pp. 55-56.

[42] *Ibid.*, p. 54.

[43] *Ibid.*, pp. 54-55.

[44] *Ibid.*, p. 56.

[45] *Ibid.*, p. 57.

[46] *Ibid.*, p. 58.

[47] *Ibid.*, p. 58.

[48] *Ibid.*, p. 58.

[49] *Ibid.*, p. 61.

[50] *Ibid.*, p. 61.

[51] *Ibid.*, p. 61.

[52] *Ibid.*, p. 62.

[53] *Ibid.*, pp. 61-62.

[54] *Ibid.*, p. 62.

[55] *Ibid.*, p. 63.

56 *Ibid.,* p. 63.
57 *Ibid.,* p. 63.
58 *Ibid.,* p. 64.
59 *Ibid.,* p. 64.
60 *Ibid.,* p. 64.
61 These figures are drawn from the Report of the Chief Electoral Officer, *Twenty-Eighth General Election 1968,* the Queen's Printer, Ottawa, 1969.

PART IV
CONCLUSION

TEN

DEMOCRACY AND THE PROBLEM OF PARTY FINANCE*

An adequate appreciation of the issues discussed in the foregoing pages, and the problems these present for the democratic process in Canada, is beclouded by the persistence of certain myths concerning parties, political finance, and the cost of elections. The Canadian electoral and parliamentary system become intelligible only through an understanding of the diverse roles played by each political party as a cohesive group with its own structure and leadership. Yet Canadian law in its majesty takes no cognizance of parties, and goes to elaborate and absurd lengths to pretend that these collectivities do not exist. Clinging to the residue of an outdated individualistic ideology, its proponents would subsume parties in the category of voluntary associations with no distinctive will or action of their own, other than those of their separate and disparate members. The channels through which access to leaders and influence on policy are procured are thus obscured. A realistic assessment of the problems presented by election funds and the roles of collectors and contributors implies the recognition of the existence of parties; without it soundly based reform is not possible.

Political analysts and the public alike must also accept the notion that election campaigns cannot be fought nor won without the expenditure of large amounts of money. Given the structure of the modern Canadian electorate, current campaign styles, and the means available for mobilizing

---

*Some of the notions expressed in this chapter were first developed by the author in an address, "Democracy within the Parties: The Problem of Party Finance," delivered at a Conference of the Exchange for Political Ideas in Canada (EPIC), at Glendon College, York University, Toronto, June 4-6, 1966.

support and communicating with the voters, it is clear that the cost of elections will continue to increase. The summary study of Canadian party finance patterns, prepared by the research staff of the Committee on Election Expenses, decries popular fallacies in the following terms:

> There is a myth often accepted in Canada that there once existed in Canadian history a golden age when elections were relatively inexpensive, but this idyllic period of innocence has been corrupted by increasing expenditures of money in an ascending spiral. The historical record gives no support to this notion. In fact it is clear that elections have always seemed relatively costly to those who participated in them.[1]

Indeed, overall campaign costs have risen steadily since the end of the Second World War. The party data presented in Part II and the declared expenditures of candidates summarized in Appendices A and B combine to support this assertion. The only breaks in these ascending curves become visible when two general election campaigns occurred within a brief time-span as in 1957-1958 and 1962-1963. The individual patterns of the three Canadian parties which claim a nation-wide following, the Liberals, the Progressive-Conservatives, and the CCF/NDP, demonstrate similar increases.

Comparisons with other democratic countries do little to mitigate either the burden or the implications of Canadian election costs. On the surface the estimated expenditures of $16 million and $25 million made during and prior to the federal general election campaigns of 1965 and 1968 compare favourably to those made elsewhere. Using Heidenheimer's formula for calculating comparative Expenditure Indices,[2] one arrives at a Canadian index of .88 for 1965 and 1.08 for 1968. These figures are well below the American, Japanese, Italian and Israeli indices for 1960, which were 1.12, 1.36, 4.5 and 20.5, respectively.[3] Canadian costs also appear to be in line with the $200 million and $300 million which Alexander estimates were spent in the U.S. campaigns of 1964 and 1968.[4] However comforting such parallels may be, they are invalid; the size of the electorate and national income are not the only factors that must be considered. Nearly all Canadian election costs are incurred in the eight- or nine-week period between dissolution of Parliament and polling day in a campaign to win a majority of the 264 (formerly 265) seats in the House of Commons. On the other hand, the American estimates cover the cost of campaigning at all levels of government — Presidential, Congressional, State, County, and local — for about 500,000 posts filled by election in a four-year cycle. Obviously, the inclusion of the often extremely costly provincial and municipal election campaigns in the total would place Canada among the higher cost countries.

Despite the rising cost of election campaigns it would be rash to conclude that there is a direct relationship betwen the amounts spent by a party or candidate and success at the polls. The evidence on this point is contradictory. The availability of funds and electoral success have usually gone hand-in-hand. Nevertheless, incumbent parties and candidates, such as the Liberals in 1957, have been defeated by opponents with lesser resources. The experience of the minor parties both at the federal and the provincial levels indicates, too, that given the proper social context and alternative supports the lack of money can be overcome; the history of Social Credit, the Ralliement des Créditistes, and the CCF/NDP are ample warrant for this statement.

However, the expansion of the CCF was hampered by chronic shortages of funds and it is equally clear that financial blockades have seriously embarrassed the Conservative Party at various periods.

The winners in Canadian elections do tend to spend more money than their rivals at the party and constituency level; and winning candidates of a particular party tend to spend more than their losing colleagues. In the

Table 10 - I
EXPENDITURES OF WINNING CANDIDATES IN THE 1968 FEDERAL GENERAL ELECTION

Party	Total Amounts Declared by:		Average Amounts Declared by:	
	All Candidates	Winning Candidates	All Candidates	Winning Candidates
	$	$	$	$
Liberal*	3,510,437	2,437,978	14,270	15,734
Progressive Conservative	2,464,092	820,146	12,508	11,391
CCF/NDP	680,711	185,422	4,264	8,428
Social Credit	47,500	0	2,065	0
Ralliement des Créditistes*	56,153	38,388	1,755	2,953
Communist	9,852	0	895	0
Others	3,853	0	963	0
Independents	54,691	0	2,188	0
Total*	6,827,289	3,481,934	9,753	12,908

*Only 262 winning candidates reported. One Liberal and one Créditiste did not submit a report. The Speaker's declaration was included in the Liberal column — although in 1968 he ran formally as an Independent, he had been a Liberal M.P.

Source: Sessional Paper prepared by the Chief Electoral Officer and tabled in the House of Commons on November 7, 1968. Reproduced with the permission of the Queen's Printer for Canada.

1968 campaign the Liberal Party spent more than any of its rivals. Furthermore, 246 Liberal candidates spent more than half the sum declared by all candidates; 155 winning Liberal candidates spent more than two-thirds of the sums expended at the constituency level by that party, and 70 percent of the total declared by winning candidates of all parties. Table 10-I establishes this relationship for all parties.

Only the general average for Conservative candidates exceeded the average spent by its winning candidates, a phenomenon accounted for by high overall expenditures and significant losses of seats in Ontario, Manitoba and Alberta in the 1968 election.

If the declared expenditures made by candidates of all parties in the 1968 election are taken into account, it would appear that about $26,000 was spent at constituency level to fill each seat in the House of Commons. The cost to each party of each seat won is portrayed in Table 10-II.

Table 10 - II
AVERAGE COST PER HOUSE OF COMMONS SEAT BY PARTY IN THE 1968 ELECTION
(declared constituency expenditures only)

Party	Cost	Seats Won
	$	
Liberal*	22,648	156
Progressive-Conservative	34,262	72
CCF/NDP	30,941	22
Ralliement des Créditistes*	4,318	14

*Liberal and Créditiste figures are based on 155 and 13 M.P.'s respectively, as one candidate from each failed to report in time for publication.

Obviously there are candidates who spent far more than these sums; one Liberal, Robert P. Kaplan M.P. for Don Valley (Toronto), reported expenditures of $68,369, and one Créditiste, Henry Latulippe M.P. for Compton, reported costs of $11,475. But a definitive statement of the cost of filling each seat would require the inclusion of party costs at the national and provincial levels. If such expenditures were added, then Liberal costs per seat won would be three to four times higher, Conservative costs more than twice, and NDP spending per member elected about double those given in Table 10-II. In 1965 overall party spending per seat was more than $60,000 and in 1968 these combined costs rose to over $90,000. The total outlay on the federal electoral process, however, would have to include the general election costs assumed by the federal government through the Office of the Chief Electoral Officer which amounted to $13,841,484.08,[5] and the costs of the "free time" valued at $350,000 provided to political parties and candidates by the Canadian Broadcasting Corporation,[6] as well as the costs of the Representation Commissioner.

The problem of money for the parties is determined by the amounts required, the sources and the means employed to gather these funds. The influence of money, contributors and collectors can only be assessed if one is prepared to dispose of the myth that no price need be paid by a political party for the acquisition of financial resources. Canadians continue to cling to the idea that campaign contributions are a private affair, a matter of secrecy, something between the giver and the party of which the public should remain ignorant. The financial history of Canadian parties, however, is singularly devoid of acts of altruism. All the evidence is to the contrary. Material gain, policy decisions, the choice of leaders, and the general course of government activity have all been counters in the effort to provide funds for the parties. At the lowest level the price has been concessions, dispensations, and specific acts of patronage; at a higher level the aim has been to "stabilize the field for corporate activity."[7] In both cases contributions have assured access to the decision-making authorities in party and government. Collectors have fulfilled an important intermediary role in this system of exchange; one that has been facilitated by the special place accorded to them in the organizational structures of the two older parties. In the NDP the situation is somewhat different but an important feature of the evolution from the old CCF structure is the enhanced role in organizational matters of spokesmen of the trade unions to which the party is now beholden for funds.

Money is a necessary resource for modern Canadian parties. The peculiar advantages of this resource lie in its transferability and convertibility.[8] Money can be moved around from area to area and from one social level to another. Money can be exchanged and used to purchase other resources such as manpower and command over the communications media; it can and has been used for the outright and direct buying of votes. If not obtained legitimately, it will be sought in other ways. The giving or withholding of campaign funds, as in the case of other supports be they personal, group or institutional, depends on the symbolic, ideological or material gratification of the contributor by the receiving party. Overdependence of parties on any single source or socio-economic group inevitably narrows the freedom of action of political decision-makers. Such parties tend to become the spokesmen of narrow social interests losing the aggregative function attributed to parties in liberal-democratic thought. An examination of policy outputs in relation to the fund-raising structures of the dominant parties casts light on the nature of the polity and its principal beneficiaries. Continued secrecy as to the size and provenance of such contributions may inhibit such studies but is itself a commentary on the relationship between donors and those who depend on their support.

The review of the legislative effort to control election expenses by the federal Parliament and the provincial Legislatures presented in Part III demonstrates that such controls may be approached from a number of standpoints. In an exercise such as this, stress may be placed on the form, the structural impact, or the rationale of the systems which have been established or proposed. Each approach assists in the formulation of policy by highlighting some of the problems involved in this difficult area.

A formal analysis would distinguish between various types of control. It would emphasize the nature of the restraints imposed, whether these be statutory, voluntary (resting on inter-party agreements), or normative (rooted in the political culture and attitudes of the citizens of the jurisdiction under consideration). These schemes might be analyzed further in terms of the activities subjected to regulation, such as the permitted sources and amounts of income, or the allowable amounts and objects of expenditure.

Control systems may be studied also in the light of their effect on the internal structure of parties and the relations between parties. This would involve an examination of the degree to which existing and proposed regulations contributed to increasing or decreasing the centralization of political parties, the relations between candidates in the constituencies and the party leadership, and the relationship between the parliamentary factions and the extra-parliamentary party organizations. A related matter would be the extent to which control system furthered the *institutionalization* of the existing party system or encouraged the formation of new groups and their entry into the electoral arena. Studies might also be made of their effect on the style of election campaigns.

The motives of the proponents of any one or a combination of control systems may also be examined. Regulations on election finance have been imposed with a view to the purity, the equity or the monetary cost of the democratic electoral process. The goal might have arisen out of a desire to "clean up" political finance. There may have been a fear that, in the absence of regulations, donors of funds or their agents might gain undue influence over political parties, legislators and public officials; or that the voter would sacrifice his freedom of choice and long-run interests in favour of a short-run monetary gain. A belief in equity and equality of opportunity coupled with a liberal distaste for "unfair competition" has apparently been at the root of some attempts to equalize chances amongst rival candidates and parties through a reduction in the advantages which allegedly accrue to those able to dispose of massive financial resources. Controls directed at the financially strong have been justified in order to maintain the electorate's freedom of choice in the age of the mass media and the "hidden persuader." Finally, controls have also stemmed from a feeling that inflated election expenditures are morally wrong in themselves, or because certain groups and individuals may be excluded from participation in the electoral process. That is, concern about costs may itself have been a motive for control or it may reflect feelings regarding the equity or purity of the political process.[9]

The half-hearted attempts made in the last one hundred years by Canadian legislators to deal with the problems associated with campaign funds have been limited to the behaviour and expenditures of candidates at the local level. The issues presented by the existence of parties, their solicitors and the sources and size of campaign funds have been bypassed. Legislation has been concerned with the definition and prohibition of certain corrupt practices by candidates and the assurance of a minimum amount of publicity for their expenditures. The proposals of the Committee on Election Expenses would strengthen these features by providing enforcement machinery and by recognizing the role of parties; a small step would be made in the direction of greater equity by providing additional opportunities to communicate with the electorate at public expense, and by providing some incentive to individual small contributors. However, the Committee's proposals do little to lessen the continued dependence of parties and candidates on the traditional sources of campaign funds in Canada.

It is clear that no fundamental changes in the financial aspects of Canadian election campaigns will occur unless an alternative source of funds is provided. Quebec has pointed the way with a system of subventions from the public treasury, adapted to our parliamentary system. Coupled with the enforcement machinery proposed by the federal advisory Committee, and provided that subsidies were extended to political parties as well as to candidates, the Quebec scheme may well serve as a model for future federal and provincial legislation. The federal Parliament could also legislate concerning the use of facilities which fall within its competence, and thus permit a reduction of the burden on federal parties and candidates through the transfer of certain indispensable costs to federal crown agencies such as the Canadian Broadcasting Corporation and the Post Office. Additional broadcasting and mailing privileges could thus be accorded to parties and candidates.

Two fundamental democratic goals may be achieved by reducing the dependence of political parties and candidates in this manner. Government subsidies would reinforce the capacity of political decision-makers to resist the importunate demands of contributors whose threats to withhold funds might otherwise limit the freedom of party leaders to act in the public interest. Substance may also be given to the right of the electorate to be fully informed about alternative policies and leaders prior to making its decision at the polls. By assuring that parties and candidates are given adequate facilities to present their programs and spokesmen through access to the communications media, the range of political choice may be widened. Those who might otherwise avoid the electoral process may thus be encouraged to participate.

Disenchantment with the failings of the electoral process has helped to promote the sense of political inefficacy that has contributed to the growth of extra-parliamentary oppositions of the Right and Left with their common proclivity to violence. Reform in the vital area of party finance might well assist in restoring faith in the possibilities of democratic control.

FOOTNOTES

1 *Report of the Committee on Election Expenses,* The Queen's Printer, Ottawa, 1966, p. 229.

2 This formula is based on dividing the expenditure per vote cast by the Average Hourly Wage of Male Industrial Workers. See Arnold J. Heidenheimer, "Comparative Party Finance: Notes on Practices and Toward a Theory," in a symposium on Comparative Political Finance, Richard Rose and Arnold J. Heidenheimer, eds., *Journal of Politics,* Volume 25, August 1963, p. 797.

3 *Ibid.,* p. 798.

4 For detailed studies of the 1964 and 1968 American election campaigns, see Herbert A. Alexander, *Financing The 1964 Election,* Citizen's Research Foundation, Study No. 9, Princeton, N.J. 1966, *passim;* and his *Financing Parties and Campaigns in 1968: A Preliminary Report,* Citizen's Research Foundation, Princeton, 1969, (mimeo).

5 See Appendix C, p. 194.

6 See Chapter 5, p. 88.

7 John Porter, *The Vertical Mosaic,* University of Toronto Press, Toronto, 1965, p. 296.

8 The implications of money as a *transfer support* are detailed in Heidenheimer, *op. cit.,* pp. 801-807.

9 For a comparative analysis of control systems, see Study No. 1, "Control and Limitation of Election Expenses in Modern Democracies," prepared under the direction of the author by the research staff of the Committee on Election Expenses, *Report of the Committee on Election Expenses, op. cit.,* pp. 85-111.

APPENDIX A

**DECLARED ELECTION EXPENSES BY POLITICAL AFFILIATION
1949 — 1968**

Table A - 1
CANADA

Total Amounts Declared by Candidates of Each Party
(in thousands of dollars, rounded to nearest thousand)

Political Affiliation	1949	1953	1957	1958	1962	1963	1965	1968
Liberal	1,013	1,284	1,674	1,118	2,115	2,094	2,616	3,510
Progressive Conservative	899	891	1,260	1,872	2,299	1,405	1,779	2,464
CCF/NDP	177	156	219	201	391	288	516	681
Social Credit	24	81	141	70	269	227	143	47
Ralliement des Créditistes	—	—	—	—	—	—	60	56
Union of Electors	9	—	—	—	—	—	—	—
Labour Progressive	24	42	5	8	—	—	—	—
Communist	—	—	—	—	9	6	8	10
Other Parties	8	4	*	1	—	*	4	4
Independents	50	71	97	6	13	19	33 ⎫	55
Other Independents	—	—	—	—	—	—	15 ⎭	
Total	2,204	2,528	3,396	3,276	5,096	4,040	5,173	6,827

Number of Candidates Filing Returns

Political Affiliation	1949	1953	1957	1958	1962	1963	1965	1968
Liberal	255	257	245	203	238	232	232	246
Progressive Conservative	215	212	236	259	229	214	216	197
CCF/NDP	152	134	135	129	177	164	175	162
Social Credit	24	64	95	56	155	149	60	23
Ralliement des Créditistes	—	—	—	—	—	—	37	32
Union of Electors	16	—	—	—	—	—	—	—
Labour Progressive	14	77	7	13	—	—	—	—
Communist	—	—	—	—	10	9	8	11
Other Parties	5	2	3	1	—	1	5	4
Independents	24	22	26	12	10	11	16 ⎫	25
Other Independents	—	—	—	—	—	—	9 ⎭	
Total	705	768	747	673	819	780	758	700

Political Affiliation	Number of Seats Won								Number of Candidates Not Filing Returns							
	1949	1953	1957	1958	1962	1963	1965	1968	1949	1953	1957	1958	1962	1963	1965	1968
Liberal	190	171	106	49	100	129	131	156	5	8	20	62	26	33	33	18
Progressive Conservative	41	51	112	208	116	95	97	72	35	37	20	6	37	51	49	66
CCF/NDP	13	23	25	8	19	17	21	22	28	36	27	40	41	68	80	101
Social Credit	10	15	19	—	30	24	5	—	4	9	18	26	75	75	26	7
Ralliement des Créditistes	—	—	—	—	—	—	9	14	—	—	—	—	—	—	40	40
Union of Electors	—	—	—	—	—	—	—	—	39	—	—	—	—	—	—	—
Labour Progressive	—	—	—	—	—	—	—	—	3	23	3	5	—	—	—	—
Communist	—	—	—	—	—	—	—	—	—	—	—	—	2	2	4	3
Other Parties	—	—	—	—	—	—	—	—	2	5	9	10	5	8	5	10
Independents	8	5	3	—	—	—	1	—	28	15	24	14	12	11	7	22
Other Independents	—	—	—	—	—	—	1	—	—	—	—	—	—	—	11	—
Total	262	265	265	265	265	265	265	264	144	133	121	163	198	248	255	267

*Less than $1,000.

Source: The information contained in Tables A-1 to A-12 inclusive has been derived from eight **Sessional Papers** prepared by the Office of the Chief Electoral Officer. The **Sessional Papers** were tabled in the House of Commons on February 15, 1950, January 13, 1954, August 12, 1959, November 26, 1959, November 27, 1962, September 26, 1963, March 18, 1966, and November 7, 1968.

Table A - 2
BRITISH COLUMBIA

Political Affiliation	Total Amounts Declared by Candidates of Each Party (in thousands of dollars, rounded to nearest thousand)								Number of Candidates Filing Returns							
	1949	1953	1957	1958	1962	1963	1965	1968	1949	1953	1957	1958	1962	1963	1965	1968
Liberal	112	154	179	69	137	154	206	252	16	22	22	22	21	20	22	22
Progressive Conservative	112	75	140	141	184	117	131	141	15	16	22	22	22	21	21	19
CCF/NDP	14	23	38	35	56	53	80	125	15	21	21	22	22	21	20	22
Social Credit	*	32	62	22	40	30	43	35	2	20	21	20	19	17	16	15
Labour Progressive ⎫	1	5	1	1	—	—	—	—	3	16	2	3	—	—	—	—
Communist ⎭	—	—	—	—	4	2	2	3	—	—	—	—	3	2	2	4
Other Party	—	—	—	—	—	—	*	—	—	—	—	—	—	—	1	—
Independent	4	*	*	—	—	7	*	1	1	1	1	—	1	2	1	1
Other Independent	—	—	—	—	—	—	1	—	—	—	—	—	—	—	1	—
Total	244	289	420	269	421	364	464	557	52	96	89	89	88	83	84	83

Political Affiliation	Number of Seats Won								Number of Candidates Not Filing Returns							
	1949	1953	1957	1958	1962	1963	1965	1968	1949	1953	1957	1958	1962	1963	1965	1968
Liberal	11	8	2	—	4	7	7	16	—	—	—	—	—	2	—	1
Progressive Conservative	3	3	7	18	6	4	3	—	3	1	1	—	—	1	1	4
CCF/NDP	3	7	7	4	10	9	9	7	—	2	—	2	3	1	2	1
Social Credit	—	4	6	—	2	2	3	—	—	1	—	2	—	5	6	4
Labour Progressive }	—	—	—	—	—	—	—	—	—	—	—	—	—	—	—	—
Communist }	—	—	—	—	—	—	—	—	—	—	—	—	—	—	2	—
Other Party	—	—	—	—	—	—	—	—	—	—	—	—	—	—	—	2
Independent	1	—	—	—	—	—	—	—	1	—	1	—	—	1	1	1
Other Independent	—	—	—	—	—	—	—	—	—	—	—	—	—	—	—	—
Total	18	22	22	22	22	22	22	23	4	4	2	4	3	10	12	13

*Less than $1,000.

Table A - 3
ALBERTA

Political Affiliation	Total Amounts Declared by Candidates of Each Party (in thousands of dollars, rounded to nearest thousand)								Number of Candidates Filing Returns							
	1949	1953	1957	1958	1962	1963	1965	1968	1949	1953	1957	1958	1962	1963	1965	1968
Liberal	46	72	120	67	77	92	116	224	17	17	16	16	17	15	14	18
Progressive Conservative	55	37	75	127	166	162	141	216	14	10	17	17	17	17	17	18
CCF/NDP	11	8	17	9	22	14	18	20	13	12	15	14	16	13	12	15
Social Credit	20	32	39	37	65	57	82	9	17	17	17	16	17	15	15	3
Labour Progressive	2	6	*	1	—	—	—	—	2	12	1	2	—	—	—	—
Communist	—	—	—	—	—	1	2	1	—	—	—	—	—	2	2	1
Independent	1	*	*	*	*	1	—	27	2	1	2	2	1	2	—	5
Total	136	155	252	243	332	327	358	497	65	69	68	67	68	64	60	60

Political Affiliation	Number of Seats Won								Number of Candidates Not Filing Returns							
	1949	1953	1957	1958	1962	1963	1965	1968	1949	1953	1957	1958	1962	1963	1965	1968
Liberal	5	4	1	—	—	1	—	4	—	—	1	1	—	2	3	1
Progressive Conservative	2	2	3	17	15	14	15	15	—	2	—	—	1	—	—	1
CCF/NDP	—	—	13	—	—	—	—	—	—	1	—	1	1	4	5	4
Social Credit	10	11	—	—	2	2	2	—	—	—	—	1	—	2	2	—
Labour Progressive ⎫	—	—	—	—	—	—	—	—	—	—	—	—	—	—	—	—
Communist ⎭	—	—	—	—	—	—	—	—	—	—	—	—	—	—	1	—
Independent	—	—	—	—	—	—	—	—	—	—	—	—	2	—	—	1
Total	17	17	17	17	17	17	17	19	—	3	1	3	3	8	11	7

*Less than $1,000.

Table A - 4
SASKATCHEWAN

Political Affiliation	Total Amounts Declared by Candidates of Each Party (in thousands of dollars, rounded to nearest thousand)								Number of Candidates Filing Returns							
	1949	1953	1957	1958	1962	1963	1965	1968	1949	1953	1957	1958	1962	1963	1965	1968
Liberal	49	47	75	48	69	77	98	126	20	16	16	15	16	17	16	13
Progressive Conservative	55	37	53	78	131	95	95	121	20	15	16	17	17	17	17	13
CCF/NDP	52	51	66	56	76	50	83	129	19	17	16	15	16	16	17	13
Social Credit	3	5	18	2	17	8	5	—	4	11	14	1	13	10	10	—
Labour Progressive ⎱ Communist	3	4	*	1	*	1	*	1	2	9	1	2	1	2	1	1
Other Parties	—	—	*	—	—	—	—	—	—	—	—	—	—	—	—	—
Independent	—	—	—	*	—	*	—	—	—	—	1	1	—	1	—	—
Total	161	144	214	185	294	201	281	377	65	68	64	51	63	63	61	40

Political Affiliation	Number of Seats Won								Number of Candidates Not Filing Returns							
	1949	1953	1957	1958	1962	1963	1965	1968	1949	1953	1957	1958	1962	1963	1965	1968
Liberal	14	5	4	—	—	—	—	2	—	1	1	2	1	—	1	—
Progressive Conservative	1	1	3	16	16	17	17	5	—	—	—	—	1	—	—	—
CCF/NDP	5	11	10	1	1	—	—	6	1	—	1	2	1	1	—	—
Social Credit	—	—	—	—	—	—	—	—	—	3	2	—	2	6	2	—
Labour Progressive	—	—	—	—	—	—	—	—	—	—	—	—	—	—	—	—
Communist	—	—	—	—	—	—	—	—	—	—	—	—	—	—	—	—
Other Parties	—	—	—	—	—	—	—	—	—	—	—	—	—	—	—	—
Independent	—	—	—	—	—	—	—	—	—	—	—	—	—	—	—	1
Total	20	17	17	17	17	17	17	13	1	4	4	4	4	7	3	1

*Less than $1,000.

Table A - 5
MANITOBA

Political Affiliation	Total Amounts Declared by Candidates of Each Party (in thousands of dollars, rounded to nearest thousand)								Number of Candidates Filing Returns							
	1949	1953	1957	1958	1962	1963	1965	1968	1949	1953	1957	1958	1962	1963	1965	1968
Liberal	40	43	55	43	76	84	99	199	16	14	13	10	12	12	10	13
Progressive Conservative	42	35	54	78	114	77	105	123	15	14	13	14	14	13	12	11
CCF/NDP	18	11	16	20	33	17	32	28	14	10	13	13	14	11	14	8
Social Credit	—	5	7	1	15	14	4	3	—	6	11	4	12	11	7	3
Ralliement des Créditistes	—	—	—	—	—	—	—	—	—	—	—	—	—	—	—	—
Labour Progressive	5	5	1	1	—	—	—	—	2	6	1	1	—	—	—	—
Communist	—	—	—	—	3	—	—	2	—	—	—	—	2	—	—	1
Independent	2	*	*	—	—	*	*	4	2	2	1	—	—	1	1	3
Total	107	99	134	144	242	193	241	359	49	52	52	42	54	48	44	39

Political Affiliation	Number of Seats Won								Number of Candidates Not Filing Returns							
	1949	1953	1957	1958	1962	1963	1965	1968	1949	1953	1957	1958	1962	1963	1965	1968
Liberal	12	8	1	—	1	2	1	5	—	—	1	4	2	2	4	—
Progressive Conservative	1	3	8	14	11	10	10	5	—	—	1	—	—	1	2	2
CCF/NDP	3	3	5	—	2	2	3	3	—	—	1	1	1	2	—	5
Social Credit	—	—	—	—	—	—	—	—	—	2	3	2	1	2	4	1
Ralliement des Créditistes	—	—	—	—	—	—	—	—	—	—	—	—	—	—	—	1
Labour Progressive }	—	—	—	—	—	—	—	—	—	1	—	—	—	—	—	—
Communist	—	—	—	—	—	—	—	—	—	—	—	—	—	—	—	—
Independent	—	—	—	—	—	—	—	—	1	1	2	—	1	—	—	—
Total	16	14	14	14	14	14	14	13	1	4	8	7	4	7	10	9

*Less than $1,000.

Table A - 6
ONTARIO

Political Affiliation	Total Amounts Declared by Candidates of Each Party (in thousands of dollars, rounded to nearest thousand)								Number of Candidates Filing Returns							
	1949	1953	1957	1958	1962	1963	1965	1968	1949	1953	1957	1958	1962	1963	1965	1968
Liberal*	330	389	488	312	743	651	891	1,237	82	83	79	68	84	77	79	85
Progressive Conservative	311	359	470	500	657	481	717	884	82	81	85	84	76	74	71	66
CCF/NDP	72	56	75	73	159	138	245	315	70	57	52	51	68	60	66	67
Social Credit	**	6	14	5	31	31	9	**	1	9	30	10	46	45	11	2
Ralliement des Créditistes	—	—	—	—	—	—	—	—	—	—	—	—	—	—	—	—
Labour Progressive }	13	16	1	3	—	—	—	—	5	27	2	5	—	—	—	—
Communist }	—	—	—	—	4	2	4	3	—	—	—	—	4	3	3	3
Union of Electors	2	—	—	—	—	—	—	—	3	—	—	—	—	—	—	—
Other Parties	4	**	—	**	—	**	3	3	2	1	2	—	—	1	3	3
Independent	2	3	5	**	**	2	9	15	4	3	3	3	2	1	5	9
Other Independent	—	—	—	—	—	—	**	—	—	—	—	—	—	—	1	—
Total	735	829	1,053	894	1,594	1,304	1,879	2,457	249	261	253	221	280	261	239	235

Political Affiliation	Number of Seats Won								Number of Candidates Not Filing Returns							
	1949	1953	1957	1958	1962	1963	1965	1968	1949	1953	1957	1958	1962	1963	1965	1968
Liberal*	56	51	21	15	44	52	51	65*	1	2	6	17	1	8	6	3
Progressive Conservative	25	33	61	67	35	27	25	17	1	4	—	1	9	11	14	21
CCF/NDP	1	1	3	3	6	6	9	6	6	8	8	12	13	20	18	21
Social Credit	—	—	—	—	—	—	—	—	4	1	8	8	24	23	8	1
Ralliement des Créditistes	—	—	—	—	—	—	—	—	—	—	—	—	—	—	—	—
Labour Progressive	—	—	—	—	—	—	—	—	2	2	—	1	1	—	—	—
Communist	—	—	—	—	—	—	—	—	—	—	—	—	1	1	—	3
Union of Electors	—	—	—	—	—	—	—	—	1	—	—	—	—	—	—	—
Other Parties	—	—	—	—	—	—	—	—	1	—	3	1	—	1	1	—
Independent	1	—	—	—	—	—	—	—	1	1	1	—	1	6	3	1
Other Independent	—	—	—	—	—	—	—	—	—	—	—	—	—	—	1	—
Total	83	85	85	85	85	85	85	88	17	18	26	40	50	70	52	50

*The Liberal Party figures for 1968 include the Speaker, Mr. Lucien Lamoureux, M.P., who formally was not affiliated with any party.

**Less than $1,000.

Table A - 7
QUEBEC

Political Affiliation	Total Amounts Declared by Candidates of Each Party (in thousands of dollars, rounded to nearest thousand)								Number of Candidates Filing Returns							
	1949	1953	1957	1958	1962	1963	1965	1968	1949	1953	1957	1958	1962	1963	1965	1968
Liberal	361	450	618	477	845	847	967	1,133	72	71	71	50	64	66	68	69
Progressive Conservative	255	239	336	747	779	314	375	642	41	46	52	70	53	46	47	42
CCF/NDP	3	2	3	6	26	36	45	50	9	10	11	11	26	31	29	22
Social Credit	—	—	—	1	96	82	—	—	—	—	—	3	40	44	—	—
Ralliement des Créditistes	—	—	—	—	—	—	60	56	—	—	—	—	—	—	37	32
Labour Progressive	—	5	—	—	—	—	—	—	—	6	—	—	—	—	—	—
Communist	—	—	—	—	—	—	—	*	—	—	—	—	—	—	—	1
Union of Electors	7	—	—	—	—	—	—	—	12	—	—	—	—	—	—	—
Other Parties	4	3	—	1	—	—	—	1	3	1	—	1	—	—	—	1
Independent	30	63	91	4	10	8	22	5	7	13	19	5	6	4	8	4
Other Independent	9	—	—	—	—	—	13		7	—	—	—	—	—	7	
Total	669	763	1,049	1,236	1,755	1,287	1,482	1,887	151	147	153	140	189	191	197	171

Political Affiliation	Number of Seats Won								Number of Candidates Not Filing Returns							
	1949	1953	1957	1958	1962	1963	1965	1968	1949	1953	1957	1958	1962	1963	1965	1968
Liberal	66	66	63	25	35	47	56	56	1	4	4	25	11	9	7	5
Progressive Conservative	2	4	9	50	14	8	8	4	28	26	16	5	23	29	28	32
CCF/NDP	—	—	—	—	—	—	—	—	11	19	11	18	14	29	42	51
Social Credit	—	—	—	—	26	20	—	—	—	—	4	12	35	31	—	—
Ralliement des Créditistes	—	—	—	—	—	—	9	14	—	—	—	—	—	—	38	38
Labour Progressive	—	—	—	—	—	—	—	—	1	19	3	2	—	—	—	—
Communist	—	—	—	—	—	—	—	—	—	—	—	—	1	1	2	—
Union of Electors	—	—	—	—	—	—	—	—	38	—	—	—	—	—	—	—
Other Parties	—	—	—	—	—	—	—	—	1	5	5	9	2	7	4	8
Independent	4	5	3	—	—	—	1	—	12	12	20	13	8	3	1	} 18
Other Independent	1	—	—	—	—	—	1	—	11	—	—	—	—	—	9	
Total	73	75	75	75	75	75	75	74	103	85	63	84	94	109	131	152

*Less than $1,000.

Table A - 8
NEW BRUNSWICK

Total Amounts Declared by Candidates of Each Party
(in thousands of dollars, rounded to nearest thousand)

Political Affiliation	1949	1953	1957	1958	1962	1963	1965	1968
Liberal	24	35	30	26	51	37	40	72
Progressive Conservative	24	29	33	46	62	35	46	73
CCF/NDP	2	*	*	*	3	3	5	6
Social Credit	—	—	*	*	1	4	—	—
Ralliement des Créditistes	—	—	—	—	—	—	—	—
Union of Electors	*	—	—	—	—	—	—	—
Independent	*	3	—	—	—	—	—	2
Total	50	68	64	73	117	79	91	153

Number of Candidates Filing Returns

Political Affiliation	1949	1953	1957	1958	1962	1963	1965	1968
Liberal	8	10	9	8	9	8	6	7
Progressive Conservative	9	9	9	10	9	6	9	7
CCF/NDP	4	2	1	1	4	4	6	5
Social Credit	—	—	2	2	3	5	—	—
Ralliement des Créditistes	—	—	—	—	—	—	—	—
Union of Electors	1	—	—	—	—	—	—	—
Independent	1	1	—	—	—	—	—	2
Total	23	22	21	21	25	23	21	21

Number of Seats Won

Political Affiliation	1949	1953	1957	1958	1962	1963	1965	1968
Liberal	7	7	5	3	6	6	6	5
Progressive Conservative	2	3	5	7	4	4	4	5
CCF/NDP	—	—	—	—	—	—	—	—
Social Credit	—	—	—	—	—	—	—	—
Ralliement des Créditistes	—	—	—	—	—	—	—	—
Union of Electors	—	—	—	—	—	—	—	—
Independent	1	—	—	—	—	—	—	—
Total	10	10	10	10	10	10	10	10

Number of Candidates Not Filing Returns

Political Affiliation	1949	1953	1957	1958	1962	1963	1965	1968
Liberal	2	—	1	2	1	2	4	3
Progressive Conservative	1	1	1	—	1	4	1	3
CCF/NDP	2	5	1	2	3	3	4	5
Social Credit	—	1	—	1	5	5	1	—
Ralliement des Créditistes	—	—	—	—	—	—	1	1
Union of Electors	1	—	1	—	1	—	—	—
Independent	—	—	—	—	—	—	—	—
Total	6	7	4	5	11	14	11	12

*Less than $1,000.

Table A-9
NOVA SCOTIA

Total Amounts Declared by Candidates of Each Party
(in thousands of dollars, rounded to nearest thousand)

Political Affiliation	1949	1953	1957	1958	1962	1963	1965	1968
Liberal	17	35	42	16	29	35	46	77
Progressive Conservative	18	31	53	58	53	77	86	96
CCF/NDP	4	4	4	*	8	6	8	6
Social Credit	—	—	—	—	*	*	—	—
Labour Progressive	—	*	—	—	—	—	—	—
Communist	—	—	—	—	—	—	—	—
Independent	—	—	—	—	—	—	*	1
Total	38	70	99	75	91	118	140	180

Number of Candidates Filing Returns

Political Affiliation	1949	1953	1957	1958	1962	1963	1965	1968
Liberal	12	11	8	5	7	6	6	7
Progressive Conservative	10	10	11	12	9	12	12	10
CCF/NDP	7	5	4	2	5	6	7	5
Social Credit	—	1	—	—	3	1	—	—
Labour Progressive	—	—	—	—	—	—	—	—
Communist	—	—	—	—	—	—	—	—
Independent	—	—	—	—	—	—	1	1
Total	29	27	23	19	24	25	26	23

Number of Seats Won

Political Affiliation	1949	1953	1957	1958	1962	1963	1965	1968
Liberal	10	10	2	—	2	5	2	1
Progressive Conservative	2	1	10	12	9	7	10	10
CCF/NDP	1	1	—	—	1	—	—	—
Social Credit	—	—	—	—	—	—	—	—
Labour Progressive	—	—	—	—	—	—	—	—
Communist	—	—	—	—	—	—	—	—
Independent	—	—	—	—	—	—	—	—
Total	13	12	12	12	12	12	12	11

Number of Candidates Not Filing Returns

Political Affiliation	1949	1953	1957	1958	1962	1963	1965	1968
Liberal	1	1	4	7	5	6	6	4
Progressive Conservative	3	2	1	—	3	—	—	1
CCF/NDP	2	—	2	2	7	3	5	6
Social Credit	—	—	1	—	4	1	—	—
Labour Progressive	—	—	—	—	—	—	—	—
Communist	—	—	—	—	—	—	—	—
Independent	—	—	—	—	—	—	—	—
Total	6	3	8	9	19	10	12	11

*Less than $1,000.

Table A - 10
PRINCE EDWARD ISLAND

Total Amounts Declared by Candidates of Each Party
(in thousands of dollars, rounded to nearest thousand)

Political Affiliation	1949	1953	1957	1958	1962	1963	1965	1968
Liberal	6	15	5	6	—	13	19	45
Progressive Conservative	4	13	12	21	45	22	42	35
CCF/NDP	—	—	—	—	5	—	*	*
Social Credit	—	—	—	—	*	—	—	—
Total	10	28	17	27	50	35	61	80

Number of Candidates Filing Returns

Political Affiliation	1949	1953	1957	1958	1962	1963	1965	1968
Liberal	4	4	2	2	—	2	2	4
Progressive Conservative	3	3	4	4	4	3	4	4
CCF/NDP	—	—	1	—	3	1	1	1
Social Credit	—	—	—	—	1	—	—	—
Total	7	7	7	6	8	6	7	9

Number of Seats Won

Political Affiliation	1949	1953	1957	1958	1962	1963	1965	1968
Liberal	3	3	—	—	—	2	—	—
Progressive Conservative	1	1	4	4	4	2	4	4
CCF/NDP	—	—	—	—	—	—	—	—
Social Credit	—	—	—	—	—	—	—	—
Total	4	4	4	4	4	4	4	4

Number of Candidates Not Filing Returns

Political Affiliation	1949	1953	1957	1958	1962	1963	1965	1968
Liberal	—	—	2	2	4	2	2	—
Progressive Conservative	1	1	—	—	—	1	—	—
CCF/NDP	2	1	2	1	1	3	3	3
Social Credit	—	—	—	—	—	—	—	—
Total	3	2	4	3	5	6	5	3

*Less than $1,000.

Table A - 11
NEWFOUNDLAND

Total Amounts Declared by Candidates of Each Party
(in thousands of dollars, rounded to nearest thousand)

Political Affiliation	1949	1953	1957	1958	1962	1963	1965	1968
Liberal	21	33	48	44	81	88	104	111
Progressive Conservative	25	33	25	55	65	10	19	115
CCF/NDP	—	—	*	—	2	*	*	1
Social Credit	—	—	—	—	—	—	*	—
Independent	—	—	—	—	—	—	—	—
Other Independents	—	—	—	—	—	—	—	—
Total	46	66	73	99	148	99	124	227

Number of Candidates Filing Returns

Political Affiliation	1949	1953	1957	1958	1962	1963	1965	1968
Liberal	7	7	7	6	7	7	7	6
Progressive Conservative	6	7	5	7	6	3	4	6
CCF/NDP	—	—	1	—	3	1	3	3
Social Credit	—	—	—	—	—	—	1	—
Independent	—	—	—	—	—	—	—	—
Other Independents	—	—	—	—	—	—	—	—
Total	13	14	13	13	16	11	15	15

Number of Seats Won

Political Affiliation	1949	1953	1957	1958	1962	1963	1965	1968
Liberal	5	7	5	5	6	7	7	1
Progressive Conservative	2	—	2	2	1	—	—	6
CCF/NDP	—	—	—	—	—	—	—	—
Social Credit	—	—	—	—	—	—	—	—
Independent	—	—	—	—	—	—	—	—
Other Independents	—	—	—	—	—	—	—	—
Total	7	7	7	7	7	7	7	7

Number of Candidates Not Filing Returns

Political Affiliation	1949	1953	1957	1958	1962	1963	1965	1968
Liberal	—	—	—	—	—	—	—	1
Progressive Conservative	1	1	1	1	1	4	3	1
CCF/NDP	1	—	—	1	1	2	—	4
Social Credit	—	—	—	—	—	—	—	—
Independent	—	1	—	1	1	1	3	1
Other Independents	—	—	—	—	1	—	1	—
Total	2	2	1	3	4	7	7	7

*Less than $1,000.

Table A - 12
YUKON AND NORTHWEST TERRITORIES

Total Amounts Declared by Candidates of Each Party
(in thousands of dollars, rounded to nearest thousand)

Political Affiliation	1949	1953	1957	1958	1962	1963	1965	1968
Liberal	8	10	13	10	7	16	30	35
Progressive Conservative	—	6	10	20	44	15	22	19
CCF/NDP	1	—	—	—	—	—	—	1
Social Credit	—	1	—	—	1	1	—	—
Independent	—	*	—	*	—	—	—	—
Total	9	17	23	31	53	32	52	55

Number of Candidates Filing Returns

Political Affiliation	1949	1953	1957	1958	1962	1963	1965	1968
Liberal	1	2	2	1	1	2	2	2
Progressive Conservative	—	1	2	2	2	2	2	1
CCF/NDP	1	—	—	—	—	—	—	1
Social Credit	—	1	—	—	1	1	—	—
Independent	—	1	—	1	—	—	—	—
Total	2	5	4	4	4	5	4	4

Number of Seats Won

Political Affiliation	1949	1953	1957	1958	1962	1963	1965	1968
Liberal	1	2	2	1	1	—	1	1
Progressive Conservative	—	—	—	1	1	2	1	1
CCF/NDP	—	—	—	—	—	—	—	—
Social Credit	—	—	—	—	—	—	—	—
Independent	—	—	—	—	—	—	—	—
Total	1	2	2	2	2	2	2	2

Number of Candidates Not Filing Returns

Political Affiliation	1949	1953	1957	1958	1962	1963	1965	1968
Liberal	—	—	—	1	1	—	—	1
Progressive Conservative	—	1	—	—	—	—	1	1
CCF/NDP	—	—	—	—	—	—	—	—
Social Credit	—	—	—	—	—	—	—	—
Independent	1	—	—	—	—	—	—	—
Total	1	1	—	1	1	—	1	2

*Less than $1,000.

APPENDIX B

AVERAGE DECLARED EXPENDITURES PER REPORTING CANDIDATE
BY PARTY: CANADA AND THE PROVINCES 1949-1968

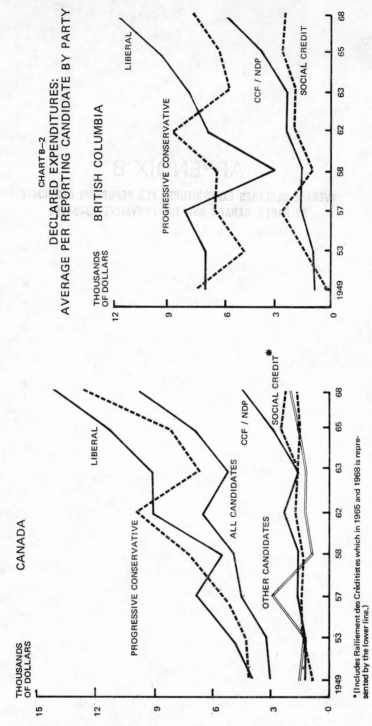

CHART B–1
DECLARED EXPENDITURES:
AVERAGE PER REPORTING CANDIDATE BY PARTY

CANADA

THOUSANDS
OF DOLLARS

LIBERAL

PROGRESSIVE CONSERVATIVE

ALL CANDIDATES

CCF / NDP

OTHER CANDIDATES

SOCIAL CREDIT *

*(Includes Ralliement des Créditistes which in 1965 and 1968 is represented by the lower line.)

CHART B–2
DECLARED EXPENDITURES:
AVERAGE PER REPORTING CANDIDATE BY PARTY

BRITISH COLUMBIA

THOUSANDS
OF DOLLARS

LIBERAL

PROGRESSIVE CONSERVATIVE

CCF / NDP

SOCIAL CREDIT

Source: Based on Information Found in Sessional Papers tabled February 15, 1950, January 13, 1954, August 12, 1958, November 26, 1959, November 27, 1962, September 26, 1963, March 18, 1966 and November 7, 1968.

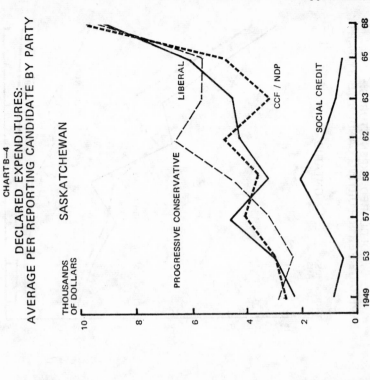

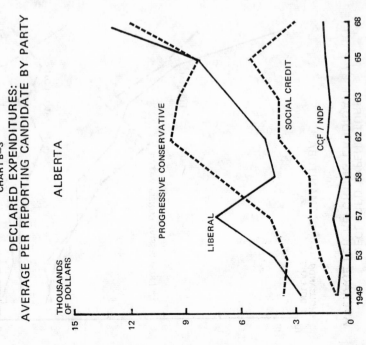

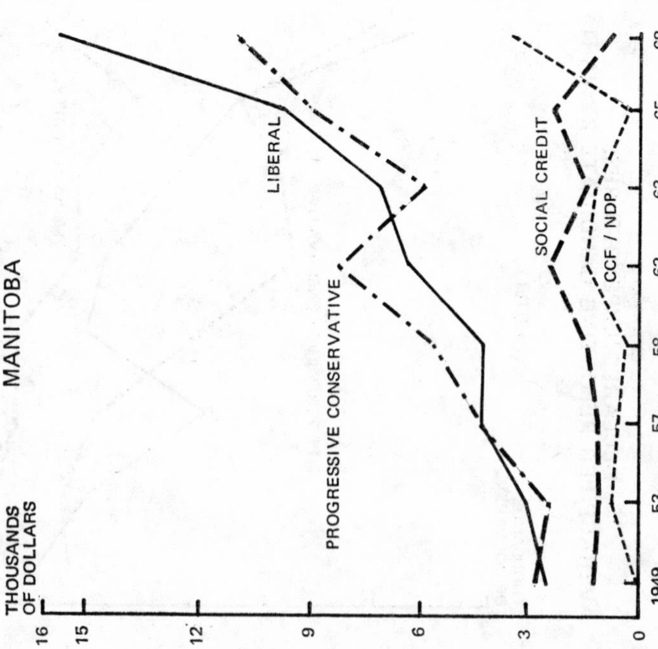

CHART B-6
DECLARED EXPENDITURES:
AVERAGE PER REPORTING CANDIDATE BY PARTY

ONTARIO

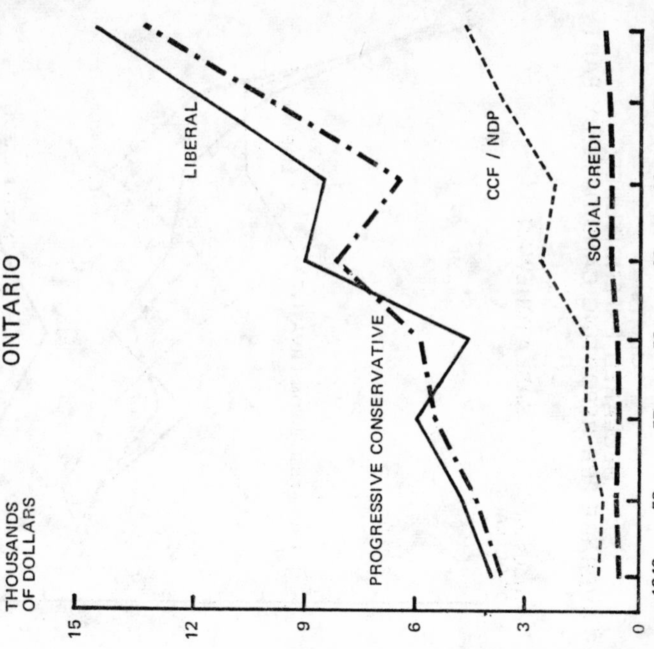

CHART B-5
DECLARED EXPENDITURES:
AVERAGE PER REPORTING CANDIDATE BY PARTY

MANITOBA

CHART B–7

DECLARED EXPENDITURES: AVERAGE PER REPORTING CANDIDATE BY PARTY

THOUSANDS OF DOLLARS
QUEBEC
17
16
12
8
4
0
LIBERAL
PROGRESSIVE CONSERVATIVE
OTHER CANDIDATES
RALLIEMENT DES CREDITISTES
CCF / NDP
1949
53
57
58
62
63
65
68

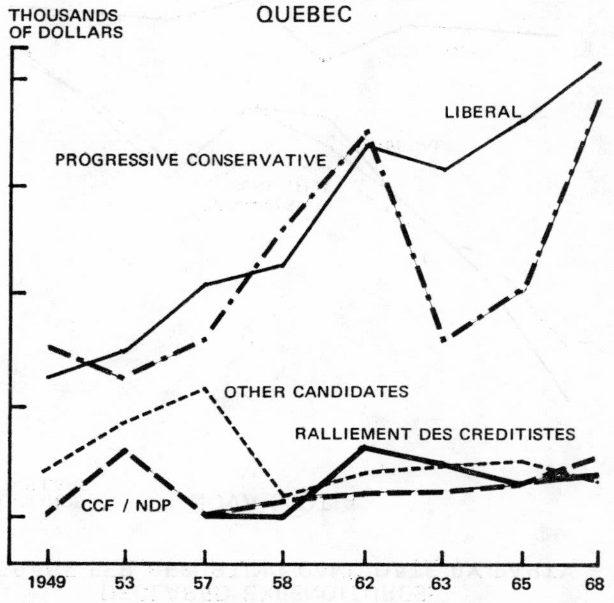

N.B. (Ralliement des Creditistes includes Social Credit prior to 1965.)

CHART B–8

DECLARED EXPENDITURES: AVERAGE PER REPORTING CANDIDATE BY PARTY

THOUSANDS OF DOLLARS
NEW BRUNSWICK
12
9
6
3
0
LIBERAL
PROGRESSIVE CONSERVATIVE
CCF / NDP
SOCIAL CREDIT
1949
53
57
58
62
63
65
68

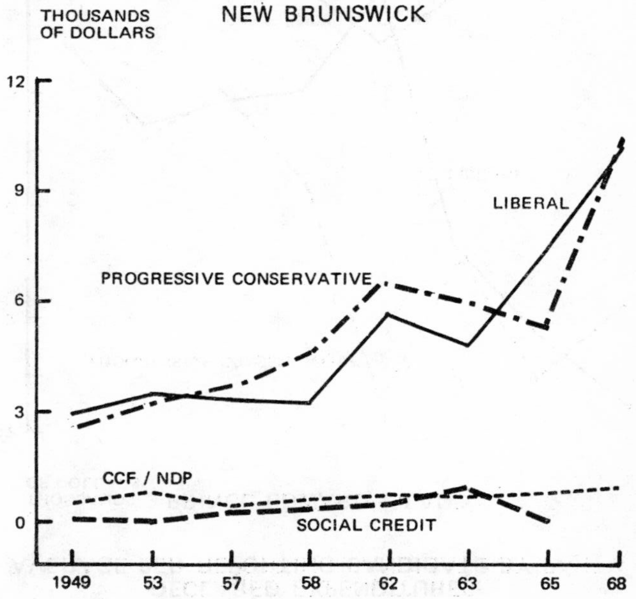

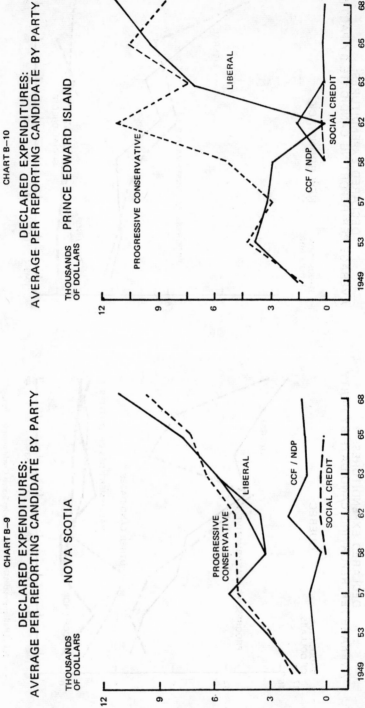

CHART B–9

DECLARED EXPENDITURES:
AVERAGE PER REPORTING CANDIDATE BY PARTY

NOVA SCOTIA

THOUSANDS
OF DOLLARS

CHART B–10

DECLARED EXPENDITURES:
AVERAGE PER REPORTING CANDIDATE BY PARTY

PRINCE EDWARD ISLAND

THOUSANDS
OF DOLLARS

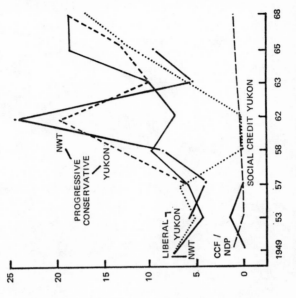

CHART B–12

DECLARED EXPENDITURES:
AVERAGE PER REPORTING CANDIDATE BY PARTY

YUKON — NORTH WEST
TERRITORIES

*After 1949 the single constituency of Yukon McKenzie River was divided into the Yukon and the North West Territories.

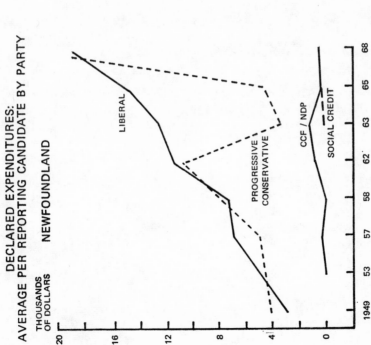

CHART B–11

DECLARED EXPENDITURES:
AVERAGE PER REPORTING CANDIDATE BY PARTY

NEWFOUNDLAND

APPENDIX C

GENERAL ELECTION COSTS ASSUMED BY THE FEDERAL GOVERNMENT
1930-1968

Table C - 1

GENERAL ELECTION COSTS PAID BY THE CHIEF ELECTORAL OFFICER
IN TWELVE GENERAL ELECTIONS 1930 - 1968
(Election Years Only)

Year	Number of Electors on List	Number of Votes Cast	Total Cost	Cost per Elector	Cost per Vote Cast
1930	5,153,971	3,922,481	$2,127,893.60	$.4128	$.5424
1935	5,918,207	4,452,675	2,978,881.27	.5033	.6690
1940					
Civilian Vote	6,588,888	4,606,364	2,651,244.99	.4023	.5755
War Service Vote	—	66,167	51,758.95	—	.7820
Total	6,588,888	4,672,531	2,703,003.95	.4023	.5784
1945					
Civilian Vote	6,952,445	4,946,115	2,859,023.32	.4112	.5780
War Service Vote	—	359,078	251,480.55	—	.7003
Total	6,952,445	5,305,193	3,110,503.87	.4112	.5863
1949					
Civilian Vote	7,893,629	5,880,878	4,419,884.00	.5633	.7515
Defense Service Vote	—	22,694	26,953.00	—	1.1877
Total	7,893,629	5,903,572	4,446,637.00	.5633	.7532
1953					
Civilian Vote	8,401,691	5,648,156	5,767,993.00	.6967	1.0212
Canadian Forces Vote	—	53,807	85,305.00	—	1.5850
Total	8,401,691	5,701,963	5,853,298.00	.6967	1.0265
1957	8,902,125	6,680,690	7,164,514.00	.8048	1.0725
1958	9,131,200	7,357,139	9,451,076.00	1.0353	1.1486
1962	9,700,325	7,772,656	10,898,486.00	1.1234	1.4021
1963	9,910,757	7,958,636	12,463,203.00	1.2575	1.5661
1965*	10,274,904	7,796,728	12,974,456.35	1.262	1.6640
1968*	10,860,888	8,217,916	13,841,484.08	1.2744	1.6847

Table prepared from information supplied by the Office of the Chief Electoral Officer.
*Statement of Actual Cost as of December 31, 1968.

INDEX

Aberhart, William, 66
Advertising agencies:
  reason for working for political
    parties, 73
  role of, 77-78
Aird, John B., 35
Alberta:
  legislation re political finance, 118
  and the Social Credit Movement, 69
Alberta Social Credit League, 67
Allan, Sir Hugh, 21
Atkinson, Joseph E., 25, 77

Baie des Chaleurs Railway
  scandal, 22-23
Bain, Rupert, 31
Ballantyne, C. G., 31, 32
Bank of Montreal, 31
Barbeau, Alphonse, 135
Beatty, Edward, 30
Beauharnois affair, 7, 25-27
Beauharnois Power Company, 25
Bell, Richard A., 41
  role of in Conservative party
    finance, 32-33
Bennett, R. B. 7, 25, 26, 28, 29, 33
  and Conservative party finance, 29
Blair, Andrew, 23
Blake, Edward, 133
Board of Broadcast Governors, 86, 91
Borden, Robert, 29

Bourassa, Henri, 28
Bracken, John, 32-33
Brewin, Andrew, 134
British Columbia:
  growth of the CCF, 49, 50
  Labour Relations Act, 119-20
  legislation on political finance, 118
  prohibits "check-off" system to
    parties, 119-20
  and the Social Credit Movement, 69
Brown, George, 21
Business community:
  and Conservative party finances
    1920-1948, 28-33
  financial role with older parties, 20
  and the 1911 election, 24
  and political finance, 6-8

Camp, Dalton, 76
Campaign expenditures:
  shift in objects of, 19-20
Canada Elections Act, 114-17
Canadian Broadcasting Corporation:
  allocation and value of time in the
    1966 Quebec election, 130
  conditions for "bona fide national
    parties" for free-time political
    broadcasts, 86-87
  percentage of free time allocated to
    political parties in federal
    election campaign, 84, 86-88

194

Canadian Labour Congress, 59
Canadian Pacific Railway, 30-31
Canadian Radio-Television
   Commission, 86, 91
Canadian society, bureaucratic
   structure of, 8
Caouette, Réal, 67, 71, 72, 74, 135
Cartier, Sir Georges Étienne, 6, 21
Cockfield, Brown advertising
   agency, 77
Coldwell, M. J., 52, 135
Committee on Election Expenses, 4,
   11, 133-51
   establishment of, 134-35
   estimated cost to federal treasury of
      Committee proposals, 150
   evaluation of Committee's
      proposals, 149-51
   inquiry of, 136-37
   1965 federal general election,
      campaign costs, 9
   recommendations, 138-49
      by-elections, 149
      control and enforcement—the
         registrar, 145-47
      duties—reports and
         audit, 145-46
      payment of subsidies, 147
      power to recommend
         changes, 146-47
      publication, 146
      report to Parliament, 146
   disclosure and reporting, 143-45
      candidates, 143-44
      fund-raisers, 145
      mass media expenditure, 145
      parties, 144-45
   enforcement, 147
   flexibility in broadcasting, 148-49
   limitations on
      expenditure, 141-43
   limitations on income and
      expenditure, 141
   no restrictions on donors, 141
   recognition of political
      parties, 138-39
   sanctions, 147-48
   subsidies to candidates and
      parties, 139
   subsidized broadcasting for
      parties, 139-40

Com. Election Expenses—*contd.*
   tax credit for contributions to
      candidates and parties, 140-41
   terms of reference, 135-36
Conservatives (includes Progressive
      Conservatives):
   and advertising agencies, 77-78
   under Bennett, 29-30
   under Bracken, 32-33
   business community:
      influence of, 28-33
      and 1911 election, 24
   calculation of cost of 1968 federal
      election, 9-10
   campaign costs:
      1957, 1958, 41
      1962, 1963, 41-42
      1965, 1968, 42
   cost of 1967 leadership
      convention, 9-10
   "democratization" of party
      finances, 32-33
   and the depression, 29-30
   under Diefenbaker, 41-42
   distribution of activists
      (percentage), 98
   donors, numbers of, 11
   under Drew, 41
   fund-raising:
      changes in allocation under
         Diefenbaker, 41
      emergence as a specialized
         task, 22
      structure of, 11-12, 20, 40-41
   under R. B. Hanson, 32
   the McGreevy Scandal, 22
   Manion and St. James Street, 30-31
   under Meighen, 29
   National Policy, 22
   and 1940 election, 31
   Pacific Scandal, 6, 21, 111
   political finance:
      compared with the Liberal
         party's, 7
      conclusions, 42
      early post-Confederation
         period, 6
      pre-1920 pattern, 20-22, 24
      1920-1948, 28-33
      1949-1968, 40-42
      and the role of the business
         community, 20